HARPSTRINGS AND CONFESSIONS

MART BAX

Harpstrings and Confessions

Machine-Style Politics in the Irish Republic

1976

VAN GORCUM, ASSEN/AMSTERDAM, THE NETHERLANDS

The publication of this book was made possible through a grant from the Netherlands Organization for the Advancement of Pure Research (Z.W.O.).

ISBN 90 232 1481 1

Printed in The Netherlands by Van Gorcum, Assen

Contents

Tables

Maps

TO THE MEMORY OF MY FATHER, FOR MY MOTHER

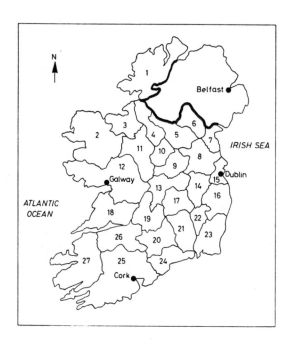

Map I. The 27 Administrative Counties of the Irish Republic

1 Donegal	8 Meath	15 Dublin	22 Carlow
2 Mayo	9 West Meath	16 Wicklow	23 Wexford
3 Sligo	10 Longford	17 Laoighis	24 Waterford
4 Leitrim	11 Roscommon	18 Clare	25 Cork
5 Cavan	12 Galway	19 Tipperary N.R.	26 Limerick
6 Monaghan	13 Offaly	20 Tipperary S.R.	27 Kerry
7 Louth	14 Kildare	21 Kilkenny	

Preface

This essay about politics in rural Ireland is the outcome of some 14 months' field work which I conducted from July 1968 until September 1969. My wife and, at that time, our only son were with me during the entire period. Their encouragement and interest in my activities as well as the friends they made were of great help.

In order to protect the identity of my *personae dramatis* I have changed names of persons, places, and areas. I have also blurred some historical facts to avoid easy recognition of the actual events. For the same reasons I have not given a map of Ireland indicating the general location of my research area.

I am indebted to many persons for practical and scientific help prior to, during, and after my field work period. To acknowledge them all is practically impossible; indeed, many names must remain unwritten for reasons of protection. My visit to Ireland and the publication of this book was made possible by a grant of the Netherlands Organization for the Advancement of Pure Research (z.w.o.). The Free University of Amsterdam enabled me financially to make a trip to the Irish Republic in 1967.

I also wish to thank the following persons who helped me in various ways: Professor Conrad M. Arensberg, Columbia University; Professor F.G. Bailey, University of California; Dr. R.H. Buchanan, the Queen's University of Belfast; Professor Basil Chubb, Trinity College Dublin; Dr. Kenneth H. Connell, the Queen's University of Belfast; Professor J.R. Fox, the London School of Economics and Political Science; Professor Ronald A. Frankenberg, University of Keele; Professor Art Gallaher, Jr., University of Kentucky; Dr. Rosemary Harris, University of London; Drs. Ed Koster, Free University of Amsterdam; Dr. Elliott Leyton, Memorial University of Newfoundland; Professor John C. Messenger, Indiana University; Professor Gordon F. Streib, Cornell University; Dr. John H. Whyte, the Queen's University of Belfast.

To Professor Jeremy Boissevain, University of Amsterdam, I owe an especial debt. He stimulated my field work and the writing of the manuscript, and helped me on many other fronts. My main intellectual debt is to him.

Finally, and most of all, I must thank my wife and my two sons for their forbearance in putting up with some long and many shorter periods of disruption in the life of the family.

Leiden, Holland   Mart Bax

Introduction

To many the Irish are almost a byword for political irrationality. They are said to throw themselves into causes, heedless of the consequences, with much bravery and immense spirit and very little calculation. This is not entirely a stereotype. Ireland's history demonstrates this in detail. The many risings and fights against the English establishment during the 18th and 19th centuries, and the almost hopeless fight of a handful of men who tried to throw off the English yoke in 1916 and establish the Republic, are clear examples. It is also demonstrated in the events reported every day in the newspapers for Northern Ireland. More intriguing, however, this same militant idealism is also still alive in the southern part of Eire which obtained independence more than 50 years ago. The wild idealism of republicanism, the attraction that the IRA has to many young men in the Republic, the political attention paid to the anniversaries of the late freedom fighters, and the importance of kinship relations with these late national heroes in political alignments, are but a few examples.

But there is another, less well known, side to Irish politics which has been growing in importance in the South since this gained its freedom early this century. For underneath the wild idealism there goes on a highly self interested and rational political operation, punctuated occasionally by bombs or fistfights, but mostly a highly orderly game in which people know when they have been beaten, when to retire, how far to push the other man, and so on and are not, at every setback, reaching for their pistols.

These two sides, on the one hand idealism, irrationality and heroism, on the other extreme pragmatism, rationality and self interest, constitute an intriguing and fascinating paradox. It forms the basis of the present study, which focuses on constituency politics. At that level traditional party loyalty and shrewd manipulation and calculation go hand in hand, and give the on-going fight for support between individual politicians its specific Irish colour.

A fair amount of research has been done, mainly by Irish political scientists, on the "formal" side of politics and government. Information on the field that I cover here, however, is almost completely lacking or at best impressionistic. Partly this is the result of the disciplinary tradition of Irish political scientists, but it may also be caused by a vague fear of political and other unpleasant consequences. In their circles this subject is almost

1

considered as unworthy of intellectual attention, as "muck-raking", which might even lead to job suicide. Foreign social scientists, on the other hand, have shown little interest in Irish politics, or have suppressed their data in order to be able to return there for further research. Although I agree with these Irish scholars that much peering behind the scenes is involved, I disagree with them about the value attached to the subject. If one realizes that the majority of the Irish politicians, especially the rural ones, are predominantly concerned with small local affairs and problems of individual electors, one cannot deny that this theme is very much worthy of intellectual attention. Irish politicians toil to keep together their flock of voters, upon whose support they depend, and attempt to subvert those of others.

In order to appreciate the present study one should know how I undertook my task, and how my initial plans changed early during my stay in Ireland. When I prepared my field work I had a vague idea of studying politics in a rural parish. However, I did not want to tie myself down in advance to a village-oriented or a "village-outward" type of study.[1] Once in the field, the relationship between parochial politics and some larger political structure might well appear to be a more interesting subject. If I came to decide upon this, however, I would be confronted with analytical problems. It will be clear that parish politics, competition in a sporting club or a local community development organization, is in a way different from politics in a county council. Yet, if I intended to study the interaction between these two structures, I would have to do that with a single framework of concepts. Even up to the present day,however,politics is in the last resort often considered as a matter of governments. What goes on in arenas of sporting clubs, villages, or trade unions is at best looked upon as "parapolitical".[2] Bailey is the first anthropologist who has provided a single model for studying both "real" politics and parapolitics.[3] Bailey, many of whose ideas are used in this book, looks upon politics as a competitive game. There is a certain agreement about the prize, the rules relating to who may play and who may not play, and the type of strategy the players use. With this analytical framework of Bailey I went to Ireland in July 1968.[4]

During the first three months of field work in a town, here called Patricksville, I obtained enough information to decide which type of study would be the most interesting. Indeed, an investigation of a type of political structure different from the ones mentioned herefore began to assume more contours, though this did not cause me to abandon Bailey's analytical framework. Remarks like "this bloody whole place is rotten with politics", stories about parliamentary representatives, county councillors, and local "hatchetmen" who were competing for voters by means of gifts, promises, and bribes, made me decide to put this competition in the centre of my analysis. Special words like "pulling strings" (asking for help or favours to a politician) and "hearing confessions" (the politician makes regular tours along all the places in his area to hear the population's complaints and problems) convinced me that this was an important field for research. In-

2

deed, it became the basic theme of my work. Pulling strings and hearing confessions appeared to be of paramount importance in Irish rural politics. "It's not for nothing that our national emblem is the harp", some people explained me. Hence the title of this book: Harpstrings and confessions.

The next logical step was to delineate my field spatially. At first glance it seemed that two fields with two different types of games could be delineated. Members of the county council, MCCs for short, compete with each other within the boundaries of a County Electoral Area (CEA). TDs, an abbreviation of the Irish *Teachta Dala*, members of parliament, on the other hand fight for voters in the far larger territory of the constituency. Initially I dealt with these two games separately, but after some time I discovered that the two were so closely interconnected and overlapped so strongly that treating them as one game was closer to reality and provided better insights. A seat in the county council is a highly attractive prize for both TDs and MCCs. Indeed, the power basis of any politician lies in his position in the county government, because the majority of the voters' problems (their prizes) must be resolved here. The most suitable way of attracting voters is by obtaining a seat in the county council. Consequently, not only MCCs and would-be MCCs compete with each other, but also TDs attempt to obtain a seat in the county council, and once obtained they do their utmost to remain in that office. On the other hand, MCCs are a potential threat for the TD's position in parliament, for many of them consider a TDship a valuable prize and attempt to obtain it. Thus an intricate picture resulted of various sorts of politicians competing with each other in the same field of which the outer boundaries are demarcated by those of the constituency. Each politician attempts to build up a support of voters by means of persons who are able to provide prizes for the electorate. Together, these voters and prize producers constitute the political machine of the politician.

Not all political leaders within the constituency fight with each other for voters. Competition takes place mainly between members of the same party because the electorate votes predominantly along party lines. Although this fact is of basic importance for my argument, I must emphasize that I did not attempt to study systematically the cause of this party loyalty. I treated this as a given, as an element of the paradox mentioned before, and from that point my exploration started. Again, this fact enabled me to confine my analysis to competition between members of a single party. I selected the *Fianna Fail* party, the largest of the three, and made a detailed study of machine politics between its politicians in one constituency. Although this is a rather small segment of the total field, information about other constituencies and parties convinced me that my picture is not unique.

Thus the present study differs from my initial plans. It is neither a village-oriented study nor a "part-whole" analysis, but a description of machine-style politics and its constituent groupings. It follows that, although I lived almost exclusively in one small town, I did not consider this community as my object or sample. It was simply a convenient place from where I

3

could operate and where certain elements of the process of machine politics could be studied in more detail. The main point of my argument is that machine-style politics is the outcome of a paradox in Irish political culture: on the one hand strong and traditional party loyalty, on the other extreme pragmatism and self interest. This cultural paradox is maintained by the implications of a peculiar electoral system which functions in a predominantly preindustrial society of small farmers who set great store in face-to-face relations and who have a strongly particularistic attitude.

Conducting this sort of "muck-raking" field work entails serious technical problems. No politician, of course, is instantly prepared to disclose his confidential activities. On the other hand, since the Irish politicians are accustomed to be approached by ordinary people, I had no problems in contacting a number of them. Moreover, it must be borne in mind that Ireland is a small country of only some three million inhabitants, of whom the majority live in the countryside, in villages and small towns. The political and administrative top of this society as well as many lawyers and businessmen constitute as it were a small community and have a fund of common knowledge about many of its members. Many of them see each other at the Royal Dublin Society, and belong to the same golf clubs, and friendly societies. It was really astonishing to realize how many people know each other and how rapidly news travels. After only a few weeks in the field, I was contacted by an American political scientist, living some 120 miles away from me, who had heard from a politician about my research plans. Again, several politicians in other corners of Ireland whom I interviewed had long since known who I was and what I was going to study.

The existence of these effective communication networks has advantages: it is not too difficult for anyone to have access to the common fund of knowledge referred to above. The Irish situation could be compared with life in a small village in which it is hard to keep "dirty news" under the table, even from the outsider-anthropologist.[5] On the other hand, it has certain disadvantages to work in a situation in which everybody knows much about the affairs of many others. I felt this especially following my field work, after I had left the Irish scene. A few articles on the subject which I sent to friends in Ireland have resulted in some persons boycotting me. Indeed, several people in Patricksville are no longer prepared to funnel news to me.

However this may be, during my field work period the disadvantages of living in a "small community" did not outweigh the advantages. I had regular and in some cases frequent contact with 32 politicians of whom seven were retired. Because I was introduced to them by some politically influential persons, most TDs and MCCs were prepared to talk about their daily activities. After some time, some confided me how they had been treated by colleagues. The tactics of telling a particular politician what opponents had said about him frequently resulted in very much information about these opponents. Thus, playing off one against the other provided me much valu-

4

able information. The readiest response came, of course, from defeated candidates. By checking and cross-checking information I gathered much of my data. A few civil servants and local government officials whom I befriended told me about activities and pressures of politicians in their offices. Of vital importance for understanding machine politics were some persons who acted as local intermediaries between the electorate and the TDs. They were key-informants, though their information cost me "a world of porter" (i.e. beer), and other small services and rewards. A lawyer who was very well informed in regional political circles because he was a general adviser to some politicians constituted a vital link in my communication network. At least twice a week we discussed my findings and ideas. Indeed, after having provided him with some anthropological literature on politics, he was able to solve my problems even quicker, and he brought others spontaneously to the forefront. Furthermore, many voters in Patricksville informed me about the ways in which they had been helped, or sacked, by politicians and local intermediaries.

By means of a taperecorder I was able to record many discussions with the persons mentioned above. Indeed, since my recorder was small and portable, I could use it sometimes unobtrusively during meetings and personal interviews. In some cases I told the persons afterwards that I had taped the discussion. Usually they did not mind as long as I did not quote them in my discussion with others. In only a few cases this secret taping cost me my rapport with the interviewees. But I feel that many modern anthropologists are familiar with these consequences, though almost none will openly admit this. Anyway, using a taperecorder enabled me not only to write down my data in great detail, but it also provided verbatim cases a number of which are used in this book.

I also sent a questionnaire to 70 per cent of the TDs and to all the members of four county councils. Approximately 50 per cent of the whole sample returned the questionnaire after having filled it in. Their answers gave me sufficient information to compose a general picture of the Irish rural politician and his daily activities.

I also used printed materials, such as publications about constituency and CEA politics, party organization, election literature, and one parish register. Apart from the techniques listed above, I read as much about politics and history as I could lay my hand on. Throughout my field work I kept a file of newspaper cuttings from two regional dailies and a national one.
The year 1969 was an interesting one, for general elections were held then. This enabled me to check my findings; indeed, I could make a close study of one machine in operation. These elections were of particular importance because the boundaries of the constituencies had just been changed. Consequently, the balance of power in "my" constituency shifted considerably.

Part one: Background and Setting

CHAPTER ONE

The National Context

I. SOME GEOGRAPHICAL NOTES

Eire, or Ireland is part of the British Isles, separated from Britain by the Irish Sea. The island covers a total area of about 32,500 square miles. Due to its eccentric location, the country has been isolated from the many cultural and social waves which have spread over the continental part of Europe. Small wonder then that Ireland's influence on the Continent has nearly always been practically nil. There is however one exception: it is widely accepted that Christianity came to Ireland first and spread from there to Northern and Western Europe. The Irish are proud of this fact and many consider Ireland as today's last stronghold of the true faith.

Morphologically Ireland is often compared to a saucer: the interior is essentially a lowland with an altitude of around 200 to 400 feet; the ring of coastal highlands is composed of gently undulating mountains, rising to 600 and sometimes 1,000 feet.

Ireland has a mild, moist, and changeable climate; extreme frosts, heavy snows in winter, and very warm and dry days in summer are exceptions. The abundant rainfall throughout the year has widely differing effects on this predominantly green-coloured country. The limestone areas of the central plane, the South, and the South-East have many rich farming areas. The entire agriculturally poor Western seabord has many bogs, marshes, and lakes.

II. THE PAST

Of the processes which have contributed to the shaping of present-day Ireland two deserve special attention: the struggle for land and nationalism, culminating in the fight for independence. These two reached their climax in the nineteenth and early twentieth century. The present Irish Republic only attained full independence in 1949 and consequently many of the old issues are still alive in present-day politics. It is therefore useful to give a brief outline of Ireland's history so that the reader will have the background information necessary to understand the present political system. In this historical outline, based on well-known publications listed in the bibliography, I deal predominantly with the nineteenth and early twentieth century.

Moreover, since this book examines politics in the Republic, the historical sketch deals mostly with that part of the island. The chapter concludes with a broad survey of the Ireland of today.

For about seven centuries Ireland was connected in one way or another with the British Empire. After a long series of battles between Irish feudal chiefs and the British Crown, Cromwell finally brought the "rebels" to their knees in the seventeenth century. Ireland became an English colony. Many of the old Irish nobility saw their lands taken from them and given to Englishmen who had helped the British government financially in its wars against Ireland. In addition, many army officers and thousands of common soldiers received Irish land as their pay was in considerable arrears.

The result of Cromwell's settlement policy was the creation of a new class of landlords. Although the Irish had been familiar with a feudal type of social and political structure for ages, the socio-economic dichotomy which followed the Cromwellian wars, was in many respects different. The landed gentry, popularly called the Ascendancy were often irresponsible landowners who paid little or no attention to the welfare of their tenants. Traditionally English, and often absentee, they formed a caste differing from the peasants in nationality, station, and religious persuasion. The Irish were predominantly Catholic, the Ascendancy mainly Protestant.

The Irish were also discriminated against by legal means. The Penal Laws, introduced in the first quarter of the eighteenth century, were essentially designed to preserve the recently renewed land settlement by preventing Catholics from obtaining land. Ownership of land in those days meant power, and in its anglicization policy England tried to keep this power basis out of the hands of the Irish.

During the larger part of the eighteenth century, because of the Penal Code, Catholics were discouraged from tilling the soil. The landed proprietors had no choice but to let their lands in large holdings to capitalists. These men turned the land into pasture, since there was a steady demand in England for grazier's produce. The "cattlemen" prospered, but the population as a whole suffered as fewer hands were needed to care for the stock. There was an abundancy of poorly paid labour on the one hand, and a scarcity of tillage land on the other.

This situation changed by the end of the eighteenth century with the abolition of the Penal Laws, when Catholics were given access to the soil again. As a result of the many wars in which she was engaged, England needed much grain. The landlords were now allowed to rent out their estates in small parcels to the peasantry, who were ably to make a living on very small plots of land. They cultivated grain to pay the rents to their landlords and fed themselves with potatoes. A process of letting and subletting developed, which brought about a progressive fragmentation of the holdings.

Another characteristic feature of this period was the rapid expansion of the population. In 1800 there were about 5 million people, in 1820 6 million. This process continued until about 1850; by then Ireland had about 8 million people of whom the great majority was dependent on the land. Steady employment, wages, and a strip of land to till were within reach of many, and this situation certainly favoured the rapid population increase.

This period of relative prosperity was brought about by Britain's war economy; it came to an end when England ceased to be at war, and when she began to import cheaper grains from America. As a result a fundamental element of Ireland's economic structure was destroyed. The cottiers, as the very small peasants were called, who made up about ninety per cent of the farming population, were no longer able to pay their rents. The big landlords were deprived of their steady and rich incomes and began to clear the cottiers and small farmers from their estates. They turned the land back from tillage to pasture. This meant that labourers lost their employment and tenants were evicted. The small farmers, once fairly certain of long leases, now became tenants dependent on the whims of their landlords. Because of the increased population the situation was worse than in the eighteenth century. Moreover, as England suppressed the development of industry and commerce the towns could not develop as industrial centres and provide an alternative way of making a living. Emigration was an answer to this problem. A steady stream of emigrants, mainly to America, began to develop and reached large proportions after 1850.

The struggle for land now began in earnest. On the one hand there were the landlords, eager to clear their estates from the many tiny peasants with uneconomic holdings, and let the land in large holdings to dairy farmers and graziers. On the other hand there were the masses of cottiers and small farmers, afraid of being evicted when their rent was in arrear. This situation of a diminishing supply of holdings and a steady rising demand for them led to abuses. Under these circumstances the landlords were all powerful; they screwed up the rents to the point that they became extortionate. They also evicted tenants living under marginal circumstances at any moment, as there were always legal reasons for doing so.

It will be clear that under those circumstances a failure of the potato crop, the staple food of the peasantry, would have disastrous effects. This is what happened in the middle of the nineteenth century. The Great Hunger, together with the many evicted peasants who went to America and Canada, diminished the population by about two and a half million. Since then emigration has become a regular phenomenon and it continues to this day.

It needs hardly any comment that various sorts of reactions followed this "grave injustice' of the evictions, which was accelerated by the famine. The peasantry itself reacted at various places in the country by setting up secret societies: Whiteboys, Threshers, Defenders, Shanavats, Rocketies were a few. These associations were local and often short lived. Their purpose was to punish evicting landlords, their underlings, and "grabbers" (people who took up the holding of an evicted peasant). The punishment was often rough: property was burned and people were killed.

The primary aim of these secret societies was to settle local abuses; they had no revolutionary intentions. The secret articles of some even included an oath of allegiance to the king.[1] Nationalism and republicanism had an old tradition in Ireland, but it was town-based and, though nationalistic feelings undoubtedly existed among the peasantry, they were not yet strong enough at this time to form a basis for organization and action.

A "New Departure" started in the last quarter of the nineteenth century, when various groupings and organizations combined to form a strong front against their common enemy, England. This New Departure movement consisted of three elements: the Land League, a country-wide organization of peasants; the Fenian Movement, an amalgamation of previous republican movements; and a number of politicians of the (Irish) Home Rule Party. The founder of the Land League, Michael Davitt, a former Fenian, realized that only by organizing the peasantry on a nation-wide scale together with the Fenians, could they form a strong counter-force against the all powerful landlords. His "the land for the people" ideology attracted many of the population. Together with Fenian leaders and members of local peasant secret societies he founded the first local branch of the Land League. The purpose of the League was to do away with evictions and rack-rents, as the extortionate rents were called, and eventually to found a landed peasantry. Davitt propagated a "moral force" policy against the "physical force" tactics of the secret societies. People should gather in big protest meetings at the houses of peasants who were threatened with evictions. Lists of "grabbers" should be published so that any one would know them and give no help whatsoever to them. Through this ostracizing, grabbers would be prevented from taking up land from evicted tenants. Tenants who were the victims of evictions should be helped financially. The tenants should pay a fair rent but no more than was agreed initially. In this way Davitt hoped to bring the landlords to their knees, it should bring down the rents to normal proportions and prevent evictions. Huge amounts of money were needed for these plans. They came from the numerous Irish migrants in America who hated the landlords bitterly.

Davitt was going to test his doctrine of moral force in county Mayo, one of the poorest parts of Ireland that suffered severely from landlordism. He contacted local leaders, priests, and members of secret societies. The first meeting was a huge protest demonstration. It was held in Irishtown, a place where a number of tenants were threatened with evictions, since they could not pay the increased rents. It was a radical outburst of "the land for the people". The landlord was a Catholic priest. Under the impression of the great numbers of protesting people he withdrew the eviction proceedings and even reduced the rents by 25 per cent. This was the first big victory of the Land League and local branches sprang up throughout Ireland.

Boycotting became another effective weapon of the Land League in the struggle against the landlords. The very word boycott is derived from an Irish case. Captain Boycott, Lord Erne's landagent, would not accept the low rents which the tenants offered him. He demanded full payment and threatened with evictions. As a consequence his servants left him, the shop-keepers refused to deliver foodstuffs, and he was soon completely isolated. He ordered labourers from another place to do the work on his land under military protection, but as Pomfret observes: " ... every pound of potatoes and every turnip cost him a shilling".[2]

In the meantime action was also undertaken on the parliamentary front; a Home Rule Party was formed. By the Act of the Union (1800) Ireland had lost its own parliament and since then Irish representatives had been obliged to go to Westminster. Now, under the leadership of Isaac Butt, many Irish members tried to re-establish their own parliament, and the Home Rule Party was set up for this purpose. Although the bulk of the population was not directly interested in Home Rule, many voted in favour of the party, since it was against England and the extreme eviction policy of many landlords (who belonged nearly exclusively to the Conservative Party, then in power). The landlords were no longer able to exert pressure on their tenants in the polling booth as the introduction of the secret ballot made it possible to vote according to their own choice. Under the strong leadership of Charles Stewart Parnell the forces of the Home Rule Party and the Land League were combined. While Davitt agitated on the home-front against the landlords, Parnell and his party pressed for Home Rule and tenant rights in Westminster. Parnell's party won a great victory in 1880 and many a landlord was defeated as Member of Parliament (M.P.). In those days it was rather expensive to be an M.P. and only landlords could afford to stay for long times in England. Now, with the help of great sums of money, mainly from America, other candidates could be put up; men who had no vested interests in Irish land, and consequently could fight against Irish landlordism. The political and economic power of the land-lords crumbled after their defeat in 1880. With the help of the Home Rulers, the Liberal Party under Gladstone's leadership pushed the Conservative government out of power. A liberal government was formed which began to introduce a series of remedial measures by which the greatest excesses of the Irish land system were removed and a new system eventually estab-lished. Gladstone's first "Act to amend the law relating to the occupation and ownership of the land in Ireland" which had become law prior to his gaining power, in 1870, had stopped evictions by making it costly for the landlord. Another Land Act (1881) gave the tenants security of tenure and fair rents. Other Acts contained provisions enabling the tenants to purchase their holdings with government aid, and later to borrow the whole purchase price from the state. Acts of the first decade of the present century further encouraged land purchase by offering the sellers-landowners a bonus on the purchase money.

Thus by the beginning of the twentieth century landlordism had almost come to an end and the power of the Ascendancy was broken. After a long period of agrarian struggle, the Irish tenantry had become owners of their farms for as long as they could pay the annual interest to the state. Ireland now was a country of peasant proprietors of whom the greater number had but a modest acreage.

THE FIGHT FOR INDEPENDENCE

While the struggle for land had come to an end early in the twentieth century, a free and independent Ireland had not yet been achieved. The country was politically still a part of the British Empire.

Irish nationalism, from the time it first emerged in the sixteenth century, was never exclusively materialistic and did not remain long without some spiritual aim which placed it high above politics and material wrongs.[3] Ireland had for long been preoccupied by politics, often rough politics, but by the end of the last century the old Gaelic idealism gained rapidly in importance. Its inspiration did not primarily come from the peasantry but from the urban population, scholars, historians, poets, all lovers of the Gaelic language and tradition. By the end of the nineteenth century this old Gaelic idealism found expression in nationalistic ideas propagated by new movements, such as the Gaelic League, *Sinn Féin, Cumann na nGaedheal*, to mention but a few. Of all these nationalistic organizations, the Gaelic Athletic Association was virtually the only one which reached the mass of the people. Founded in 1884 with the aim of revitalizing the old Gaelic sports, it spread rapidly to every parish and became an important reservoir for any national movement which demanded active, militant, and loyal supporters.

Although none of these nationalist movements planned armed rebellion against England, all to a greater or lesser extent were infiltrated by an organization which did: the Irish Republican Brotherhood (IRB). The Fenians, as their members are often called, were more interested in politics than in culture. The IRB, which was founded just after the famine, aimed at establishing the national independence of Ireland through armed rebellion. In the early decades of this century this movement became the basis of an Irish underground army, the Irish Volunteers, later called the Irish Republican Army (IRA).

While the star or Irish nationalism was rising, the Home Rule Party, following Parnell's death, split into various factions which competed over small and sometimes personal issues. The driving force of land reform diminished as the farmers got land, often with the help of state loans. A good number even became a rather conservative factor in Irish political life, for they took little interest in the republican ideal.

From 1895 to 1906, the Conservatives were back in power in Westminster and Home Rule was shelved. This party had supported the Liberal policy of land purchase but it was firmly against Home Rule for Ireland. It was an opposition cause. But apart from that, the Conservatives were strongly entrenched in both imperialistic and Protestant England and in the Northern part of Ireland (Ulster), where Protestants dominated. If Home

14

Rule for Ireland were accepted, the Protestants in Ireland feared they might be dominated by a Catholic majority in an Irish parliament. For the Protestants in Northern Ireland Home Rule meant "Rome Rule".

In 1906 the Liberals came back, formed a government, and Home Rule became again a parliamentary issue in Westminster. The Liberals were supported again by the Home Rule Party, now called the Irish Nationalist Party. The Nationalists voted in general with the Liberals, for these were democratic and popular in Catholic Ireland, and their record in supporting humanitarian legislation in parliament was a very creditable one. The leaders of the Nationalist party had hoped to attain victory by means of parliamentary politics through a renewed alliance with the Liberals. But it turned out differently.

In 1912, a Home Rule Bill was introduced which was the subject of furious debate up to the outbreak of World War I. Particularly in Protestant Ulster there was fierce opposition to the idea of a separate parliament for the whole of Ireland. The Bill passed the Commons, was rejected in the House of Lords, but it automatically became law in 1914.[4] Though the Bill was passed at the outbreak of the war it did not come into force until the war was over.

Events now began to take a serious turn. In Ulster the population began to arm a volunteer force as part of a programme to employ "all means which may be found necessary to defeat the present conspiracy to set up a Home Rule Parliament in Ireland".[5] In Dublin the Irish Republican Brotherhood began to organize the National Volunteer Force and a Citizen Army. The numbers of local branches of the Volunteer Force increased rapidly in the country under the threat of Northern Ireland's drilling. The Force was primarily intended as a defensive body. The IRB, however, had always propagated revolution by force in order to make Ireland independent from Britain. It was mainly a Dublin-based organization but a number of branches existed in the countryside as well. Some leaders of the Nationalist party controlled the Volunteer Force, but a split within the organization became inevitable when, with the outbreak of World War I in 1914, the Nationalist party at Westminster joined the Liberals and Conservatives in agreeing to postpone the implementation of Home Rule for the duration of the War. The Force's section wich supported the Nationalist party was convinced that Ireland's full cooperation with England in the war would bind the existing and any future government to Irish autonomy. The IRB on the other hand, was convinced that "England's difficulty was Ireland's opportunity". This extremist wing in the Irish Volunteers broke decisively with the Nationalist party's section when the latter began to campaign in the country in favour of recruiting soldiers for the British army. In January 1916, the Supreme Council of the IRB decided on a rising for April 23 (Easter Sunday), and empowered a military council to plan it. It had chosen this date because the next day would be a Bank Holiday, on which the officers and many soldiers of the Dublin garrison would be at the races, safely out of the way. Arrangements were made for gunrunning from Germany but soon many members of the local branches were imprisoned, betrayed by pro-English "informers". Some of the military council's members argued that it was time to strike now, since the round-ups throughout the country made arrest of the leaders a near-certainty. Others contended that in the circumstances it would be suicidal to go into action now. They sent messages through the country countermanding the insurrection. A smaller faction, however, voted in favour of rebellion on April 23. On Easter Sunday a handful of Volunteers turned up, they captured a number of buildings in Dublin and proclaimed the Irish Republic.[6] England sent a force which bombarded the strongholds for four days, after which the rebels surrendered. Fourteen leaders were executed. One of the commanders who escaped the death penalty was Eamon de Valera, who was to become prominent in the next era of Irish political history.

Although this rebellion was a rather small affair, it served as a blood sacrifice to the country. Because of this "bloody murdering" in Dublin, nationalism became a vital force again in Ireland. This time it aroused people's interest not because of reasons related to the land, but because of England's brutal reactions to their case. Thousands of suspects throughout the country were imprisoned by the British and many others were cruelly mistreated. But all this came to the credit of the now rapidly growing nationalistic movement of the Sinn Féin. This organization became a leading force as a political party. The old Nationalist party now steadily disappeared and made room for this new militant one which was no longer content with mere Home Rule. Nationalism had now got a strong Republican flavour.

Sinn Féin's popularity increased rapidly; it captured seventy-three out of 105 Irish seats for Westminster, which had formerly belonged to more moderate Nationalists. When the World War ended in 1918, it was certain that Sin Féin would claim the right of nationhood for the whole of Ireland at a time when the Allies were setting so many free. They took the step immediately: in 1919 the Sinn Féiners established *Dáil Éireann* (the Assembly of Ireland) and proclaimed *Saorstát Éireann* (the Free State of Ireland).

The Home Rule Act had not been put into effect after the war. England was faced with the problem of Protestant Ulster which did not want to become a small minority governed by a majority of Catholics from the South. But in 1920 the North got its own parliament, and Partition became a fact. It took some time however before the British government handed the South over to the militant Sinn Féin.

The War of Independence, which in fact had started some years before, now began to reach its climax. The Republicans organized a kind of guerrilla war against everything British. The Irish Republican Army (as the Volunteers now came to be called) killed members of the Royal Irish Constabulary police force, burnt police barracks and English military garrisons, and raided ammunition and guns. The IRA shot many people who were suspected of acting as informers on behalf of Britain or interned them

16

at secret places, they burnt big houses of former landlords and killed or mutilated their inhabitants. The IRA "flying columns" were most feared for their ambushes in the countryside.

England decided to meet this ruthless policy of the Republicans in the same way. It sent a select force of ex-officers, the Auxiliaries, and others, just back from the War. Because these latter still wore their emergency dress, they received the name of Black-and-Tans. It was no longer a war between two armies, it was "between expert gunmen on both sides".[7] England realized that it could never win the war and by the end of 1921 a treaty was proposed and signed under English pressure by an envoy of the Irish Provisional Government. By this treaty the Irish Free State was recognized as a Dominion with full powers of self-government.

Although Irish self-government had been restored in 1922 after more than hundred years, it was still a far cry from a peaceful Ireland. Events that occurred in the next few years brought a complete rift in the Free State.

THE CIVIL WAR AND ITS AFTERMATH

Ireland again became deeply involved in war. This time it brought a deep cleavage in the Southern part of the country. The main reason was the difference of opinion over the terms of the Treaty. By the middle of 1921, both camps in the Anglo-Irish war were in search of a settlement. After various negotiations which failed, England proposed a treaty. The Treaty set up the Irish Free State as a self-governing unit with Dominion status, within the British Empire. The representative of the British Crown was to be an appointed governor-general, and the members of the *Dáil*, the Parliament, had to take an oath of allegiance to the British Crown. The Treaty also provided for the right of Northern Ireland to remain independent from the rest of the island and continue to be politically a part of Britain, be it with its own administration of internal affairs. The Free State had to pay land annuities to England.[8] By the end of 1921, England and an envoy of the Irish provisional government met in London and tried to come to terms with each other over the treaty. Britain threatened the Irish envoy with "immediate and terrible war" in case the two parties would not come to an agreement, and under this pressure the Irish representatives signed the Treaty at last. When they came back in Dublin their decision caused great controversy in the Dáil. A number of deputies were for and others were against accepting the Treaty. Those who opposed it, of whom De Valera was the most notable, saw acceptance as betrayal of the 1916 Rising. It meant that partition of Northern and Southern Ireland would be definite, and that Ireland as a whole would continue to be part of the British Empire. In short, that it would not be a free and independent republic. Taking the oath of allegiance to the British Crown was a slap in the face of Irish republicanism. Those deputies who supported the Treaty accepted it as the best possible bargain that could be obtained. In their opinion the Irish army was worn out and the population longed for peace. They hoped to reunite Northern and Southern Ireland through a commission, proposed by England, which would investigate the possibilities of doing so. Moreover, they believed that the country would be helped more by good relations with England, since Ireland was economically still closely connected with Britain. On January 7, 1922, the Dáil ratified the Treaty by sixty-four votes to fifty-seven. On January 10, 1922, the pro-Treaty group formed a government and the anti-Treatyites, led by De Valera, left the Dáil in protest.

There was no single principle that decided which side the population would choose. The IRA element were for the most part soldiers who depended not primarily on the national political or military leaders who had figured so largely in the fight against England. Rather, they followed their own brigade officers. Many of these local leaders with their following chose the pro-Treaty side. One of the main reasons for this was that the newly established government started to build up a paid national army. Many of the old IRAS suddenly found themselves with uniforms, regular pay, and increased opportunities for a better career. This new and unexpected circumstance decided a good number of IRAmen to accept the Treaty. Als aligned with the pro-Treaty side were those people who wanted not so much a Republic or a Free State but peace. Among those the middle classes and many large farmers were strongly represented, since they were in many respects dependent on the British markets for their produce.

On the anti-Treaty side were many politicians, headed by De Valera. Many other IRA leaders and soldiers were against the Treaty because it denied the Republic, recognized the British Crown, and enshrined Partition. Also many small farmers from the poorer areas in the west and south, who were not dependent on English markets, farm labourers, and many of the urban working class followed the anti-Treaty line.

Trouble flared up in various parts of the country when pro- and anti-Treaty sections of the IRA seized parts of towns, English barracks, and ammunition. On April 13, 1922, the Four Courts in Dublin (the former seat of British justice) was seized by a group of Irregulars, as the anti-Treaty element of the IRA now was called. They sent a letter to the Dáil which demanded among other things that the Republic, proclaimed in 1916, should be maintained.

At a peace conference in Dublin the Archbishop of that city tried to mediate between the political sections of the pro- and the anti-Treaty groupings, but the conference broke down. The pro-Treaty section was adamant that a general election must be held on the issue of the Treaty. The Republican nationalists, on the other hand, objected as they thought that the general desire in the country for peace would result in a vote favourable to the Treaty.

However it may be, voting took place in June 16, 1922. The election campaign was a torrid affair. Pro- and anti-Treaty speakers were fired upon, some of them wounded, and in Cork, while the votes were waiting to be counted, a band of anti-Treatyites eluded the armed guard of the counting place, got in through the roof, and altered 4,000 ballots. The results of the election were however strongly in favour of the Treaty: 486,419 votes to 133,864.

In the mean time the situation in the country had deteriorated beyond the point where a peaceful solution was possible. The assassination by some Republicanists of a prominent English politician on the steps of his London home, turned the Irish political struggle into Civil War. England intended to intervene in Ireland as a reaction against this brutal murder but gave it up when the Free State government started shelling the rebels in the Four Courts. By this time the Irish government had formed a war council which dealt with crimes in a ruthless way.

From the bombarding of the Four Courts on June 28, 1922 until May 24, 1923, when the Civil War officially ended, terrible things were done by both sides. In one town a group of Free State soldiers raided various houses and shot suspects. In another town an anti-Treaty group set a booby-trap which killed a number of Treatyites. In reprisal some Free State soldiers chained a group of Irregulars together and set them to dismantle a barricade which had been mined; the men were blown to pieces. All anti-Treaty men in one prison were castrated during interrogations.

Many people became involved in the war not so much because of their political allegiance but for reasons of personal loyalty. One woman, for example, took in some hunted Irregulars, because she knew some of them very well. A personal enemy of hers informed a group of Free State soldiers who shot both her and the Irregulars. In reprisal some relatives of the killed Irregulars strangled the informer and his family, and burnt his farm.

On October 25, 1922, a number of anti-Treatyites elected De Valera as president of "the Irish Republic" and the Irregulars founded the army of the Republic. As part of their policy they intended to liquidate prominent political and military leaders of the pro-Treaty camp. Any Dáil-deputy who had voted for the Treaty, and every member of the Free State army was to be shot. At this time all members of the government lived in government buildings and slept with revolvers by their beds. Both camps undertook actions of shootings and reprisals. Their acts were no longer legal; terror was met with terror.

The Irregulars, headed by De Valera, were in an unfavourable position and they soon became disorganized. They were not only fewer in numbers than the Free State army but were also constantly short of arms and ammunition. It is no wonder then that they had to surrender when a number of their most prominent leaders were shot or imprisoned. The anti-Treaty forces stopped their military operations on May 24, 1923, and with this the Civil War was ended officially.

When the Free State government, the pro-Treaty element, started its administration it had to cope with enormous problems. The two wars had dislocated the country economically and had divided it deeply. Both sides mistrusted each other, and this has bedevilled Irish life upto the present day. The anti-Treaty side regarded the Free State government as an unlawful junta, and its army and police as instruments of a political clique rather than of the nation. Later, when the anti-Treaty element formed the government, the other side in turn regarded all government activity as suspect. This intensified the existing hostility towards authority, which is a legacy of British rule. After the war lawlessness was widespread. The government had to solve this problem first. It established a civil guard, later called *Garda Siochana,* to cope with the crime explosion in a country where it had become normal to settle quarrels with violence.

The government pursued an economic policy of free trade. The country's basis was agriculture; more than 50 per cent of the population were engaged in agriculture. Obviously then, the first thing for a government to do was to make agriculture prosper. The benefits of this would then filter through to everybody else: to the small industrialists, the shopkeepers, the professions. But given the small size of the home market, it was clear that farmers could prosper only if they were able to export. To make the farmers competitive on the British market, it was not only necessary to improve their technical standard, it was also of vital importance to produce as cheaply as possible. For this purpose it was preferable to import maize rather than to produce homegrown feeding stuffs. Again, wheat could better be imported cheaply than produced at home. Thus Irish farming was to be geared to the export market; it should not be protected in its own market. The government pursued the same policy towards industry. It did not protect industry by tariffs since these would cause higher purchase prices for the farmers. Similarly, it kept the rates and taxes as low as possible. All this could be achieved only by extreme prudence in public expenditure, which meant that social expenditure was heavily limited.

The medium and large farmers prospered from this policy; they were supported by the government in their export of meat and dairy products. Numerous other people, however, were antagonized. The small farmers from the West and the South who were not dependent on export, the small businessmen, shopkeepers, labourers, and farm hands were the victims of the government policy. The professions, old age pensioners, and civil servants saw their salaries or pensions reduced as the cost of living rose. As a consequence of this policy emigration, rural depopulation, and unemployment went on as before.

Important developments were also taking place in other sections of political life. An Act in 1925 made employment in the civil service, local government service, and a variety of professional and other occupations dependent on signing a declaration of allegiance to the Free State Constitution. Moreover, the allocation of government grants to local authorities was made conditional on their giving jobs on road repair and similar work to adherents of the pro-Treaty cause. The lines of division among Irishmen, drawn in the war, were hardened through this government patronage and live on to the present day.

Many sections in the country, and especially the ultra-nationalist political element under De Valera, reacted strongly to this pro-Treaty policy. De Valera and his followers realized that they would probably never reach their goal of a free and independent republic by abstaining from the Dáil. However, entering the Dáil would bring them into conflict with the Sinn Féin ideology which aimed at ending Partition by force of arms. This party had already lost out of its ranks the pro-Treaty men who had organized their own party, *Cumann na nGaedheal*, and now another split in Sinn Féin was pending. When the De Valera faction could not come to an agreement with the rest of Sinn Féin, they withdrew from the party and started their own party, *Fianna Fail*, in 1926.

Owing to the widespread disappointment with the present government and particularly, because of its own policy, Fianna Fail attracted many followers, especially from the lower middle and lower classes. In addition to its intention of establishing a free and independent republic, the party also aimed at protection on all fronts in order to revitalize the country's rural economy. But most of all, De Valera attracted many from the farming community by his promise to withhold the land annuities which had to be paid to England as a compensation to the loss of revenue from the land.

During successive elections Fianna Fail increased its number of seats in the Dáil that counted 153 seats in those years (from 44 in 1927 to 72 in 1932), mainly at the cost of smaller parties. The present-day political polarization into pro- and anti-Treaty camps became ever clearer. In the 1932 election Fianna Fail, together with the tiny Labour Party, won an absolute majority and formed a government. From then until 1948 a Fianna Fail government was returned and had either an absolute majority in the Dáil or something quite near to it. Indeed, apart from two short periods of unstable coalition government, it was in power from 1932 to 1973.

On becoming prime minister, De Valera immediately ran into trouble with England. The main cause was the withholding of the land annuities. A period of economic warfare started between the two countries. England retaliated with a bill whereby extra duties were imposed on imports from Ireland. The Irish government responded with a similar bill. Though many small farmers, shopkeepers, small industrialists, and labourers benefited from the Fianna Fail administration, most of the bigger businessmen and the medium size and large farmers, who supported Cumann na nGaedheal, were the victims of the protectionist policy, since their exports to England were curbed.

Fianna Fail's policy brought much good to the nation, but the country had not yet settled down to tranquil, constitutional politics. Violence flared up particularly during elections. It was not unusual for a candidate to surround himself with a team of "bully boys" to protect him against attacks from the other party's candidate. Knuckledusters were even dealt out to the election workers.[9]

Many of the hard core IRA voted for Fianna Fail. Their attitude towards *Fine Gael*, as Cumann na nGaedheal, came to be called, was one of unrelenting hostility. Under the slogan "No Free Speech for Traitors", the IRA systematically broke up Fine Gael election meetings. This provoked a reaction from Fine Gael and the Blueshirt movement was set up. Organized by ex-Free State soldiers, it was a body set up to defend free speech. The men wore blue shirts to recognize each other at election meetings. The movement became particularly popular with certain segments of the farming community as it, too, opposed the paying of the land annuities. While Fianna Fail, of course, had a mandate from the electorate to withhold the annuities from the British government, the Blueshirts proposed withholding them from the Irish government as well. They intervened at sales to prevent the selling of cattle seized at the government's behest from farmers who defaulted on their payments of rates of land annuities, which were still collected though withheld from Britain. The Blueshirts organized campaigns for the non-payment of rates during which furniture and other property was hidden from the bailiff. These incidents, the conflicts with the law and between IRA and Blueshirts, as well as the constant parades, drilling, and various other sorts of obstruction by the rival groupings, gave one the impression of being back in the Civil War period.

Although the Blueshirt movement lasted for only a few years (1931-1935) and then disintegrated rapidly, it has left the country with a fairly strong social and political cleavage, which went far to destroy the old ease and familiarity of rural Irish relationships.

With the eclipse of the Blueshirt movement Ireland's turbulent past was closed. During the next decade and a half De Valera directed his government towards constitutional developments. Though largely autonomous since 1932, the Southern part of Ireland finally became a Republic in 1949, ironically enough under a pro-Treaty administration! At last, after a long period of struggles and wars, the Southern part of Ireland had reached its goal: a free and independent Republic. The country had gained freedom but only at the cost of a deep and bitter cleavage, which has determined Ireland's political, economic, and social relations ever since.

III. A SHORT SKETCH OF PRESENT-DAY IRELAND*

AN EMPTY COUNTRY

A traveller to Ireland is immediately confronted with the consequences of the turbulent past. Ireland today is a thinly populated, almost empty country. The decrease in population by more than one-half since the Famine has left this country – roughly three times the size of Holland, which has a population of more than thirteen million – with slightly less then three million inhabitants.[10] The picture of the country's emptiness is made more extreme if one considers that more than one quarter of the Republic's population is concentrated in the two big cities, Dublin and Cork, of which the latter in actual fact is but a provincial town. Over half of the people live outside towns and villages, scattered over the countryside.

Though Ireland's population has remained almost stable the last few years, rural depopulation continues. Only Dublin, the capital, and some other large towns show an increase, but the smaller towns and villages provide at best a stable demographic picture.

The cause of this rural depopulation is certainly not a low reproduction rate. Ireland has in its rural parts a fairly old population, and the proportion of bachelors and spinsters ranks higher than in any country from which reliable data can be drawn; but the natural increase is high: eleven per 1,000 per annum. The main cause of this depopulation is emigration.[11] Many emigrate to England; since 1926, every year some thousands cross the Irish Sea. It has become a kind of *"rite de passage"* to try your luck in "glamorous England". "Ireland is a reservoir of cheap labour on which Britain can draw at will", as Freeman crisply puts it.[12] Many Irish communities have developed as a consequence in the cities of England. The exiles, as the emigrants are called, as a rule keep in close touch with their relations at home. Often they visit Ireland during Christmas and summer holidays and thus open the horizon of those who stay at home.

Certainly an important key to this demographic problem lies in the failure to provide enough new jobs in the towns and countryside. An unemployment rate of seven to nine per cent is not unusual for rural Ireland. However, this figure gives a too flattered picture if one realizes that many have employment for only part of the year. For the rest of the time they have to look for all sorts of odd jobs, or are dependent on Home Assistance or the dole.[13] Moreover, a good number are dependent on their employers' whims, who can and often do fire them whenever they like. There is a country-wide cry for steady and stable employment.[14] The employment opportunities in the countryside are limited and are even decreasing. Each year more small farms are united and mechanical methods reduce the demand for labour. Moreover, the rural towns would never be able to absorb the many rural migrants. Scarcely surpassing one or two thousand inhabitants each, these towns only distribute, they have no industry. The industrial revolution passed them by. They are the institutional centres of the rural surroundings and consist usually of little more than a main street on which the shops, pubs, the church, a local bank, and the primary schools are located. The town's main function is serving the farming hinterland which provides their "life blood", as Arensberg calls it. The economic ups and downs of the farming community determine the town's position.[15]

AGRICULTURE

Despite the heavy emigration, agriculture is still one of the main pillars of

23

the country's economy. In itself it accounts for about one-fifth of the national income, and for nearly sixty per cent of total exports. About two-fifths of the employed population find their main activity in agriculture. Taking into consideration that much industry is based on agricultural raw materials, the dependency on agriculture for employment is over fifty-five per cent.

Irish farming is primarily a grass farming, with livestock providing the main cash return, primarily in the form of beef and dairy products. In the midlands, the East, and in large parts of the Southeast, the land is excellent and farms in these areas are generally larger than in the rest of the country. Farms in the whole Western part of the country are small.

Although agriculture is of basic importance to the country's economy it is still far from economically satisfactory. The small and often uneconomic holdings still dominate the scene.[16] Particularly on the poor soils of the Western seaboard counties and in some inland areas small farms are the rule. People here live on little more than a subsistence basis. This is a very large problem area.[17] Since these areas in particular have lost so many of their inhabitants through emigration, and are consequently no longer over-populated, it is legitimate to ask: What then is the problem? One might be more surprised to hear that the government in fact stimulates depopulation by inducing small farmers to sell their holdings to make more large ones. The problem is, of course, complex, but according to many experts the root is social and psychological.[18] There is a lack of initiative to improve one's standard of living. There is no incentive to make the home more agreable for the family, as more than sixty per cent of all Irish farms are but run by bachelors, widows or widowers. A farmer's existence is sparse enough, but few seem to want more. He has no family to feed, clothe or educate, no son to inherit a going concern. Moreover, if his land is below a certain rateable value, he is allowed to draw the dole twelve months a year. Even if he has a family, his sons and daughters will leave the dull and dreary country life. Often the future heir does not want to wait until his ageing father is inclined to retire: he goes to England where his relatives and friends have found good jobs. And if he does not take up the courage to leave, the son in his fourties when succeeding his father, will find it hard to get a spouse, and often he will stay bachelor for the rest of his life.[19]

On the industrial front the picture is slightly more optimistic now, despite the fact that Ireland has always suffered from a lack of minerals, especially coal and iron, so vital for industrial development. After a period of protectionist policy, the boundaries were opened to foreign business. They were attracted by offers of factory sites and new buildings, a rich source of labour, grants and alluring tax concessions on all money made by exporting. Besides these foreign industries the Irish government set up a number of semi-state factories. But industry, despite its spectacular growth, is producing only one job for every three to four people who leave the farms. Moreover, the factories are concentrated around Dublin and Cork, in the Shannon area and some other larger towns, thus leaving the rural towns with the same old problem: lack of steady and secure employment.

Almost as typical as the country's rural character and its emptiness is Ireland's religious structure. The Republic is predominantly Roman Catholic; about 95 per cent of the population belongs to this Church, while the rest is made up mainly of Protestants, of which the Church of Ireland claims about four per cent. Although Catholics have always been more numerous, the number of Protestants was previously larger. The Protestant Ascendancy gradually lost its power and their numbers declined; most of them emigrated to England or Northern Ireland.

The organization structure of the Catholic Church in Ireland deviates not much from that in other countries; thus some general remarks will suffice here. The whole island is divided into four ecclesiastical provinces: Armagh, Dublin, Cashel, and Tuam. At the head of each province is an archbishop. The incumbent of the see of Armagh, roughly corresponding with Protestant dominated Northern Ireland, is the Primate of All Ireland, while the metropolitan of the Dublin archdiocese is the Primate of Ireland. The provinces are subdivided into 26 dioceses, an unusually high total for so small a country. Each diocese is headed by a bishop. Together the bishops form the highest authority of the Church, the Hierarchy. This body meets twice yearly at Maynooth; they form in fact the "board meetings" at which the organization of the Church is planned. The bishop, as head of the diocese, is assisted by a number of advisers, canons, who also run the Curia, the administrative headquarters of the diocese. The bishop nominates the canons whose status is mainly honorary. Although they constitute a body they have no special authority or revenues attached to their functions. They all have a parish from which they derive their incomes. Each bishop is in charge of appointing the parish priests and curates within his diocese. The parish is the Church's basic social and territorial unit. Head of the parish is the parish priest; he is assisted by one or more curates in his care of the souls of the Catholic residents in the parish. All these constitute the secular or diocesan clergy, 3,798 in numbers.[20]

There are also the regular clergy, the members of the various orders and congregations who live in their own premises under the discipline of their order and are subject only to the authority of their provincial or superior. They are mainly engaged in charitable and educational functions. A number of them also work abroad as missionaries. The total number of regular clergy, friars, monks, and nuns, who work and live in Ireland, is slightly under 9,000.[21]

In comparison to European Churches the Irish Catholic Church is not a rich body. Before the Reformation (1534) the Church had very extensive possessions and abundant regular revenues from glebe land, tithes, and voluntary offerings from various sources. The Reformation cut off all but the last; the bishops lost their vast domains, some of which extended to 10,000 acres. After the Penal Laws had been revoked and the Catholics rehabilitated, the Church once more began to acquire property, but she was the Church of the poor classes and therefore the contributions were meagre. Consequently, unlike other European Catholic countries, she has scarcely any revenues from landed interests.[22] The Irish Church is not subsidized by the state, but she depends and lives entirely on the generosity of the faithful. This is practically her only source of revenue, but it is regular and generous.[23] The parish priests and curates live from offerings at the church door, from offerings for marriages, funerals and baptisms (the stole fees), and from Christmas and Easter dues. Private mass offerings for the rest of the souls of deceased relatives are another important source of income. Indeed, this often forms the financial basis for many curates. Testamentary donations are also important elements in the incomes of the secular and regular clergy. The bishops and other secular clergy are titulars of one or several parishes (mensal parishes) from which they derive their main source of income. In addition, the bishops receive money from the Cathedratum, an offering from each parish priest in his diocese, from delevering holy oils to the parish priests, and further from a special collection, usually held at the first Sunday in Lent.

As a rule the Irish are faithful, loyal churchgoing Catholics; about 90 per cent attend mass regularly on Sundays. The year around social life is scheduled after the various religious ceremonies of which the May procession, dedicated to the Blessed Virgin Mary, and the Corpus Christi procession in June, are the most prominent. Apart from the Sunday mass there are the monthly Evening Devotions, and further religious summits are Lent, Christmas, and Easter. In the countryside, town and country "stations" are important events. This institution is a survival from the days of the Penal Laws, when Catholics were forbidden to congregate. In those days the priest held mass with a number of people at various places in the countryside. At present the same is done; after a short mass, often at the house of a prominent local person, the faithful have breakfast together.

Going to mass on a Sunday is an important event in rural Ireland. People come from all corners of the parish by bicycle, car, or pony and trap. The chapel, as the Catholic church is called, is more than a religious meeting place. Here people exchange local news, hear the dates of meetings of the various local associations, and they are even told that the dust collector will do his round on Thursday instead of Tuesday. Outside the chapel's gates the voluntary associations hold their annual collections, and after mass the politicians make speeches during election time. When mass is over the population does some shopping and takes some pints of beer before going back home.

Irish religious ceremonial life is rather poor and it stands in sharp contrast to the number of faithful and to the situation in many Southern European countries. The churches are simple and sobre structures, sung masses are rare exceptions and there is no High-Mass exept at Christmas and Easter. Despite their large numbers, the Irish saints do not have a central place in ceremonies and in the lives of the faithful. Apart from Saint Patrick, the national patron saint whose anniversary is celebrated yearly, the many other saints are not much worshipped. There are a few exceptions: in some rural places the local patron saint's birthday is celebrated and individually people will go to its sacred place, a blessed well or so, and pray for all sorts of help. The numerous lay apostolate associations and devotional societies lead an anemic life in many rural communities. They are often dormant until some newly appointed curate brings them to life again for some time.

According to the popular view Ireland is a priest-ridden country in which the Hierarchy dominates all sectors of public life, even the state. As in all stereotypes, there is some truth in this one, but careful examination is demanded. In so Catholic a country one might think the Church would have a privileged legal status, but this is not the case.

Up until 1973, the Constitution contained an article in which "The Church recognizes the special position of the Holy Apostolic and Roman Church as the guardian of the faith professed by the great majority of the citizens."[24] But in actual fact this was a dead clause. Blanchard in dealing with the Church-State relationship observes that there is "separation of the two powers, but interpenetration of the systems, and co-operation".[25] The state has neither a ministry for religion nor a religious department to look after the relations with church authorities. In contrast to practice in a number of European countries, the Irish state does not endow religion or its ministers in any way.

The Church takes no official part in politics, in the sense that her clergy do not sit in the houses of parliament. The parish priests, who played a vital role in politics during the time of English domination, have long since been advised by their superior not to be active in party organizations or during election time.[26] On other occasions and in different circumstances, however, prelates and clergy do clearly and publicly expose their views, which have great influence. Also, there is hardly any politician who will openly oppose the local clergy for fear that it might cost him support. Thus, although officially separated, the Church penetrates in all sectors of life.

Clashes between the Church and the government seldom come into the open, but if they do, one may be fairly sure the Church will win. The famous Noel Brown case illustrates this. Noel Brown, Minister for Health, proposed to introduce a scheme to provide a comprehensive free (state) medical help for mothers and children. The Catholic Hierarchy announced its opposition to the scheme, a major complaint being that the right to provide for the health of children belonged to parents, not to the state.

Religious staff the hospitals, county homes, and similar institutions. Indeed, they occupy in fact more than 40 per cent of the professional class. The managers of the primary schools are the parish priests, who also appoint the teaching staff. Many girls' schools are run by nuns, and the majority of secondary schools belong to religious orders or congregations. The university colleges are also staffed by a considerable number of secular clergy.

Ireland has a state censorship on books, but the Catholic Church has a strong influence in the censorship board. Small wonder then that so many famous writers, like Samuel Becket, James Joyce, George Russell, Sean O'Faolain, Brendan Behan, and Edna O'Brien had to go abroad to publish.

At the local level, the parish priest in rural Ireland exercises a powerful influence over his flock. His wishes often carry the weight of orders. His private life is normally comfortable, no matter what degree of poverty exists in other houses. Nevertheless parish priests can rely neither upon a state pension nor a house of retreat if they retire. They are then dependent on diocesan funds, which in turn are based in some measure on the congregation's generosity. A result of this is that parish priests are often in office until they die, and this slows up promotions, so that as a rule the minimum age of parish priests on appointment is about fifty-seven.[27] Certainly an important effect of this is the fact that many rural parish priests are old-fashioned and reactionary in their behavior and attitudes. As manager of the primary schools and president or chairman of many voluntary associations, the parish priest is a powerful leader, often ruling in an authoritarian way. Though no longer active in politics with a capital P, he is certainly involved in local faction fighting, and not a few coalitions can be grouped according to the stand of the clergy.

NATIONALISM

Many newly independent countries develop nationalism. Much has been done in Ireland in this respect to revive the old Irish or Gaelic language. Irish was made the "official language" when the state was founded in 1922, and in the 1937 Constitution it became "the first official language". At that time, the position of Irish was deplorable. Its use had steadily fallen under Britain's policy of anglicization. Irish was still in use in the Western seaboard counties and in a small part of the Southeast, together known as the *Gaeltacht*. The new government took it up on itself to revive Irish, but particularly the later Fianna Fáil administrations did much in this respect. The language became a compulsory subject in all schools. Henceforth students who failed Irish in their state examinations would fail the whole examination. Those who wrote their papers in Irish would receive ten per cent higher marks. In addition, the government encouraged schools to teach all subjects through the medium of Irish, and many teachers were rashly sent to the Gaeltacht to refresh their knowledge of it. The language was made obligatory for anyone wishing to join the civil service, the police, and the army. Promotion within the public services often is still bestowed less on merit than on proficiency in Irish. Even medical appointments within the public service are dependent on knowledge of the language. The government set up a Gaeltacht department, which is in charge of developing these areas. Various voluntary associations, such as the Gaelic League, *Comhaltas Ceoltóirí Éreann, Gael Linn,* to mention only a few, were established or revived to restore old Irish culture. Signposting, stamps, government printing are now either in Irish or bilingual.

Yet the language movement has not been an unqualified success, and next to Partition, it is the most controversial subject in Ireland.

The two main political parties, Fianna Fail and Fine Gael, blame each other for the failures. During its administation, Fianna Fail was accused by Fine Gael of making the whole scheme compulsory, and therefore unpopular; Fine Gael is said to be involved in subversive activities relative to the revival movement.[28] Despite the many endeavours to make it the first language, only 21 percent of the population is able to speak Irish according to the 1946 Census. However, this statement does not imply that 21 percent of the population speaks Irish in day-to-day contacts.[29] The key to the problem, of course, is that there is no *practical* use for the language. Contrary for instance to the new Hebrew State of Israel, where people came from countries with widely differing languages, most Irish have spoken English fluently for generations.

Nationalism is alive in still another, more underground and militant way. The hard core of it is the Irish Republican Army, the "New IRA". The Army, once a strong arm of the Republicans in their fight against England, was officially abolished after Southern Ireland's independence in 1922. However, since Partition is still a fact, and thus the Republican ideal of a united Ireland completely independent from England was never fully reached, the Republican movement has continued its militant activities.

During its administration, Fianna Fail has always pursued a rather shadowy policy towards the New IRA, an illegal organization since 1922 and sometimes referred to as the Irish Mafia. Certainly, if Fianna Fail had taken a more severe attitude towards the movement, it would have lost much popularity, for in many parts of the country the IRA is still somewhat sacred. Having been a member of the "Old IRA" (1916-24), still gives considerable prestige. Marches are organized to funerals or anniversaries of old comrades-in-arms. On the death of an old freedom fighter, the local and national press recalls in lengths the deceased's activities during the Troubles, as the turbulent period is often called. The Fianna Fail party annually commemorates their late leaders of the war period with big meetings, and so does its main opponent, Fine Gael. Each has its own saints-of-the-recent-past. Thus not only the history of the civil war is kept alive, but also the heroism of physical violence.

Although it is very hard to give accurate information on the organization's numerical strength, some sources estimate a number of some thousands of hard core soldiers, but the number of sympathizers and supporters is much larger.[30] The IRA has its headquarters in Dublin, the names of the leaders are known to many and its newspaper, the United Irishman, albeit branded as illegal is sold openly in shops in Dublin and the countryside. The IRA aims at the destruction by force of foreign influence in te Republic and at ending Partition. In recent times it has undertaken various sorts of obstructive activities in England, and the consequences of its shooting and bombing in Northern Ireland are well-known from the newspapers. Again, its actions on the homefront have never stopped. During 1968 and 1969 , for example, several Germans who had bought big farms on the West coast were threatened with shooting and damage to their property. The government should not permit foreigners to buy land while Irishmen were in need of it. In 1968, lobster fishermen in County Galway were not pleased at the sight of highly equiped Americans coming into their fishing grounds. In August, the American company's equipment was blown to bits. Soon afterwards, the IRA announced that one of their units had been responsible for the explosion. The statement concluded: "The IRA, conscious of its duty as the revolutionary army of the Irish people, will continue to defend the rights of the Irish people, whenever these rights are attacked by foreign opportunists".[31] To conclude the story: The judge who had to handle the case was put under heavy pressure by some regional men of influence and dismissed it.

CHAPTER TWO

Government, Parties, and Electoral System: the Political Setting

I. GOVERNMENT

Central Government

From the start the Irish state adopted the political institutions and procedures of Britain. The state is constitutionally embodied in the *Oireachtas* (parliament) and the president. Parliament has two houses; the *Seanad* (second chamber) and the *Dail* (first chamber). The president and the Dail are elected under universal suffrage, the Seanad by various sorts of groupings and by the prime minister (always referred to in Irish as *Taoiseach*) from a number of panels. The Seanad consists of 60 members and the Dail has 144 seats at present, filled by TDs.[1]

Although the president has not the type of control of the head of state of France or of the USA, his office is more than ceremonial. No bill may become law without his signature. He summons and dissolves the Dail on the advice of the prime minister whom he formally appoints after the Dail has nominated a head of government. Subject to the prior approval of the Dail and on the nomination of the prime minister, the president appoints the members of the government.

Although the president has thus more than ceremonial powers, the prime ministers has always been the most important figure on the Irish political scene. As head of government, he decides whether to call an election before the expiration of a parliament's five year constitutional term. He selects his cabinet ministers and the secretaries to the departments (in effect junior ministers) from amongst the TDs, and he is entitled to ask for their resignation. Also, the prime minister finally determines at cabinet meetings, usually held twice a week, what action the government will take in day-to-day and long-term questions.

Each minister is the head of his department and he is assisted in his administration by civil servants, recruited by open competitive examination.

The Dail is the most spectacular national arena. Its task is, generally speaking, to make laws for the country and to scrutinize policy, but only ministers, some outstanding TDA, usually referred to as "front-benchers" because they occupy the first rows in the house, and staff members of the departments are involved in this work. The majority of the TDs, and this holds particularly for the rural deputies, are only slightly involved and interested in national affairs, and they seldom make speeches in the Dail on those issues. They come, when called by the chief whip to take their seats when it comes to the division lobbies, and almost invariably they vote as the party dictates. Problems of small local and individual nature are more important for these "back-benchers", and most of their time is consumed by solving these problems.

The Dail is often a colourful debating place. Speeches are made in strong local accents, and personal "mud slinging" frequently takes place during the rather undisciplined discussions which stand in contrast to the debates in the English House of Commons.

The Seanad, it has often been alleged, fills the gap caused by the absence of an honour's list in the Irish republic. This body was intended as a platform for the sort of thinking which does not conform with the more rigid party discipline in the Dail. However, this has been a failure; party divisions dominate the scene there as well. Coogan puts it rather bluntly and humorously though in many cases correctly when he compares the Seanad with the catechism definition of purgatory: ... "some souls suffer for a time before they are translated to the Dail; or, alternatively, if they have lost their seats in the Dail, a place wherein they suffer until restored to electoral felicity".[2]

Local Government

Next to central government there is formally also local government. This term is somewhat misleading: Ireland has never had any form of local government based on the grass roots system of the parish, the real local unit.[3] Under British legislation in 1889, many specialized local authorities were concentrated in the major local government unit, the county. Since then, though some important reforms have taken place, basically the system has remained as it was. In addition to this country government, usually referred to as "the county council", there are some other sorts of local authorities: borough councils, borough corporations, urban district councils, and "councils" of town commissioners. These, however, are in effect all dependent upon the county council. An exception is the borough council which has the same status as the county council. Thus, local government has become to a great extent county government.

The republic consists of 27 administrative counties, each with its own council (See Map I.). The members of the county council, referred to as MCCs, are elected by universal suffrage. The number of MCCs per county ranges from 21 to 46, depending on size and number of inhabitants of the county.

Although second in rank from a national point of view, the county council is certainly the most important for the average citizen. It provides the basic environmental services: roads, public health and sanitary services, personal health services, housing, physical planning, public assistance, and a great number of "miscellaneous" services. Moreover, on the fringe of the county councils are two other county authorities, the Vocational Education Committees and the Committees of Agriculture. County councils appoint members to them and they exhibit many of the essentials of the former. It may be evident then, that these services are of very great importance for the population. "They provide citizens with most of the essential help which they are likely to need, literally 'from the womb to the tomb' ".[4]

The administrative part of the local government has one head office per county and a number of regional offices in charge of the day-to-day acitivities. Its senior posts are filled by competitions conducted by the Local Appointments Commission; lower clerical posts are filled by competitive examination or interview board procedures; while labourers and other manual workers are engaged by the professional officers.

Since the foundation of the state, local government has been related to and formally dependent on the central government through the latter's departments, particularly the Department of Local Government. Generally speaking, the central-local relationship is the following: the central government makes the general schemes relative to local matters through its departments of state. The county council acts as government agent for the expenditure of the state grants and local public moneys. So the basic link between people and administration begins at county level.[5]

Despite this relationship of dependency, the council had a considerable measure of power up until recent times. The councillors decide in their various committees how the public money for the year, derived partly from state grants and partly from the local rates, should be divided over the various services, and which areas should get priority in the public schemes.[6] They also had considerable influence in the appointments of local government servants. Up until the early 1940's there was no rigid division between policy making and administration. The council dealt with almost all administration itself. Of course, this gave rise to abuses, such as nepotism, bribery, patronage.

In 1942, this "public scandal" was done away with in principle, by the introduction of the Managerial Act. The MCCs power was curbed. Through this act the county manager and his officers have inevitably become the major initiators of policy, as the well springs of new policy are often to be found to a large extent in the administration of existing services. Besides for some smaller reserved powers, the council approves the estimates and votes the rates, but the manager prepares the budget. On him rests the burden of producing workable schemes and adequate solutions to problems; the council has the final authority.

II. POLITICAL PARTIES

Just as Ireland adopted the British governmental tradition, so too, it developed a party system which could be characterized as polar. Although the republic has always had more than three political parties, the two or three biggest of them took up attitudes of responsibility to form a government for the country, whether they were in power or in opposition. Each party tries to win enough support to form a government of its own leaders. Up until 1973, apart from only two short periods of coalition government, Ireland has shown a picture of stable one party government throughout the years.

The principle cause of the polarization of Irish politics and the emergence of two large parties was the split of Sinn Fein over the terms of the Treaty with England. This has been described in chapter one. It has divided the country clearly until today. The parties which emerged from the Treaty-issue are Fianna Fail and Fine Gael. The Labour Party, third in rank, though the oldest party in the state, has never been able to attract an average support of more than a tenth of the electorate.[7] So it could be maintained that the Irish political system, like that of England and the USA, has many characteristics of a two party system. In local government one finds the same picture; here Fianna Fail and Fine Gael also dominate the scene.

The two large parties do not differ much in outlook; both are rather conservative and each of them has reactionary and progressive elements in its ranks. The differences in ideology are equally small; stemming from the one nationalistic Sinn Fein movement, one could hardly expect something else. Chubb describes the present character of the parties as "non-ideological, broad-based, pragmatic, welfare-oriented . . . engaged in the producer and consumer politics typical of the prosperous and satisfied western communities".[8] However, the images which the parties generated in the past are still alive, and in the rural areas the differences are still often explained in terms of their stands in the past. To many, Fine Gael is the party of the well-off people, the establishment, while Fianna Fail has a broader support.

Although it is impossible to explain party support entirely in general socio-economic or cultural and historical terms, some broad general observations can be made. In former days the division was more clear cut. Fianna Fail, due to its policy, attracted many of the poorer classes: small farmers, landless labourers, urban workers, and some of the lower middle classes. Fine Gael (then called Cumann na nGaedheal) was the party of the Treaty and Commonwealth status, of peace and stability. It attracted the medium size and large farmers, the business community, and the industrialists. This picture has changed. Fianna Fail, which was in office from 1932 till 1973 with only two small interruptions, has attracted many of the commercial and industrial classes. However, as a recently published Gallup Poll has proved, the original appeal of Fianna Fail to the smaller farmers and of Fine Gael to the more prosperous in the farming and business communities are still reflected in the social composition of the parties' support today.[9]

The formal organization of the three parties is about the same, so I can confine the description to one, Fianna Fail. The party is hierarchically or-

34

ganized. At the bottom are the local clubs, based on the parish in rural Ireland, on the ward in the larger towns and cities. The number of these clubs ranges from a few hundred in the case of Labour to about two thousand for Fianna Fail. As a rule the clubs are small, each with about ten to thirty members. The functions of the club are to recruit new personnel, nominate candidates, and fight elections. Activities like political education, fund raising, and even recruitment of new members, which could be considered as basic to winning elections, are not undertaken on any regular basis. Nor does the club *as organization* act to any great extent as an information channel between the people and the centre. Communication is kept alive through the "parallel structure" of the personal networks of local influentials, politicians, and others. Congruent with this is the small number of individual party members.[10] The main activity of the clubs during elections is door-to-door canvassing. Between elections they often become dormant though the principal members are known and if necessary they can be approached. There is a board of officers consisting of a chairman, vice-chairman, secretary, and one or two treasurers. The secretary is usually the key to the whole local organization. Often he is better educated than the others and more active in party work.

All the clubs of a County Electoral Area, which is an administrative unit for county council elections, send three delegates each, including the secretary, to the regional organization. This body must supervize, direct, and advise the local clubs, arrange public meetings, conduct propaganda, and arrange conventions for the nomination of candidates for local government elections. Above this body is the constituency organization. It consists of a secretary and two other delegates from each regional organization in its area. This body has powers and duties similar to the regional one in relation to the selection of Dail candidates at a convention. Each local club is also entitled to send (and actually does so) three delegates who have the power to vote to these constituency conventions. It will be noted that the local clubs have considerable influence in the nomination process. They are preoccupied in getting their own local nominees accepted, for everybody believes and knows that it is important to have a man from the area in office in order to obtain maximal benefit of public money and services. In spite of party leaders presiding over the national and local conventions for the selections of candidates, the centre by no means controls nominations.

The National Executive is the top organization of the party, and its members are elected at the annual convention. Finally there is National Headquarters, the party's central office. It is a tiny body with limited functions and staffed with about five persons, including the secretary. There are no paid party organizers. The central office produces and distributes handbooks, notes for speakers and publicity material during elections, though even then its acitivities are limited.

From this outline it will be clear that though the official organization structure is hierarchical and centralized, the actual system is more "feudal".

Each nominee or candidate is a feudal prince in his own area. With his own small cluster of clubs, and through intricate bargaining, he seeks the support of other nominees in order to oust rivals. Once nominated, he works with club canvassers for his election.

III. THE ELECTORAL SYSTEM

Electoral systems can be studied from two distinct though connected points of view. One can study a particular type in order to see how it influences the way a representative body is composed. Political scientists, among others, have investigated the "mathematics" of the system, the relationship between a particular type of system and the stability and strength of government, to what extent the democratic ideal of fair representation for all groupings of the community is attained in government, and so forth.[11] These are all questions on a macro scale, so to say.

The other angle from which an electoral system can be studied focuses on its implications for the voters and politicians. Questions about the extent to which the system determines the role of the politicians, the way leaders recruit support, the degree of the electorate's involvement and interest in politics, the relationship between individual politicians and voters are all covered when studying an election system from the second angle. They all deal with politics *not* in the highly institutionalized arenas of the Dail and county council but with politics at the grass roots. To my knowledge this field has hardly been explored in a systematic way; even Irish authors have paid little attention to this field.[12] The first range of questions is less important for my purposes. The second, however, is of great importance as it bears on politics behind the scenes.

The Mechanics of the System

Before expounding how and to what extent the Irish election system determines politics in Ireland, I first give a description of its mechanism as many readers may not be familiar with it.[13] In combination with universal suffrage the Irish have an election system of proportional representation by means of the single transferable vote, here shortly referred to as PR. It is operated for Dail, county council, and Seanad elections. The country is divided into multi-member constituencies for the Dail, reliable to revision each twelfth year so that the ratio between the number of seats and the electorate stays roughly the same. For local government elections each county is divided into County Electoral Areas, CEA for short, also multi-member units. Thus, TDS are elected from the constituencies and MCCs from the far smaller CEAS. The organization of elections is in the hands of a Returning Officer, a local government official. He accepts nominations, arranges polling places, election machinery and personnel, he presides over the poll and supervises the count. A candidate is not required by law to reside in the constituency or CEA he contests though almost all do. However, he may not contest in two or more districts. On the polling day at the booth each voter receives a ballot paper with the names in alphabetical order of all candidates standing in his district. There are always more candidates on each paper than seats to be filled. In a "five seater" as a five member district is popularly called, there may be as many as 15 names on the ballot paper. Each voter then may give as many preference votes as there are names on his ballot paper. He ranks them according to his own personal choice; "1" against the name of Mr. X, his first preference, "2" against Mr. Y, and so forth. When the pollings is finished all ballot boxes of a particular area are opened simultaneously and the votes are counted. As each paper is opened a single vote is given to the candidate to whom the voter gave first preference. The first count is ended. A candidate is declared elected if he has obtained a certain proportion of the total number of valid votes cast. A quota is calculated for this.[14] Now, if a candidate is elected and received more than the quota, his surplus is divided among those mentioned on his papers as second preference. On the other hand, if, as is more common, none of the candidates obtained the quota on the first count and consequently none is elected, the candidate with the lowest number of votes is eliminated and his votes are redistributed in accordance with the second preferences. This means that in effect most candidates are elected by means of second or lower preference votes of others. A fair number of first preferences is necessary to prevent elimination in the first count, but second and lower ones are vital to get elected. The whole process of transferring surpluses or votes of eliminated candidates goes on until either the total number of seats is filled or, and this often happens, only two candidates are left over, none of them with a quota In that case the candidate with the highest number of votes is declared elected without having reached the quota. Often eight or nine counts are made, sometimes as many as 15.

Fair Representation

Although it is not my intention to judge whether PR is good or bad, it is interesting to mention the current debates when PR is compared with other types of election systems. With the help of this background information we can see then to what extent politics in Ireland is determined by the type of electoral system.

Britain introduced PR in Ireland in 1918 to safeguard minority rights, particularly those of the Protestant minority. Another reason was that many people ware dissatisfied with what they considered the manifest imperfections of the British system. The main criticisms were tyranny of the parties over both the individual politicians and the rights of the voters, great chances of a government ruling with a minority of support in the country, and of frequent changes of government. In 1923, the Free State government accepted PR as the best of all systems and embedded it in the constitution.

The basic assumptions underlying the acceptance of PR were, to give fair representation to all shades of political thought, greater freedom of choice to the individual voters, and less power to the parties as such.

These principles are not realized by the majority, or first-past-the-post system, used in Britain and other countries. In this system each constituency returns one candidate and each voter has a single or straight vote. The imperfections of the majority system will be clear from an example. In a constituency of 46,000 electors the shares of the votes for each party are like this:

Conservative Party – 20,000 votes
Labour Party – 19,000 votes
Liberal Party – 7,000 votes

The Conservatives win the seat. This result may be considered as fair or unfair, depending on what the 7,000 Liberals thought of the relative merits of the Conservative and Labour candidates. However, we do not know this, for under the majority system the voters cannot express their second preferences; they have a single, *non-transferable* vote. This means that in fact the 7,000 Liberals and the 19,000 Labour electors have wasted their votes. They also have enabled a minority of their fellow constituents (20,000 out of a total of 46,000) to elect their M.P. If this pattern repeats itself in other constituencies it can result in a government that is elected by a minority of the voters. This is exactly what happens sometimes in England. If the multi-member constituency and the single transferable vote were used, the elector could indicate his order of preference, therewith ensuring each grouping in the community of a representation proportionate to its following.

Various countries use a mixture of the majority and the Irish PR system in the form of a party list system. In this the voter can give his (straight) vote to a party, but he can also indicate his views on other matters, particularly on the relative merits of individual candidates *within* his chosen party. However, as Lakeman observes, the various types of list systems "have this feature in common: that every vote (whether or not given in the first instance to an individual candidate) is, automatically and without further reference to the voter's wishes, added to the total of the (party) list in which that candidate appears".[15] So even in this system the party's powers are great and the individual voter's influence is curbed.

The major criticisms of protagonists of the Irish PR of both the majority and the various types of list systems are: 1) Fair representation is not reached and the voter does not have the democratic power necessary to see his preference elected. 2) The voter is primarily concerned with the support of a party. 3) Most of the time the link between the electorate and the individual politician is not close; often the voters do not even know him. 4) The party leaders decide which candidates will be nominated and thus the electorate has hardly any influence on the nominations.[16]

What about the Irish PR? For this system to give perfect proportionate results, the whole country would have to be treated as one great constituency. If we assume that this were practicable then a party with 15 per cent of the votes would obtain 15 per cent of the seats, and a party with four per cent of the votes would get four per cent of the seats. But of course, it is highly impracticable to treat the whole country as one great constituency: the list of candidates, arranged in alphabetical order and without reference to their party affiliation, would be so long that the voters would be bewildered. The larger the constituency the better the chance for smaller parties to win a seat. In a five-member district it must obtain about one-sixth, and in a three-member constituency one-fourth. In Ireland in 1923, there were one nine-member, three eight-member, five seven-member, nine five-member, four four-member, and eight three-member constituencies. Large-member constituencies thus dominated. Since then, the size of the constituencies was twice reduced, and now there are only two five-member, 14 four-member, but 26 three-member constituencies. This means that Ireland is now farther away from the ideal of maximal proportionality. The present set up heavily favours the larger parties, and it represents a compromise between PR and the majority system.

PR Incompatible with Stable Government?

It has often been maintained that PR militates against strong government and the development of a strong two-party system. Although the reasoning behind this seems to be sound it is contrary to experience. In the three countries which use PR, Ireland, Malta, and Tasmania, the number of parties is not great and in all of them a two-party system, or better a system of two-party groups in which two great parties dominate, is the rule. Lakeman has shown for countries which changed to any system of proportional representation that there was no real increase in the number of parties.[17] On the other hand, Duverger observes that no country with any variety of a system of proportional representation has a real two-party system, whereas this is the rule under a majority system.[18] There seems to be a confusion in the debates on this subject. The technical implications of PR are one thing, but the political climate in the country might very well militate against the tendency of party multiplication.[19] This is very clearly so in Ireland. The conflicts over the Treaty-issue and later political developments have brought a cleavage in the country resulting in only two great parties. Moreover, under these circumstances a multiplication tendency is imcompatible with small-member constituencies, and as we saw before, these dominate in Ireland at present. One thing, however, is certain: PR facilitates the breaking away of *individual* politicians from parties, whereas this is nearly impossible under a majority system.[20] Under the PR system an independent candidate may win a seat with the support of the second preference votes of other candidates, whereas his colleague under the majority system lacks these "extra" votes.

It is quite usual for Irish politicians to leave their parties and stand as independents. But most of the time this is a temporary phenomenon and independents eventually become incorporated again into one of the large parties. So in *this* way PR certainly facilitates factionalism, rivalry, and instability *within* the parties.

PR, *Individual Competition, Infighting, and "Messenger-Boys"*

More can be said about the Irish PR, particularly relative to the nature of political competition, the politician's role, and the relation between leaders and their electorate. The existence of multi-member districts and the principle of the single transferable vote, each of these separately, are important in this connection. In each constituency the parties put up as a rule more candidates than they expect to be elected. They do this to cover the area as well as possible. The exact numbers are determined by the size of the votes each party can obtain, and this is based on the results of previous elections and various sorts of "backdoor" information. Party competition in Ireland, as has been observed, is of a clear polar nature; the contests are mainly between Fianna Fail and Fine Gael. This means that in all constituencies each has a number of candidates. For the voters there is a limited choice in parties, but the range of candidates from which to choose within each party is greater. This in its turn implies that not only politicians from different parties compete with one another but also candidates from the same party. A politician can compete with candidates from another party by offering a more attractive policy, but he cannot do so towards ones from his own party, because these are all bound by the same programme. The only way he can outdo the latter is by building up a greater reputation as a worker for his electorate. This is very much the case: Irish politicians are primarily engaged in rendering services to their voters. Generally speaking, they are intermediaries between their constituents and the various offices of local and central government. I give a detailed description of their role in the next chapter. Several authors have stressed that competition between party colleagues is often more extreme and that they are a more serious threat to each other, be it all behind the scenes, than between candidates of different parties.[21] This holds not only for large districts but also for small ones. In a "three-seater" one major party will win two seats and the other one.

One may object that fellow party candidates must cooperate because under the PR system they need each other's second and lower preferences to be elected. Indeed, Boissevain observes that one of the main tactics of Maltese politicians is to exchange second preferences.[22] To some extent this holds also for Ireland. However, a candidate is *never sure* that his party colleague will keep his promise; he might promise his second preferences to more than one colleague. Indeed, he might even try to induce the electorate to give no more votes than just one for him.[23] Moreover, it is incorrect to look upon competition for voters as something taking place during election time only. In actual fact it is a long process of cultivating support *between* elections; the votes are only harvested, so to speak, at election time. The politician must not only cultivate his first preferences himself, but to a great extent his second preference votes as well, and whenever possible, try to convert these into first preferences. Furthermore, infighting, instead of cooperation, is stimulated by the procedure of putting up more candidates than can be elected, as described above. Contrary to the Maltese situation, in Ireland the "mock candidates" or dummies are more than only vote-ga-therers for their superiors who, in return for second preferences, will procure some favour for the dummy. The "sacrificial lambs", as the dummies are called in Ireland, can be a serious threat for the sitting politician. For Dail elections MCCs are nominated usually next to the sitting TDs, and these persons have already developed a considerable record of services for the electorate. They definitely may outvote a sitting TD. Finally, a TD may exchange second preference votes with an MCC and thus try to oust a colleague TD whom he considers too strong. So there is not only competition between sitting politicians but also between them and MCCs, all of which intensifies infighting.

The existence of multi-member districts stimulates the politicians to play the role of intermediaries for still other reasons. In this type of district the electorate can go for help to more than one politician. This implies that each politician has more work to do for his voters than if the constituency were a single-member unit (which is naturally much smaller). However, not only the voters take the initiative and ask for help, the politicians also stimulate this. Indeed, they sometimes create problems which they later claim to have solved, and by doing this they try to build up more credit with the electorate in order to "catch" more votes. It is not for nothing that Chubb portrays the Irish politicians as *"hawkers* of local interests".[24] It will be evident that under these circumstances politicians must be well informed about local problems, and they must have close contacts with the electorate. Most of the Irish politicians are local men, that is, they work and live in their districts. There is hardly room for "carpet-baggers" in the Irish situation. All this gives politics in Ireland a parochial character, which is also illustrated in the relative unimportance of party programmes.[25]

The mechanism of the single transferable vote itself promotes the role of intermediary from the side of the politicians and pragmatism from the voters. First preference votes are basic to the candidates; they prevent them from being eliminated in the first count but most politicians are elected on later counts. This means that second and sometimes third preference votes are also of great importance for them. As an informant put: "Today there is a rat race for second prefs in holy mother Ireland". A major way to obtain these votes is by rendering services to as many people as possible, and this again promotes the politicians playing the role of "messenger-boys". The voters are pragmatists under those circumstances. PR gives them the opportunity to decide the order of their preferences. The parties do not and cannot dictate that order, whereas under the majority and most of the list systems the party top decides who will become nominated and elected. Now, if the voters can mark their own order of preference it will be evident that they are led by pragmatic considerations. That is, they will give a higher preference to a candidate with a long record of services (or whom they *think* he has such a record), and a lower preference to a "smaller" man.

This pragmatism, however paradoxically it may be, does not lead to much voting across party lines, though the electoral system fully permits this. For Dail elections the majority of the voters give their first and following preferences mainly to candidates of the same party. The wounds and enmities originated during the Troubles and the civil war and its aftermath still seem to be important. For local government elections the picture seems to be slightly different. Here local personal contacts may sometimes override party loyalty. It is not unusual that a very popular Labour MCC obtains many votes from people who would probably never vote Labour in Dail elections.[26] Thus, in addition to factors mentioned above, this Irish pecularity of voting along party lines strongly promotes intra-party competition; indeed, it makes it to a predominant feature of Irish politics.[27]

CONCLUSIONS

From the preceding pages a picture has emerged of a very parochial Irish political system. This parochialism is reflected in the strength of local factors and personalities, in the strong influence of local political clubs, in the importance of local government in people's estimation, and in the priority in the public mind of the politician's role as a contact man. This parochialism is undergirded by the electoral system which strongly stimulates competition between individual politicians for voters, and induces the electors to be pragmatists in their electoral behavior. In the specific Irish circumstances of a political polarization, two large parties dominate the scene, the electors vote mainly along party lines. Consequently, competition between candidates of the same party is as a rule stronger than between politicians of different parties, be it that these processes are mainly behind the scenes and cover longer periods than just the election time. The following chapters take a closer look behind these scenes. They examine in detail the nature of political competition, the politician's role, and the way he builds up a following.

Part two: Politics in the Constituency

CHAPTER THREE

The Political Elite: Tasks, Personnel, and Prizes

I. TASKS

The two types of politicians, the TDs and the MCCs, have as their main official tasks legislation and scrutiny of expenditure respectively. Political practice, however, is at variance with the law. Making laws for the country, and amending and criticizing them, is left to the ministers, some front-bench members of the parties and staff officials of the departments. The ordinary rural TD – and more than two-thirds of the TDs are rural representatives – is only slightly involved and interested in national affairs. On the local government level the bulk of the work is done by the county manager and his staff, and most of the time MCCs do not interfere with his financial policy.[1]

The politicians' actual work consists mainly, if not exclusively, of looking after the personal and local interests of their voters. The professional politician is an intermediary mainly between his voters and the various administrative units of local and central government. He himself looks upon this as his main task and so do the people. When he was questioned on this point by the Attorney General, one politician declared that "it was in the very nature of a deputy's work to interview departmental officials on behalf of his constituents".[2] Politicians are obliged to do this "home work", as it is popularly called, whether they want it or not. If they do not do it they may well lose their support, and this in fact has happened various times.[3] Even ministers, who are also TDs, regularly go to their constituencies and hear all the complaints and problems.

A politician's task – providing answers to the questions of his people – includes seeking information, grants, benefits or rights, expediting a case, granting favours, jobs, licences, renting a county council cottage. Most of these questions lie within the sphere of local government administration though the offices of the central government departments are frequently bothered with questions as well.[4]

The popular word for asking for help is "pulling strings"; the people pull the string, that is the politician, and he will try to obtain what has been asked for by influencing the official in whose sphere of competence the matter lies. As a rule people have a keen idea of the amount of "pull" of the various politicians in their area. TDs are generally looked upon as having the biggest pull, they are the "number-one men" in the area; MCCs are considered to have less pull. Local jokers told me, to show the nation-wide nature of this phenomenon, "It's not for nothing that our national emblem is the harp". The following story also illustrates the important place that pulling strings has in the eyes of the public. When the statue of the English queen was removed from the square of Leinster House (the building where the Dail meets), people discussed which national emblem should be put in its place. It was widely joked that there was no need for another emblem. The word PULL was written in large capital letters on the entrance doors to Leinster House.

The voter's questions often reach the politician directly, that is, people visit him and explain their problems. In other cases they, or some local friend or relative, send him a letter in which they inform him of their complaints and problems. "Hearing confessions", as this visiting of politicians is usually called, is more or less institutionalized. Apart from certain days when they are at home or in a party office, during which they are available to their electors, the TDs and MCCs make regular tours along all the local political clubs in their electoral area. Anybody can then come and see them. Regularly one sees in the newspapers announcements like this one: Con Doherty, TD, MCC will attend at ... on Saturday, February 1. Everybody welcome. But of course, the good politician is in fact always at the disposal of his people. One sees him during door-to-door election canvassing, at hurling and football matches, at the horse races, outside the church, and at other public meeting places. He is at the beck and call of his people, listening carefully, writing down all the problems in his "prayerbook", as people sometimes call his note book, and promising to do all he can. As I often made notes in my small pocket note book during my field work, some people gave me the nickname of "our local TD".

All this work costs him very much time. Small wonder then, to hear people comment that the seats in the Dail and the county hall are so often empty. TDs and MCCs, instead of being in the house, are in the libraries, writing piles of letters, or interview civil and local government servants for their electors. It is not unusual for a politician to receive about 75 questions weekly.[5] And he has to deal with almost all the correspondence himself. Letter-writing is probably a greater chore to Irish politicians than to any other representative in the world. One TD for a rural constituency told me that he spent two-thirds of his political working time on his correspondence. Another said he wrote 150 letters a week, and a third gave the figure of 30 a day. A survey from the newspaper The Irish Times came to the conclusion that some 140 politicians between them write over one million letters a year.

Most of the politician's interventions on personal matters and many on local district business are made by letter to the county manager, or by a visit to the county offices. Both MCCs and TDs are frequent visitors, well known to the officials, and they often have personal contacts with them.

When the politician hears from an official about a decision of a case or about the state of a pending application, he may well ask "a letter to that effect". To facilitate the politicians most of the offices send out their replies with carbon copies, and the politician sends the carbon copy, together with some small personal note, to his client.

The politicians intervene not only at local government level but also in central government matters. This, of course is especially true for TDs who spend three days a week in Dublin, when the Dail meets. Their activities there are regular and continuous in any department dealing with services involving individual applications or local services. They take up all sorts of matters; housing and agricultural grants, land redistribution, compulsory purchase, old age pensions, and other social welfare benefits. The departments frequented most often are Local Government, Health, Agriculture, Lands, the Gaeltacht, and the Board of Works.[6] Where payments of grants are concerned interventions are very frequent. The office of Public Works is a case in point; here about 45 letters per day were going out to politicians in July 1962.[7]

The politician's interventions are of course not confined to these governmental offices. They make representations for their clients also in shops, factories, and private offices. They also contact locally influential persons like priests, doctors, school teachers, and lawyers. One university professor told me that he was constantly bothered by politicians who came "to put in a word" for children of constituents.

Pulling Strings: Fact or Fiction?

Does it make any difference whether or not a person asks a politician to intervene on his behalf at a particular office? A simple yes or no answer cannot be given. Much depends on the specific cases in question, but some general points can be mentioned. To begin with, people ask for a wide range of items and services but in most cases the politicians cannot grant the requests themselves. In former days, the politicians had far more power than they have now. The MCCs decided how public money should be divided over the various local services, and which areas should get priority in the public schemes. They also had considerable influence in the appointments of local government personnel. This has changed: the county manager and his staff now make the policy, the MCCs give their final approval, but in fact most of the time they leave it to the manager. Again, the ordinary TD has no influence at all on policy making in the various central departments. Although questions on jobs rank high on the list of the politicians, they have no longer a direct say in this matter either.[8] All senior local goverment posts are filled by competition, conducted by a single Local Appointments Commission, and for the central bureaucracy by the Civil Service Commission. In some other cases the county council or its committees decide who will be appointed: rate collectors, some officers in the vocational education service, the local agricultural services, and some others. The professional officers engage labourers and other manual workers, and the politicians often approach them for jobs.

In addition to the reduced statutory powers, also fixed rules for all sorts of items and services have limited the politician's leverage; rules that can only be violated with difficulty. For instance, the politician can no longer at will arrange for the county council to rent its cottages to his clients. Only persons under a certain minimal income are entitled to rent a cottage. In this and practically all cases the politician is curbed by the rules. However, this does not mean that he can do nothing at all, that he will stay idle. He still makes use of his influence by manipulating the rules and the concrete situation in his own and his client's advantage. This is of course a far more subtle business than the "straight pull" of former days, as the next case will illustrate: A businessman in Milltown wanted to build a garage and petrol station on a piece of land of his own, on the fringe of the town. The land which bordered the main road, was situated just outside the 30 miles per hour speed limit, and according to the 1963 Planning Act no petrol station may be built there because of the speed of the main traffic. The businessman, a *Taca* payer who knew about these regulations, went to his local Fianna Fail TD whom he had helped financially and otherwise during elections, and asked for his help.[9] The TD went to the Department of Local Government and succeeded in getting the 30 M/h signpost repositioned about half a mile farther on the road.

This is not a case of illegal practice because the Milltown development scheme had just been accepted and consequently the businessman's land fell within the townboundaries now. In this and similar cases the politicians, far from violating the rules, make use of these rules and combine them in an advantageous way. He might speed up a decision by urging that a particular family is in dire need of another cottage because the one in which they live now is in a dangerous condition. This might bring the family higher on the priority list.

On some matters the politician's intervention is unnecessary, for the decisions are automatic ones. At a certain age, people automatically are entitled to an old age pension. Yet they still go to their local TD and ask for his help. In those cases he only writes a letter to the department concerned and sends the answer back to his client.

In other cases it only *seems* that the politician has power and that his intervention is effective, but in actual fact the result has to do with the differential access to new information. As a rule the politician hears first of a new service for the town. He can manipulate this knowledge to his own advantage and give the population the impression that he really has "pull". I was able to trace the course of a case of his type. Sean Dwane, TD, MCC attended a meeting of a local Fianna Fail club. After the ordinary business he hemself suggested in a very subtle way that a particular place in the town was dangerous; the school children crossed the road there and traffic caused a lot of accidents. There should come some sort of a safeguard. Some members suggested a zebra crossing. Dwane said he would do his best. Some weeks later, he informed both the local club and the press that he had a letter from the Department of Local Government stating a zebra crossing would be built in the town within about two months. Later I heard from a staff officer that a plan to extend the zebra crossings to rural towns had been approved about five days before Dwane had brought the matter to the local club. Nevertheless, the local population was convinced that Sean had done "a grand job for the town".

Thus, whether or not a politician has power and influence, the people often think he has, and in many cases they have the idea that "there is no harm in trying". And, of course, it is in the politician's interest to keep this image alive. To attract voters implies doing favours for them, or anyway, to let them think that favours are done or can be done.

Sometimes though politicians really do have the powers not only to provide people with items or services but also to withdraw favours previously given. This power was publicly illustrated in a case where some local leaders objected violently to the closing of an underpopulated rural primary school. A politician who had been one of the proposers of the closure warned the objectors to stop their obstructionist activities. He had "their jobs in the palm of his hand", he said. They did not obey and some days later, they lost their jobs.[10] Whether pulling strings is fact or fiction, whether it has any success, depends in very many cases upon a number of circumstances. It depends on the politician's position relative to the case, on his relationship with those who have the final say in the matter, and also upon the relationship between the politician and the client, and between the client and the person who takes the final decision. The positional factor determines to a great extent the effect of pulling strings and stems from the individual politician's particular role. As an intermediary he brings people into contact with each other, directly or indirectly. When he helps a person he can later ask his help in another situation for another person. These transactions are based on credit; A will help B either because A owes some help or B might be able to help A in the future. The politician's power is that *he* decides at what moments and to what extent he wants to use his credit. His main object is to build up as much credit with as many people as possible. The more widespread his credit, the more effective his influence is, and the better he can help his clients. To conclude this section I give an example of the ways this positional factor conditions the effects of pulling strings.

Ted Moynihan, a Fianna Fail TD, has good connections with some businessmen. One of them, Rick Regan, deals in building materials. Regan always helps Moynihan during election time. He gives money for his election fund, provides cars for the canvassers, and he often drives the politician round the area during elections. Moynihan on his turn is often able to provide Regan with contracts from the county council for the repair of sewage systems and the delivery of various sorts of pipes. He succeeds in this with the help of the county engineer who himself obtained his job through Moynihan's influence. These two persons are of vital importance to Moynihan's political work because they can provide him with jobs for his voters. Regan always informs Moynihan of vacancies in his business, and the engineer gives him first option on county council manual jobs. Moynihan is known as the "fella with big pull" for jobs.

In a nearby town there is a big factory which always attracted many personnel from Moynihan's area. However, up until recently this politician had never been able to provide his clients with jobs there. This source had been closed to him and all jobs were given to a Fine Gael colleague who had a very good contact man high up in the factory. This man died in a road accident. Moynihan was able to get the vacancy filled by a nephew of his through contacts with the official from the Department of Agriculture, a Fianna Fail man who is charged with appointing the higher personnel of this semi-state factory. Since then he obtains a considerable share of all appointments in the clerical and labour sections of the factory through the channel of his nephew.

Thus, it will have become clear that pulling strings is both fact and fiction.

Irish Politicians as Brokers

In the preceding pages it has been demonstrated that the Irish politician's first and foremost task is that of an intermediary. He is the link between the electorate and the various offices of local and central government, and other bodies. Helping people on a particularistic basis for support or protection has often been called patronage. Sociological literature describes it in terms of making use of public resources for private purposes. Patronage, however, is a very wide concept which embraces a range of activities that should not be lumped together. Mayer and Boissevain distinguish patronage from brokerage on the point of differential access to resources which lead to differences in tactics and strength.[11] The authors point out that a patron has first order resources, that is, he controls land, jobs, scholarship funds directly. These resources are limited and consequently the following that a patron can attract on the resources is limited. A broker, on the other hand, has second order resources; he deals in strategic relations, in promises to contact other persons who control the first order resources that his followers desire. As a result of this extra link the "vagueness" is more real; the broker's strength can less easily be checked, and consequently he will attract a greater following. Of course, one must be careful to realize that patronage and brokerage are closely related; they are roles and not actual individuals. An individual may play both roles, even at the same time, but it will have become clear that the Irish politician is predominantly a broker. He deals in contacts with persons strategically situated in relation to first order resources. His basic aim is building up and expanding a network of contacts with these persons for people who, in return for his efforts on their behalf, might be induced to vote for him.

It is time to ask now: Why is brokerage so all important in Ireland? One explanation, often given, is of a historical nature. Authors like Chubb and Whyte point out that Ireland has a long tradition in this respect.[12] They have described particularistic political behavior for the country's past in general terms of patronage, and they explain it by referring to Ireland's previous economic and social structure. This type of explanation certainly has its value but it fails to answer the question: Given the disappearance of the cause, why does the effect continue to exist? Apparently then, we must seek for some other factors which might explain the phenomenon's continuation.

Boissevain and Kenny, among others, have studied patronage in Sicily and Malta, and in Spain respectively.[13] For Sicily Boissevain emphasizes that there was a need for it as people required protection against violence, insecurity, and exploitation. Both authors stress the importance of Roman Catholicism as a determining factor. According to them values and norms from the sacred world have spread out, so to say, to the other more profane sectors of life. Catholicism with its hierarchical organization and the role of the saints as intermediaries between God (the great patron) and the mortal people, stands as a model for more profane actions and gives a strong ideological basis for other social systems. One could use this idea also for predominantly Catholic Ireland. Indeed, it is striking to find more or less institutionalized words and practices as hearing confessions and prayer book in the political sphere. But however striking this correlation may be, both the link with Catholicism and the need for protection are explanatory insufficient. An explanation in terms of human needs contains an element of finality; a final explicans for behavior is given. An explanation in terms of a value system, like Catholicism, which Kenny explicitly gives, is also insufficient. It seems to suggest that people behave in a particular way *because* they value highly the rules for behavior. Again then, this approach does not provide an acceptable explanation for the importance of brokerage.

Various authors have pointed at the correlation between the occurrence of brokerage and the degree of integration of the various parts of the society into the wider whole of the nation or the state.[14] Silverman, for example, has traced this process of integration for Central Italy.[15] She observes that brokerage develops with the partial penetration of the country's central authority into the rural areas. The local population at that stage does not know how to reach the centre's bureaucracies and consequently needs the help of some intermediary. Special persons emerge, owing to their status or some other characteristic, who have a foot in both the local and the central camps. Silverman points out that brokerage will disappear, or at least assume a crippled form, with increasing integration, that is, when the centre increases its (bureaucratic) penetration into the rest of the country.

Much of what Silverman describes for Italy holds true for earlier phases of Ireland as well. However, the odd thing is that despite increasing interference of the centre into the citizens' lives, brokerage does not disappear from the Irish scene. Indeed, as the centre's services increase the Irish politician appears to become busier playing his brokerage role.[16]

This paradox can be solved if one considers integration not exclusively in terms of increasing bureaucratization from the centre. Integration is a two-way process, between at least two parties. It does not automatically follow that increasing centralization results in the population making *direct* use of the services of the centre. They might well use brokers to that end. There may be structural resistance that prevents the population from interacting directly with the centre. Brokerage militates against integration. Indeed, it is of vital importance for the Irish politician to keep integration partial; if it increased he would lose his brokerage role.

Now we seem to have arrived at the point where the arrow of causation is turned. Instead of arguing that brokerage is the effect of partial integration and that it will disappear with increasing integration, I suggest that brokerage, at a certain stage of societal integration, causes partial integration. But this means that I must give an explanation for the continuation of brokerage and in fact also for the partial integration.

I think the basic cause is the electoral system that functions in a specific political climate. Contrary to other electoral systems, the Irish PR gives the voter very much power over the election of individual political candidates. He has one vote but with this single vote he can arrange his order of preferences and express them on his ballot paper. As a rule he will give high priority to the candidate who has shown his capacities in the past, or whom he thinks will best look after his interests in the future. It will be evident that the elected politicians will do their utmost to improve their image and that they will compete with each other on this point. This is particularly so because several operating politicians compete with each other in a system of multi-member constituencies. Moreover, since the Irish vote predominantly along party lines, particularly fellow party politicians compete with each other for voters. These politicians, of course, cannot attract supporters on different ideologies; they must do so by rendering as many services as possible to the electorate.

Thus, it will be clear that brokerage does not automatically disappear when the centre increases its infiltrations into the lives of the population. Factors may be at work which constitute a resistance to integration and which foster the continuation of brokerage.

Up to this point we have been predominantly concerned with the tasks of the operating politicians. It is time to take a closer look at the persons performing these tasks.

II. PERSONNEL

When dealing with the personnel question, Irish authors give a detailed description of the composition of the various representative bodies. They provide pictures of the occupational structure, the educational level, the age structure. It is of course interesting to know that particular occupations, certain age categories, and educational levels are more represented than others, but it is not enough. One should ask: Why persons with *these* characteristics?[17] The answer to this question provides the reasons for the combination of characteristics and enables us to predict who will become politicians in the future. Consequently, my central question in analysing personnel is not: What is the actual composition of the Dail and the county council? Rather it is: What sorts of prerequisites must a person comply with to become a politician? We can then check the answers against the actual composition of the representative bodies. For this purpose I use data from one Dail only, namely the 18th Dail, which sat from 1965 to 1969. These data are set out in table I. The composition of this Dail does not much deviate from others elected after 1918 as has been amply demonstrated by Cohan, McCracken, and Whyte.[18] For local government I make use of data from one county council (table II), though information from other sources proves that this council is not atypical either.[19] Again, I do not break down the figures for the three parties because there are no striking differences between them.[20]

According to the constitution, anybody who is 21 years or older and who is an Irish citizen is eligible to become a TD or an MCC. In fact the recruitment field is smaller; no farm hands or factory labourers are TD and no university professors are MCC. Apparently then there are other prerequisites that confine the field of recruitment. Many of the prerequisites flow logically from the politician's tasks as these have been described in the previous section. Therefore, it seems useful to start with the analysis of personnel from this perspective.

Time

A politician has to do a lot of work for his constituents. Furthermore, he must attend all sorts of party meetings and make regular visits to all the local clubs in his area. In addition, a TD has to attend the Dail meetings three days a week. For that purpose many rural TDs must travel a long distance from their home to Dublin, and most of them stay there until the meetings are over. Attending council meetings is a less serious problem for the MCC; the council only meets once a month and its various committees are held about once a fortnight. Moreover, the MCCs can travel the distance from their homes to the county hall in maximally a few hours.

All these tasks together cost a lot of time. Time, then, is an important prerequisite. Much of the time has to be withdrawn from the politician's ordinary occupation, for Ireland has not many full time politicians. Politics is a hazardous business, for one runs the risk of being defeated. In that case one must be able to fall back on other sources of income.

Table I. Occupation of TDs of the 18th Dail (1965-69).

Occupation	absolute numbers	percentage
A. PROFESSIONAL		
Barristers	7	
Solicitors	7	
Medical doctors	3	
Teachers	8	
Journalists	1	
Accountants	1	
Engineers	1	
Sub-total	28	19
B. COMMERCIAL, INSURANCE, and FINANCE		
Shopkeepers	22	
Publicans	7	
Commercial travellers	1	
Auctioneers	3	
Insurance officials	1	
Garage owners	1	
Estate managers	1	
Sub-total	36	25
C. AGRICULTURAL		
Farmers	34	
Sub-total	34	24
D. MISCELLANEOUS		
Secretaries of trade and other associations	1	
Trade union officials	10	
Clerks	1	
Local government employees	1	
Building contractors	1	
Bookmakers	1	
Gas company employees	1	
Bus conductors	1	
Electricians	2	
Ambulance drivers	1	
Dental mechanics	1	
Printing works foremen	1	
Shoe operatives	1	
Housewives	3	
Sub-total	26	18
E. ENGAGED in POLITICS[1]	20	14
TOTAL	144	100

[1]) Persons "engaged in politics" are full time politicians. This category includes ministers and TDs who have not even a minimal occupation elsewhere.

Not every occupation allows the withdrawal of so much time. Table I indicates a partial explanation: almost 50 per cent of the members of the Dail are farmers, shopkeepers, publicans, and small businessmen. If we confine our picture to rural Ireland, with which in fact I am concerned in this book, it will appear that these middle class occupations are even more strongly represented. For that purpose we may subtract both the 20 "persons engaged in politics", who are almost all persons holding ministerial office and who live in Dublin, and 19 out of the 28 "persons with professional occupations", who live in and represent the urbanized Dublin area. The result is that 70 out of 105 TDs belong to this middle class. Again, it is interesting to know that 15 out of 34 farmer TDs have a pub as an economic sideline. We find the same picture for the county council (table II). Indeed, it is even more pronounced: out of a total of 46, 25 are farmers, and 17 are shopkeepers and publicans. Five of the 25 farmers could also be classified as publicans for they have a pub as well.

Why then do farmers, shopkeepers, publicans, and the others mentioned command much time for political purposes? At first glance this factor is not evident for them. There is nothing inherent to their occupations which allows them much spare-time. However, if we look at the organizational structure of their economic units, which has been amply described by

Table II. *Occupation of Members of the Tallow County Council* (1967-69)

Occupation	absolute numbers	percentage
A. PROFESSIONAL		
Barristers	1	
Sub-total	1	2
B. COMMERCIAL, INSURANCE, and FINANCE		
Shopkeepers	8	
Publicans	8	
Auctioneers	1	
Sub-total	17	37
C. AGRICULTURAL		
Farmers	25	
Sub-total	25	54
D. MISCELLANEOUS		
Millworkers	1	
Housewives	2	
Sub-total	3	7
TOTAL	46	100

Arensberg and Kimball, much will become clearer.[21] In Ireland shopkeepers and publicans leave much of the work to the housewife, some resident niece or aunt, or to a grown-up daughter or son, and many of them have a servant for the busy hours of the day. The same is true for the farmers. Partly due to the inheritance system, the children stay long at home, and they can do the work, together with some farm hands, the housewife, or an unmarried relative resident in the household. Apparently then, farmers, small businessmen, publicans, and shopkeepers do not have to invest all their time in the management of their enterprises. They can leave much of the work to others while maintaining only the direction. Thus, if they wish, they can invest the surplus time in political activities.

Money

To be a politician or to become one not only costs time, it also costs money. It is of course very difficult to obtain much information on the politician's private bookkeeping, and my information may well be incomplete and inaccurate. However, even a rough picture of the expenses will help us to see that this is a relevant factor. To begin with, there is a fairly big difference in regular expenses between TDs and MCCs; as a rule the TDs have much more costs. We may classify the expenses into three categories: correspondence, election, and miscellaneous. Letter-writing takes a very important place in the politician's work. The TD has more correspondence than the MCC because the former has a larger area to represent, with more electors, and consequently a larger number of problems to solve. However, much of his expenses are paid by the state; each TD may send up to 500 letters weekly post free, provided that he writes them on Dail paper and posts them in Leinster House. The MCC does not have these facilities, but he is regularly in the county offices for meetings and he can then handle many problems with the officials. Yet many politicians maintained that their personal expenditure on postage is still considerable.

Before and during elections a lot of expenses are made: deposits (£ 200 for general elections and £ 100 for local elections), printing material, literature, posters, cars to bring the old people to the polling booth, loudspeakers, and meeting rooms to mention but a few. However, a considerable amount of these expenses are covered by the party. Headquarters provide financial aid, part of which is derived from the annual collections of the local clubs. Moreover, regional party bodies sometimes organize "victory balls" to celebrate the victory of their candidates, and part of the procedes are used to cover election expenses. In spite of this financial support the candidate must cover a considerable amount himself. During the canvassing he and his teams of canvassers must travel throughout the area. The candidate must pay for expenses such as the hiring of cars, meals, and telephone calls. But above all he must spend much money for drinks. It is common practice for the candidate to stop at every pub on his tour and stand his team mates and all the public which happens to be in the pub a round. Indeed, it is quite normal for many people "to hang on for the next couple of pubs". Apart from the expenses involved in this ceremonial drinking, many candidates give some pounds to their canvassers "for services rendered". The politician must pay this type of expenses out of his own pocket, and according to the answers on my questionnaire they range from £ 160 to well over £ 400 for general elections, and from £ 40 to more than £ 200 for local elections.

Expenses for correspondence and canvassing are two drains on the politician's purse, but there are also numerous miscellaneous expenses about which it is almost impossible to obtain exact information. One reason certainly is that the politicians simply do not know the amounts themselves. These miscellaneous expenses include contributions to party funds and subscriptions to charities, in addition to the expense of attending meetings, dinners, weddings and funerals and the other social engagements in which a politician is obliged to take part.

Although this financial picture is rather crude it warrants the conclusion that the expenses can be considerable, and that a person who wants to become a successful politician must be able to meet them.

Social Class

Time and money are important prerequisites but they are not sufficient. People of the higher social classes, the lawyers and the landed gentry, who might in terms of their available time and money be very suitable, are actually hardly represented in rural Ireland. This is the more striking if one realizes that these categories predominate politically in countries where patronage and brokerage loom large.[22] Indeed, prior to the revolution these categories dominated in Ireland.[23] These classes have disappeared from politics since, and a strong anti-landlord and anti-intellectual mentality has developed. The few landlord families that have survived the Troubles and that are still in Ireland, together with the rural lawyers, are at a disadvantage; becoming a good politician at present requires that one is a "real local" and a "good mixer". A real local is someone who is well-known in the area, who works and lives there, and whose father and mother lived there and were born in the area. (This characteristic seems to be very important for Irish politicians. More than 80 per cent of the TDs and MCCs live and work in their electoral district, and a considerable number of them were born in the same area).

To be a real local, however, at the same time implies that one is a good mixer; that one has good contacts with all sorts of people and behaves in the same way as the majority. One should not feel "a cut above the rest" and show this attitude in one's social contacts. "You should not rub shoulders with the rich only, because the gilt might fall off them and give you a golden dress. This might blind the eyes of the ordinary Joe Soaps", was the terse way an informant put it. The landlord families do not possess these necessary attributes. Although they have lived for generations in Ireland, and sometimes on the same estate, they are not "from the area", and they are no good mixers. Both the landed gentry and the lawyers lead a life quite apart from the ordinary rural population. Their social contacts are not village-directed and their recreational activities are different. Moreover, they are not prepared to do the work which is expected from an Irish politician. They do not want to listen to all sorts of personal problems and small local gossip. They are not prepared to act as the people's messenger boys; they look down upon this work. The ordinary population, on the other hand, do not easily go with their problems to these persons because they are "strangers". In short, they are outside the moral and cultural community of the countryside and therefore cannot act as brokers.

Although lawyers are scantly represented compared to those of other developing countries, they play an important role in Irish politics, and it is well worth paying some attention to their political activities. Many became active party members after finishing their studies. All around the country, in all towns and villages, one finds lawyers who are identified with a particular political party. Many of them are a member of the regional or top-level national organizations of the party, or Members of the National Executive. A good number of them are electoral agents of individual politicians, especially to TDs. They make speeches during election campaigns on behalf of candidates, they are script writers for the party and act, generally speaking, as the politician's private legal advisers in all sorts of matters. By doing this they hope to improve their positions in two ways: by expanding their clientele and by obtaining a better job.

Many solicitors, particularly young ones, have not much business, especially when starting off. An average country solicitor earns £ 1,500 to £ 2,000 per annum (1969). Of course, some make far more, but there are many who earn less. They are always looking for clients and they feel that their talents and their intelligence can be useful to the parties and to individual politicians. As a TD's election agent, the solicitor is in a good position to expand his clientele; his name is on each election pamphlet of the politician whose agent he is. In this way his party affiliation and his close connections with a candidate become known to each family to which the candidate sends the pamphlet. He is thus advertising his name and status, and when there are legal problems people might well go to the agent of their local politician. Again, during "confessions" politicians will advise their clients to go to Mr. X, his agent. Apart from this he is paid about £ 200 to £ 300 in his function of election agent by the party fund.

Lawyers also hope that their good services will enable them to obtain a better job. Party patronage is a very important factor in the appointment of judges. All the vacancies are given to party members. Of the vacancies that arose between 1956 and 1973, all but one or two were filled by lawyers who had been active in Fianna Fail. There are also a number of other jobs for a lawyer, provided always that he has good connections with politicians and that he is known to the governing party. There are the higher legal jobs in the civil service and positions as legal advisers in semi-state bodies. Again, a lawyer can join the Land Registry and the Probate Registry, he can become a county or city sheriff (with a salary of £ 2,500 to £ 3,500 per annum), or a county registrar, a job which is worth about £ 4,000 per year.

Centrality

So far we have dealt with prerequisites for office flowing from the politician's tasks. Among these centrality in communication networks, with which I deal in this section, takes a very important place. Since this concept has been used by Boissevain for analysing brokerage in political situations, it is worth quoting this author in detail. Boissevain observes: "Every person is naturally at the centre of his own personal network.[24] But the objective position of a person in a given group or field of activity seen as a network of social relations, influences his chances of being able to manipulate people and information. The more central his position, the better able he is to bring about communication. Centrality is an index of the degree to which a person is accessible to the persons in a particular total (non-egocentric) network."[25]

As the personal approach in solving problems is important in Irish politics, it will be evident that persons with high centrality in rural Irish life are in a favourable position to become politicians. Once again particular occupations come into the forefront: shopkeepers, publicans, small businessmen, auctioneers, are centrally located in the rural communication network. Throughout the day there is a constant stream of information to and from them as they are frequented by many people from the area. They are always well-informed on everything, they hear the gossip and the news of the day from their incoming clients and pass it on to other customers. It is common practice to leave a message at the pub or shop for a friend who may well drop in for a chat and thus pick up the message. Many country journalists make regular tours in their area along these information centres to collect in an easy way the news and all the particulars of what happened the previous week.

The local clergy – the parish priests and their curates – are usually also centrally located in the rural communities. They might be very suitable for political leadership. Indeed, they were the local leaders during the era of English domination and they often acted as vote brokers.[26] Since the Troubles in the early decades of this century, however, they have disappeared from the political scene. At the time they were not permitted by the Hierarchy to be politically active, as their intervention would naturally have contributed to the then explosive controversies. Officially they are inactive eversince.

59

Persons who lack this centrality are at a disadvantage, and those who want to become politicians certainly must build up a central position in country life. It is therefore common practice to become a member of as many organizations as possible to become known and informed in the area. It is interesting to note in this respect that 15 per cent of the TDs in 1965, and 23 per cent of MCCs of the Tallow county council, entered politics after becoming prominent in sport.

Credit

Having high centrality and being well-known in one's area is important in order to play a brokerage role, but it is usually not enough. People must not only know the would-be politician, they must also know that he has the qualities to manipulate persons and situations successfully. In other words, he must have built up credit with the population. "You must show what your grapevine is worth", as a politician put it to me.[27] The usual way to do this is by getting good results from connections with persons who command first and second order resources. Obtaining some money from a sport fund for the local pitch, a departmental letter stating that the town will get an industry in due time, making the local representative promise that a public convenience will be built, are but a few examples. There are various ways for obtaining these connections with strategic people and of building up credit with the population. An important way stems from communication problems with which most politicians are always confronted. The politician must keep in touch with the people to hear all the local and personal problems. He might well be centrally located in his own small hometown-area, but it is far more difficult for him to be well-informed in the larger area he represents. To have this larger communication system function well, he needs social relays, persons who themselves are centrally located in their own local network. These persons are small local brokers themselves; they bridge the gap between the politician and part of the population. Elsewhere I have called these right-hand men broker's brokers; I deal with them in more detail in the next chapter.[28] It will be evident that these positions, born out of the need for maximal communication, are very suitable for would-be politicians. Analysing the career patterns of TDs and MCCs I found that a considerable number of them had been broker's broker before they gained office.[29]

The importance of centrality and credit as prerequisites for political office can be illustrated in still another way. Increasingly the normal path to the Dail is via service in local government. In 1965, 78 per cent of the TDs were also MCCs, and about 60 per cent became TD after having been an MCC for several years. The county council is considered as a "school" where one learns to manipulate, to extend one's contacts, and to handle officials. Here one learns about the rights and duties of the citizens, and makes oneself and one's qualities known to the general public.

60

A Revolutionary Past

Another prerequisite has to do with the revolutionary past. This is participation as a freedom fighter in the struggle of 1916-23. Such a background was an asset to any candidate, and as late as 1948, 43 per cent of the TDS could claim among others this asset.[30] Once of great significance it inevitably has become of dwindling importance; deaths and retirements have decreased their numbers. In 1965, only 10 per cent belonged to this dwindling band in the Dail, and in the county council of Tallow only two were left. But still the names of these men are well-known, and in their election publicity material many candidates claim to be a relative of and trace the relationship to a famous freedom fighter.

Kinship

This brings us to a final prerequisite, which has to do with kinship. Kinship is important in this country which is so much characterized by a personalization of social relationships. In some villages it is still a favourite pastime to trace back the genealogies of many persons from the parish, and every village has genealogical specialists to whom once can go for details on one's family's past. People are used to thinking in terms of kinship relations. Even relatives and their descendants who have lived since long in America, and whom they have never seen, are still considered as belonging to the "circle". On the death of a wealthy person some people will fairly quickly tell you which persons might inherit, even when these people live scattered over Ireland, in England, Australia or in the USA. When John F. Kennedy, and later Charles de Gaulle, visited Ireland, several people traced kinship connections to them, sometimes five, six or more generations back, and they had this news published in the local newspapers. To be related to a prominent person gives status and enhances one's opportunities in life, according to rural people. Politicians are obliged to attend the funerals of constituents and their relatives, and if they cannot go they certainly will write a letter of sympathy to the relatives. I know a TD who has these letters in print.

It is hardly surprising then that kinship is important in politics for both nomination and attracting votes. However, contrary to the situation in some other countries, Ireland has but a few families who could be described as having developed political dynasties. Irish families have not yet been able to acquire much power, for the country gained independence relatively recently. However, in a number of cases a dynastic tendency becomes manifest. In 1965, 19 per cent of the TDS were sons of former representatives, and in the county council of Tallow I traced eight such cases. But family connections are not confined to the father-son relationship. A fairly great number of persons, now active as politicians, can and do trace all sorts of kin relationships to previous and sitting TDS and MCCS. In 1965 a total of 29 per cent of

61

the Dail was connected with former or sitting representatives of their own or other constituencies.

Given the prerequisites mentioned above and the willingness to become a politician, persons like those are certainly in a favourable position. In the case where a son succeeds his father, he may inherit his father's network of contacts and probably some of his credit. Other relatives may inherit the status and share the good name. People will say he is from "good stock", that they knew the candidate's uncle or grandfather, and that this was a capable man, so he must be good, and they may well give him a vote.

In still another way kinship comes to the fore in politics. It is an unwritten law that on the death of a politician one of his close relatives will be coopted in the county council, or he or she will be asked to stand as his successor in the Dail by-election. That person makes a good chance of being elected because many people give their vote out of sympathy. This is the main reason that women are constantly represented in the political bodies. If anywhere, then it is in politics that the often quoted saying "Blood is thicker than water" determines much of the people's actions.

In the preceding pages a number of attributes have been described and prerequisites with which a person must comply in order to gain political office. Some requirements flow directly from the politician's tasks, such as time, centrality, credit, and to a lesser extent also money. Others, such as kinship and a revolutionary past, appeared to be important, though not necessary, stepping stones. Anti-intellectualism, strong egalitarianism, and a lack of informal communication between the ordinary people and persons of the higher echelons of society usually prevent the latter from acting as brokers, and therewith from obtaining a seat in the Dail or the county council.

III. PRIZES

The prerequisites dealt with in the previous section of course do not provide a full answer to the question why certain persons are more likely to be politicians than others. They only form the potential, the category from which politicians will be recruited. Even if a person possesses the necessary attributes this does not mean that he automatically becomes a politician. He must be prepared to take up the job. Therefore, *willingness* is an important factor. Prizes are important in this respect. By prizes I mean any reward that can be gained from the job, such as prestige, money, social mobility. The prizes to be won in the political arena determine to a great extent whether or not a person is prepared to become a politician. But prizes are no absolute quantities; what constitutes a prize for one category of persons is not a prize for others. A five pound note for attending a meeting of the county council does not constitute a prize for a big businessman, whereas it may be so for a small publican. Therefore, next to providing more information on politics as an enterprise, the analysis of prizes is also a means to give more details on who will likely become a politician.

Money and Kind

There is a great variety of prizes, and the first one to be mentioned is the regular salary which a politician earns. A Dail member's salary is £ 2,500 per annum (1969). He is also entitled to a pension, the amount of which depends upon the number of years he remains in office. At first sight this may not appear to be very much. However, it should be borne in mind that most TDS earn a living in some other way as well. This holds also true for ministers; apart from their Dail allowance of £ 2,500, and their salary as a minister which is £ 3,500 yearly, they own a farm, an accountants office, or a factory. These salaries must therefore be considered as an extra source of income, obtained on top of their "regular" enterprise, and in that case it is certainly an important prize. However, this prize is not safe and steady; it can always be lost in the next election. Thus, we may conclude that a TDship is a prize worth competing for, only for those who can fall back on a steady and solid economic basis which they are able to maintain even during frequent absence. Evidently then, for rural Ireland farmers, shopkeepers, publicans, and small businessmen are in a favourable position for becoming politicians. For them membership of the Dail is an extra source of income without much danger; if they lose they are able to live on as they did before they were elected. The same is true for other occupations, though not much represented: teachers and some others can get leave of absence for as long as they are in the Dail.

So far I have only dealt with TDS. But how about MCCs? They do not earn a salary, they receive £ 5 for each monthly council meeting, some pounds for county committee meetings which they attend, and a small amount of travelling allowance. What then makes people strive for this office? One factor of importance is that this office is a first and almost necessary step to membership in the Dail, where they are paid a salary.

Other reasons can be mentioned and these bring us at the same time to the next category of prizes for both TDs and MCCs. These all have to do with the politicians being "close to the fire", close to were decisions are taken and policies mapped out. As they are usually informed about such decisions before the general public, they can manipulate this information for their own benefit. The opportunities are numerous and various, but a few examples will do. Land speculation is a favourite political enterprise, particularly around the somewhat bigger country towns. I know, for example, that about one quarter of the MCCs of one county council have improved their positions through land speculation, and the farmers among them have increased their own acreage. Of that same council almost all politicians have been able to obtain personal priority for various sorts of local government services: water and sewage connections, building grants, agricultural grants,

63

the tarring of the roads to their houses, to mention but a few personal benefits they have derived from their office.

The following case is a spectacular example of political manipulation and an illustration of the prizes a politician can get out of his activities. A new quay had to be built in Ballycroom. The county engineers provided the plans and the place where it should be built. The county manager decided to put an advertisement for tenders in the various local newspapers. Eamon Cloughessy TD, MCC, happened to meet Dan Flannery, an old friend and a fellow party member who is a building contractor, and he told him about the quay plans. The man was interested and he promised that Cloughessy would receive £ 2,000 if he succeeded in getting the tender for him. Cloughessy went to work. If it came to a vote, Cloughessy's fellow party colleagues in the council would certainly vote for this party man's tender. So Cloughessy did not need to worry about that. However, his party had no absolute majority in the house, and this meant that he had to have some MCCs from the other parties across the floor on this vote. He went back to Flannery and asked him £ 250 "palm oil" for buying the votes of some other MCCs. At the same time, Cloughessy had to make sure that the assistant county manager would cooperate. This man was also bribed. Cloughessy and the assistant county mannager agreed that Flannery should send in three tenders; the official should open all the tenders just before the meeting and decide which one of Flannery's tenders should be put in between the others. So agreed, so done. At the meeting it appeared that Flannery's tender was the one but lowest, but the majority of the MCCs voted in favour of Flannery's. The latter's tender was accepted on the formal grounds that his work for the council had always been good. Moreover, he was a local man, and if possible the council should give work to the local men in order to spread the "favours" fairly over the county. Cloughessy received his £ 2,000 and bought among other things a greyhound racing track which appears to be running well.

Although this seems to be no unique case (I came across some others) it is of course very spectacular, and not all prizes are as big as this one. But a smaller steady stream of rewards may be equally attractive. Three MCCs and one TD I knew, all of whom are shopkeepers, had been able to obtain contracts to supply the groceries for some county hospitals and infirmaries. It was also alleged that friends and relatives of certain politicians regularly obtained contracts for the supply of sewage pipes and other building materials.

Again, the very institute of hearing confessions is particularly significant to shopkeepers, publicans, small businessmen, and auctioneers. Through it they can expand their numbers of customers. People seek them out in their place of work, do business with them as a preliminary to asking for a favour. One rural shopkeeper who had lost his seat in the county council, told me that since then his clientele had diminished by about one-third, whereas as long as he had been MCC it had steadily increased.

Another important category of prizes flows from the politician's broker-age role *vis-à-vis* the voters. As a broker the politician deals in contacts. He communicates on a transactional basis, that is, he brings people in touch with each other for profit. This profit may vary; he will transact for money, prestige, for votes, or even out of sheer pity for a person. But in all cases he is "paid", whether it is now or in the future. To illustrate this principle I give an example.

A businessman in Killaveen intended to establish a small factory in the town some years ago. The man had some capital himself, but to start the business he needed £ 50,000. He went to his local TD and explained his case, whereupon the TD contacted his party colleague, the minister for in-dustry. The TD argued that it would bring more work in the town and he gave some statistics on local labour potential. Moreover, he had the local party clubs write some letters to the minister. The plan was investigated and accepted. A young brother-in-law of the TD was appointed in the board of directors. This straw man receives yearly a small sum of money, while the TD cashes about £ 150 per annum.

Prestige and Mobility

Other, less material prizes have to do with prestige and social mobility. Being a TD or an MCC certainly makes the rural person – whether publican, shopkeeper, or farmer – higher in the eyes of the ordinary countryman. Once elected, the politician is always in the public limelight and his name is in the newspapers. He is well-informed of what goes on in the world, and in the pubs people speak about what he has done for their area. He is invited to all sorts of socials and public meetings where he is especially welcomed. He is asked to open a new bridge, to name a ship.

Looking like the pre-revolutionary landed gentry, emulating their way of life and habits, is still often the ideal of many a politician. The ascendancy could afford politics because they were members of the leisure class. They had much power and prestige, they made the decisions for the area and be-haved like feudal patrons towards the population. They were in all sorts of charity organizations and met the bishops and other notables. Particularly for the bigger farmers (the "new ascendancy") this old image seems still to have much attraction. They have improved their economic position, partic-ularly through the government's protectionistic policy (which is actually meant "to improve the poor farmers" of the west). They have educated their children as priests, doctors, teachers, and vets, they can leave the farm to a grown-up son. They have met all their obligations to their family and have gained prestige in doing so. Yet they still feel that they miss something themselves. They want to improve their status and they see their opportuni-ty in politics.

Although it is possible to obtain more prestige in this way, political office is not the best means of climbing high up the social ladder. Of course, MCCs may well become TDs and some politicians may even reach ministerial level. But particularly at the latter level the opportunities are limited; to become a minister it seems to be important to have a university degree.[31] Again, it is highly unusual for rural politicians to use their office as a stepping stone to a good job in the civil service. To join the higher echelons of the civil service, where payment is better than the TD's £ 2,500, one must have education qualifications (a university degree or at least a certificate of some business school), which most of the rural politicians lack.

There is another, also important, reason that bars the politician from upward mobility. Being a "real local" and a "good mixer" is not only an important prerequisite *to becoming* a politician, it is an almost necessary condition *to keeping* the position as well. The politician can and does improve his financial position as we have seen before, and this may enable him to mix with bigger businessmen and the rural clique of professionals. Indeed, he is invited to their socials, and they will try to keep in regular contact with him for future political help, but he can never really become one of them. He must watch his step, for he cannot become too much involved in the activities of their circles. This might sour the mass of the voters on whom he is predominantly dependent and who consider him as their man. He cannot abandon his electoral basis, the grass roots. A politically highly informed Irish friend of mine described this as follows: "There is a conflict inside them (i.e. the politicians), inside their own personalities. They feel that they are superior now to the ordinary voters. They feel that they are entitled to be respected and being drawn in by the class that spurned them all along. And they strive by having become TD to jump into that class. They feel that they do not belong any longer to the ordinary Joe Soaps. But they simply can't do it; they will lose the grass roots and consequently their seat".

From this short outline of prizes it has become clear that all politicians can obtain rewards from their offices. The majority of the prizes can be acquired only by those who have frequent and regular contacts with the rural population. These rewards enable the politicians to improve their own private business. Furthermore, these prizes are particularly valuable for persons who have already a solid economic basis and a regular income. Other, less tangible prizes, such as prestige and social mobility, are attractive only for those who belong to the moral and cultural community of rural Ireland. It will be evident then that shopkeepers, publicans, small businessmen, and farmers loom large among the political elite of the countryside.

IV. CONCLUSIONS

This chapter has attempted to give an outline of the political elite, that is, the operating politicians of rural Ireland. I began with a description of their tasks. A picture emerged of politicians whose first and foremost task consists of solving the electorate's individual and local problems. Both TDs and

MCCs function primarily as intermediaries between the population and the various local and central government administrative offices; they are brokers. This role is forced upon the politicians by the electoral system.

The next purpose was to explain why particular categories of persons dominate the Dail and the county council. The explanation was guided by two hypotheses. The first one suggested that persons gain political office who are good brokers. The second hypothesis presupposed that prizes constitute another determinant for the recruitment of personnel. Many prizes are not only a consequence of the politicians acting as brokers, they are also very attractive for holders of certain occupations.

It became obvious that shopkeepers, publicans, small businessmen and farmers are much more suitable than others, and that the prizes available attract them the most. Indeed, through this analysis it became clear why personnel of the higher strata of society are so scantly represented in rural Ireland, while they predominate in other countries.

Thus the most important characteristics of the political elite were stated and analysed. A picture emerged of a political elite, recruited from the middle class, and very centrally located in country life, with a strongly particularistic attitude and parochial outlook, shrewdly manipulating their environment for their own benefit and that of their clients.

CHAPTER FOUR

Leaders and Support: Political Machines *

I. THE MACHINE

Bases for Support

In most modern non-totalitarian systems both individual politicians and political parties must recruit supporters to obtain and hold power. Bailey distinguishes two ways of recruiting supporters which have important implications for the stability of the groupings attracted. They can be attracted either on a transactional basis or on a moral one. Followers are mobilized on a transactional basis when their motive is calculation of profit and advantage. In that case the relationships have to be nursed one by one. Each individual is attracted by the belief that he will obtain some tangible reward from the relationship. Supporters are recruited on a moral basis when this transactional element is absent. In this case parties or individual politicians can attract whole groups or categories whose members feel united by a common ideology. Bailey calls groupings united on a transactional basis machines, and those united on a moral basis movements.[1]

This distinction is of course an ideal one; in actual groupings one finds both moral and transactional elements. However, it appeared in previous pages that the transactional element looms large in Irish voting behavior. Therefore further attention to the concept of political machine might be fruitful.

What does a Political Machine look like?

Today there is a vast literature on machine politics. The subject has been studied especially in American cities though data have been gathered also from developing countries and new nations. There is much agreement about the nature of machine relations; the non-ideological, transactional, profit-making basis is widely accepted as the fundamental characteristic.

Despite the many studies on machine politics, however, a clear and analytically useful model of the political machine, of its structural form, seems to be lacking. Several authors have attempted to describe the machine in terms of the (American) party organization and they look upon it as a parallel structure of the governmental hierarchy.[2] Only vague references are made to the influence of the business sector and the importance of spoils and jobbery in the bureaucratic sphere. Others simply equate it with "the political party".[3] Gosnell's study of Chicago and Mandelbaum's analysis of New York provide many details about ward bosses and precinct captains, but again, a clear model of the *entire* political machine is lacking. More recent studies, like that of Banfield and Wilson, do not improve the picture.[4] Indeed, Scott's recent cross-cultural analysis of political corruption, though providing much valuable information on machine politics, systematically omits any attempt to describing the structural form of the machine.[5] Some authors seem to confine the machine to the category of leaders.[6] Although I agree that leaders play a vital role – they operate the machine – I find it rather strange to reduce a machine to its leaders. Somebody is a leader *because* he has supporters; together they constitute a group. Moreover, what about a machine that consists of only one member, namely the leader?

In short, since a complete and satisfactory model is not found in the current literature, we must build our own. After this we can analyse the competitive game of machine politics.

Towards a Generic Model of the Political Machine

The first basic characteristic has to do with the nature of the relationships between a machine's personnel. The political machine is historically a rather new phenomenon. It could only begin to flourish with the emergence of a large category of independent voters for whose support had to be competed by those who seek public office. Of course, "vote-buying" has always existed but the scale on which it exists is important. Under pre-modern or "feudal" circumstances the majority of the voters were "locked-in electors", that is, they were not free to give their votes to whom they wanted.[7] Usually they acted according to the wishes of those who controlled their means of subsistence. Thus the person who sought political office only had to "buy" the support of a few powerful patrons, who, in their turn, delivered the votes of their clients. The bulk of the voters thus had no bargaining power. Only when the mass of the electors began to obtain some of this power, that is, were freed from traditional patterns of deference and dependency, could political machines mature. The ordinary voters then came to control a valuable political resource. They realized that the giving or withholding of their votes made a difference to those who sought political office. In their turn the competitors for office began to understand that they achieved a bargaining position *vis-à-vis* a large category of voters. In sum then, political machines are social aggregates of which leaders and supporters both have power and interact with each other from bargaining positions. The two facts of mass suffrage and bargaining power have important implications for the role of the leader and the form of the machine, as will be seen shortly.

The second basic characteristic has to do with structural form. Basically a political machine is not a group with corporate features, like a political party.[8] Rather, it can best be considered as an ego-centered interaction system: a vast network in which the leader is located at the centre. Even if all the people in the machine were party members one could not call it a corporate group. It is not the fact that people are members of a particular party that makes them belong to the machine; it is their relationship with a common focus, the leader, which forms the basis of machine membership, and those relations may be structurally diverse. Thus, all the elements of this group-like phenomenon are kept together by their common orientation towards the leader. And all have in common that they are related to him, or to some other person in it, on a personal and frequently transactional basis. The leader is of course the centre of the machine; he also wants to make profit out of it. Votes are among the important resources he wants to get out of the relationships. The metaphor of a machine is therefore a good one because it reflects exactly the way in which this network functions. It is a system of wheels within wheels.[9] Each wheel needs the others to function properly and the leader is, so to speak, the pivot around which everything turns. The total machine is a prize-producing and a prize-consuming system, and in its turn each wheel is again a producing and a consuming unit.

Also, machines are open-ended and non-exclusive, overlapping entities. The machine has no fixed boundaries: some people drop out and others join it, and once the leader has some regular contacts with a "new" member, this person can be reckoned as belonging to the machine. Machines are non-exclusive in that persons can be members of several machines at the same time; machines overlap each other at various points. Bureaucrats provide leaders from the same and from different parties with services. The electors divide their votes; either on the same or on different occasions, among various sorts of leaders.

The third basic characteristic, almost logically flowing from the previous description, has to do with time. Some authors who have analysed political machines in terms of egocentric interaction systems seem to confine the term machine to that part of the network which is active only or very specifically just before and during elections. They seem to confine it to electoral machine.[10] This is an unhappy curtailment. To a certain extent it is irrelevant to fix the attention on the period of elections when studying political machines: it is certainly not possible to explain the election results on this basis only. Only part of the machine emerges then, but the whole machine is in fact responsible for the quality and the quantity of the products, that is, the number of votes. It must be emphasized that politics is a long process and not something just confined to election times: it also takes place – and often very decidedly so – between elections. If the whole machine does not function properly between elections then the results of the election will be meagre. That this large system, a politician's "total" network, is of basic importance is illustrated by the motto of Irish politicians: Win elections between elections.[11]

So far we have only dealt with some very general characteristics of the political machine. It is now time to take a closer look at its composition. All the persons with whom the leader keeps in touch for holding or increasing his power are his supporters. These supporters can be divided into two categories. The first one consists of voters. They are the very basis of the leader's power; he depends upon their votes for the continuation of his office. In order to tie this large number of persons to him he must provide them with prizes. Hence I call this category of supporters the *prize consumers*. However, since the leader does not command these prizes personally, or at best only a very small portion – he is primarily a broker and not a patron – he needs another category of supporters who can provide him with these prizes. Thus the second category of supporters consists of *prize producers*.

This distinction may seem strange since I remarked above that each element in the machine both produces and consumes prizes. This is true, the electors give their votes to the leader in return for prizes or promises. Again, those indicated as producers of prizes usually obtain help from the leader because he owes them some debt, or they build up credit with him for future services. However, if we take the long-term view on political machines as advocated here, we may argue that some persons or categories more frequently produce prizes than others. That is, we discover a more basic flow-pattern in which certain categories of persons can be considered as prize producers and others as consumers.

To summarize, a political machine may be considered as a vast egocentered interaction system which functions not only during elections but also, and more importantly, between elections. This model consists of three elements: a prize-producing part, a prize-consuming segment, and a leader who connects the former two. Basically the leader is a broker, not a patron, because both producers and consumers have bargaining power *vis-à-vis* the leader. Furthermore, he is the person for whose purposes the machine exists and who has usually built it himself. The producing and consuming parts embrace all those persons, groupings, and categories which are either directly or indirectly related to the leader on a personal and frequently transactional basis. The machine may be compared with an hour-glass as set out in diagram I.

Diagram I. Generic Model of the Political Machine.

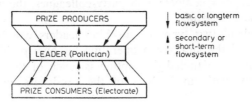

71

This is of course a very general model, that is, it describes roles and statuses and no actual individuals. Actual political machines may vary in internal differentiation and complexity; they may consist of a clique of leaders or exhibit a hierarchical leadership pattern, but the same basic model underlies them all. The model holds for small machines of precinct captains and ward bosses of American cities, but also applies to state machines in the USA, and to entire party machines in new African nations. Again, for specific situations and for particular activities certain elements of the machine may be mobilized. I call these subdivisions action sets. An action set is an egocentric interaction system of which the actors are mobilized by an ego on various bases and for a particular purpose which is decided upon by the ego. Persons mobilized during elections for canvassing constitute an action set or a combination of sets or subsets. (Detailed examples of these sets are given in chapter seven.)

With this model in mind we now take a closer look at the Irish political scene.

II. IRISH POLITICAL MACHINES

Does this model apply to Ireland? From previous descriptions it has become clear that the personal approach, and especially the transactional element, is very important in Irish voting behavior. However, much depends upon our focus. When we focus on the political parties as national bodies we may call them movements. The majority of the population votes for moral reasons for a particular party, in any event not for transactional reasons. Their parents before them voted for the party and they vote the same ticket. When rural Irish people are asked why they vote for Fianna Fail or Fine Gael, they answer invariably: "What was good enough for my parents is good enough for me". However, when we change our focus and put the party's candidates under the lens, we may conclude that very many people vote mainly for calculations of profit and advantage. In their choice they are frequently guided by their ideas of the "pull" of each candidate. In other words, the individual politician has transactional relations with many voters; they are part of his personal machine. Thus, when we study a political party from this point of view we may argue that it is an aggregate of individual machines. In short, we have a movement which consists of a number of machines. Since the present study focuses on individual politicians and the ways in which they compete with party-colleagues, the model of the political machine seems useful.

For rural Ireland two types of machine leaders can be distinguished, namely the TD and the MCC; each operating his own political machine. In the following pages a detailed description is given of these machines. The description begins with an analysis of the producers and consumers of prizes.

72

The category of prize-producers consists of all those persons who can give the politician the items and services which his clients, the voters, want. It embraces a great variety of persons: lawyers, businessmen, personnel from central and local government offices, from state and semi-state bodies, from state factories, and a number of other bodies in which the government has some sort of influence. As most of the prizes for which the voters ask are within the sphere of central and particularly local government administration, I pay the most attention to the relationships of the politician with this part of the prize-producing element.

The Bureaucracy and the Politician's Machine

The central question in this section is: Why should the officials help the politicians and give them what they ask for? Why should they give priority to a particular client of a politician whose case is at the bottom of the priority list? Why do they give jobs to his clients? In short, why and how do these persons come into a politician's machine? The general answer is that they themselves are dependent upon the politician's help for personal prizes. They help him as far as they can both in order to pay off their debts to him and to build up credit with him to ensure themselves of future services. Moreover, they are vulnerable to various sorts of pressures from politicians.

Appointments and Promotions

The bureaucracy is made dependent upon the services of politicians in a number of ways but a very important one has to do with their appointments and promotions. The reader might now immediately think of the spoils system which was – and to some extent still is – practised in the USA. America created a system of elective offices with short terms of rotation as a safeguard against tyranny and arrogance of the officialdom. This was considered a symbol of democracy. With a change of government very many positions change hands and the party then in power gives all these jobs to party members or adherents.[12]

For two reasons this spectacular "all-in-all-out" system does not exist in Ireland. The first and most important reason is a constitutional one. An Irish civil servant or local government official who has been appointed permanently cannot be fired when there is a change of government. The second reason is that few governmental changes have taken place since the foundation of the state in 1922. Apart from two short periods of coalition government, Fianna Fail was in office up to 1973. However, this does not imply that a spoils system is altogether absent. When the pro-Treaty movemet (later called the Fine Gael party) took office in 1922, it set up its own administrative bodies and staffed them with its party adherents. Since the last decade or so these persons have begun to retire and their vacancies were filled systematically by members of Fianna Fail.[13] Thus during the few governmental changes the spoils system certainly has flourished though only in cases of already existing vacancies. Very odd things happened then as the following case illustrates. A solicitor from Tipperary who had always been an active Fine Gael member, was promised the job of county registrar. He went up to Dublin to be appointed by the Fine Gael prime minister, but when he came out of the train in Dublin and heard that the coalition government had fallen, he had to return without his job.

Furthermore, the numbers of elective offices in Ireland are rather small. They are confined to advisory and governing bodies of a number of state and semi-state bodies and factories, to legal offices in these bodies, and to a few others. But in all these cases the holders of these offices keep their position irrespective of governmental changes. Legal appointments for judges and justices are made for life and the others mentioned rotate about every five years.

The distribution of these elected offices is organized roughly as follows: When there is a vacancy in one of these boards or in the legal sphere, TDs will propose names of applicants to the prime minister or the minister of the department concerned, and state what these persons have done for the party. Generally these applicants are businessmen or lawyers who have given all sorts of support to the politician. By proposing a name the politician now tries to pay off his political debts. The prime minister or the minister, together with some officials of his department, make the decisions who will be appointed.

Up to this point the Irish situation shows some features similar to the American spoils system with its elective and short term offices, but there the similarity ends. In most cases neither the Irish government nor the individual politicians decide directly about jobs and other favours. Generally the higher personnel from the governmental bureaucracies is selected by non-party commissions and boards, specifically established for those occasions. But this certainly does not mean that the political factor is absent, that politicians have no influence in the appointments at all. Indeed, it seems to be quite normal to ask a politician for help in connection with jobs.[14] Their influence, however, is of a more indirect, and covert nature.

There are various ways of appointing personnel in the bureaucracies, depending on the nature of the job and its level in the bureaucratic hierarchy. Consequently there are also various ways in which a politician can influence the appointments. Two commissions with offices in Dublin are in charge of the general organization of recruiting the officials. They are the Civil Service Commission (CSC) and the Local Appointments Commission (LAC), respectively for the bureaucracies of central and local government. They deal only with appointments of the higher officials and the professional officers. The Dublin commissions in fact do not select the candidates themselves but only check whether candidates comply with the formal requirements, such as their educational qualifications. The actual selection is done through an interview by a selection board appointed by the appropriate commission in Dublin. The procedure is as follows: When there is a vacancy in the local government service, the county manager informs the LAC, and he also advertises the vacancy in the newspapers, stating the requirements for the candidates.[15] When the applications come in he sends a copy to the LAC. The Dublin office then sets up an interview board, consisting generally of three to five members, which interviews the applicants and selects one of them. The existence of these commissions guarantees a minimum standard for personnel, but it does not mean that there is no room left for manipulation by politicians. An example will illustrate the way in which politicians manipulate the situation in their clients' (and consequently their own) advantage.

A vacancy for assistant county solicitor occurred some five years ago in Dunennis, a rather big seaport town in county Tallow. The LAC was informed and requested to appoint a selection board to interview the applicants. Mr. Gallagher, assistant county solicitor in a smaller town, was anxious to get the job: it meant a higher salary, better school and other facilities for his family. He went to see his local TD and explained his case. The TD promised to do his best.

The TD had to find out the names of the board members and see whether these persons could help him. Now there are certain rules which reduce the number of potential board members. The members have always the same occupation: they are officials who have experience with the type of work. Furthermore, the circle of potential members is made smaller by the rule that the members are always selected from a town or county which has the same sort of characteristics, or somewhat more complex, than the town or county for which the vacancy exists. The vacancy in this case was for an assistant county solicitor for a rather big town with a harbour in county Tallow. The first man in the board was the assistant county solicitor from Dublin, a city with the same sort of legal problems as Dunennis, though slightly more complex. The second board member was the assistant county solicitor from Galway, a county of roughly the same size as Tallow, and with many other similar traits. The third man was the assistant county solicitor from Tipperary, a county with the same agricultural structure as Tallow. The last member was from county Waterford which has a similar harbour.

Our TD knew these rules and decided to contact the assistant county solicitor from Waterford. He thought that this person might well be on the board. Moreover, he expected that the man would help him; he was a party member and he had been helped to his present job by an uncle of the TD. It appeared that the TD had chosen wisely. The assistant county solicitor from Waterford was indeed on the board but he did not yet know who the other members were. He expected, however, that his colleague in Dublin would be a member as well. He promised to contact this colleague whom he expected would give him the information as they were close friends. It appeared that the Dublin man was on the board as well, and also knew the names of the other members.

When the TD learned the names he had to get in touch with these persons directly or indirectly. In the Dail he approached his party colleague from Galway and asked him whether he knew the assistant county solicitor from Galway. This was very much the case: he and the solicitor were "boozing pals". The Galway TD promised his colleague to fix the case. Our TD then approached the man from Tipperary directly. This person was glad to help, for his brother, a builder and contractor, had once obtained a very lucrative tip from our TD in a case concerning the rebuilding of a county hospital.

The TD had done his work and now he had to wait for the results. He was fairly sure of the cooperation of three board members; the only one about whom he was not certain was the man in Dublin. The interview board met and Mr. Gallagher, the TD's client, was appointed. Gallagher was very grateful and promised to help the TD wherever he could. Thus, the TD had built Gallagher into his political machine, thereby creating a very important new entrance to his "store" of prizes for his clients.

Some eight months later the TD had occasion to make use of this new prize-producer. A wealthy and locally influential farmer in his area had run afoul of the law. On his own initiative the farmer had tapped a recently constructed water main to a small village, and at certain periods of the day was using the water in bulk for his stables. However, he had used poor materials and the villagers got hardly any water during those hours. The county engineer investigated the matter and found the cause. The farmer was very much afraid that he would be sentenced and fined. In great distress he went to his TD (the same man who had helped Gallagher) and asked for help. The TD promised to fix the matter. He went to Gallagher who is in charge of the preparation of this sort of legal matter and made him promise to treat his client favourably. The result was that the farmer was not fined, but compelled to have the proper materials installed at his own expense, though assisted by a grant from the government.

Thus far we have dealt with the appointment of the higher officials and the professional officers. The politician's influence was indirect then. He was dependent on the good turns of a number of other persons. His approach is more direct however when it comes to less important officials such as clerks, road workers, and other manual labourers. Personnel for these occupations are appointed as a rule by the county manager, the head of the regional office, or by the technical officers, depending upon the type of job. These persons can set up selection boards but often they themselves interview the applicants and make their own choices. The county manager or the head of the regional office selects the clerks, typists, doorkeepers, beadles, and the like. The county engineer or some other technical officer selects the road workers, engine and truck drivers, mechanics and a number of other technical and manual employees. The persons who are in charge of these appointments are usually prepared to respond to a politician's appeals. For them it is only a small service and they will do it either to pay off a debt or to build up credit with the politician which they themselves, or some relative or friend, might need in the future. They will also help because a politician can put them under various sorts of pressure, but I come to that in more detail shortly.

Again, a politician's interferences can have good results and his approach is more direct in cases of temporary employment. Particularly in local government a large number of persons are temporarily employed.[16] Most are contracted not through an interview board but by the county manager. If possible he will comply with a politician's request for the same reasons as mentioned above for other staff officials. The applicants themselves are dependent upon the politicians not only for their entry into the service, but also for their continuation in it. Their positions are particularly vulnerable, for they can get the sack at any time. Consequently, they try to make themselves indispensable in the eyes of the politicians so that these will do their utmost to keep them there.

Miscellaneous Pressures

There are still other means for a politician to make the bureaucracy help him, for the officials are vulnerable to many sorts of pressures. They derive both from the bureaucrats' official positions and roles and from positions that actually have nothing to do with their work. A first pressure has to do with publicity. When an official is not prepared to help a TD or an MCC, when he is slow in dealing with requests, or when a politician gets the impression that a particular official is boycotting him, he will complain to the man's superior, or he may even ask for information in a committee or in the council at large. This publicity can damage the official's good name and position. It may imply that his chances for promotion become smaller; indeed, other politicians might even refuse their help when a case arises because he has the reputation of not being prepared to help. This publicity or the threat to do this, is not only harmful to the official in question, it may also put his superior in a bad light. And the latter is equally vulnerable to a politician's pressures and dependent upon his services. Consequently, he will put his personnel under pressure and urge them to help the MCCs and TDs wherever possible.

Similarly the MCC who is also TD can apply more effective pressure than someone who is an MCC only. The TD has a wider network of personnel contacts because he is in Dublin every week, where he can interview key officials of the central government's departments. These persons, and particularly personnel from the Department of Local Government, can make further inquiries into the business of a particular local government. They can find out why a case has been delayed, and in various matters they can even order the local government to expedite the case. Moreover, a TD can expose the matter in the Dail by asking for information on the case. Often, however, he does not need to take all these steps: the very fact that he *can* do so, and that the officials know this, is often sufficient to make them respond to his pressure.

Party affiliation can be used as another means of pressure and it may have various results. The MCC who belongs to the party that has a majority in the council has an extra asset. If, for example, some politicians from the same party see that cases of their clients are always delayed, it can happen that all their party colleagues begin to boycott the manager on his policy proposals. The manager of course does not want this: he must have the county's administration running smoothly. He will do his best to be on good terms with all the politicians from the council. In cases where it comes to a lack of cooperation, the pressures work out again in various ways. The manager will investigate the matter and order the officials concerned to treat all politicians "fairly". And, of course, the manager himself is also under pressure: the case might be exposed in the Dail with the consequences described above. Moreover, he must remain friendly with the politicians for future private services.

In matters where the bureaucracy of the central government takes the decisions the role of party affiliation is even clearer. Politicians from the Labour Party or Fine Gael are at a disadvantage here, unless they have important personnel connections with some departmental officials. But even then their influence is only limited to cases which are entirely in the discretion of the official whom they know personally. Fianna Fail was in power for a long time and during its administration it filled all vacancies with party adherents. Partly this was done as a reward for services rendered to the party of some politician, partly to serve the interests of the party's politicians. Consequently, the interests of Fianna Fail politicians will be looked after better and their cases given higher priority than those of other parties. In addition, up to 1973, Fianna Fail politicians could bring their cases to the top men in the departments: the ministers and the secretaries who are invariably party members and also TDS. These persons of course are in the best position to help.

In addition to pressures stemming from the formal political and administrative organization, a politician can make use of his qualities and positions in still other fields of activity. Put differently: because personal networks overlap each other it is often possible for politicians to work through persons from their own networks whose own personal networks include important officials. Some examples of these important links are relatives who are high up in the religious or governmental worlds, friends or relatives important in the sphere of the news media, friends and relatives who are closely related to the county manager and other important staff officers. A politician can manipulate these contacts, thereby putting the bureaucracy under moral and other pressure to help him. This of course is the same as saying that the personal background of both politicians and officials are very important in influencing the outcome of decisions. Finally, the client's background *vis-à-*

vis the official is equally important. When there is a close relationship between the county manager and, for example, a brother of a politician's client, the former will certainly take the case in more serious consideration. In sum then, from this detailed description it has become clear that manipulating personal contacts constitutes the politician's basic strategy both for obtaining and for holding a category of prize producers.

THE PRIZE CONSUMERS

The other main part of a politician's machine consists of the prize consumers, the voters. As with the prize producers *vis-à-vis* the politician, so also here the relationship is actually a reciprocal one: the voters ask a politician for help, and in return they give him their votes. On the other hand, giving one's vote to a particular politician without a direct "repayment" is not a deed of charity or a matter of moral commitment, it is an investment against the day when one may need him. More can be said about the prize consuming segment of the machine, but this brings us to the next section.

III. COMMUNICATION PROBLEMS AND STRUCTURAL DIFFERENTIATION

Up to this point no distinction has been made between the machines of TDs and MCCs; they were lumped together, for so far there were no structural differences but only differences in size. The prize producing part of the TD's machine is larger, and it also contains a number of very critical persons. This is of course the result of the TD being a Dail representative, for as such he has more and better connections in the central government sphere than the ordinary MCC. The same holds true for the other part of the TD's machine, which consists of the prize consumers. This is also larger than that of the MCC, but the very larger number of voters results in the TD's machine differing structurally from that of the MCC. From the description that follows it will become clear that the voters in a TD's machine are differently located *vis-à-vis* their leader and therewith *vis-à-vis* the prizes.

Where a politician must attract voters on personal and usually transactional ties, there he must continuously look for new ways for creating and maintaining these ties. Ideally he must have close contact with each of the voters, and nurse this contact personally. He must always be well-informed about all the individual voter's problems and those of his village or town. In short, he must know his area as his own pocket and there must be a constant stream of information from the area to him and from him back to the area.

The voters, on the other hand, must be able to get in touch with the politician as well. It may, however, be difficult to reach him, for it must be remembered that Ireland is very sparsely populated. The rural population is often at a disadvantage when it comes to "long distance" communication. It can take a day to cover a distance of 20 miles because bus and train connections are scarce, and in some very remote areas there are none at all.

This is the same as saying that communication is of vital importance for the proper functioning of a political machine. Indeed, a fundamental task of the machine *is* communication. When this is bad the machine functions badly and may even desintegrate. For both politician and voter it is of vital importance to maintain maximum communication, and each will do his best and take steps to increase communication.

THE MCC

How serious is this communication problem for the MCC and how does he approach it? For him it is relatively small. That part of the CEA which he represents, his pocket or bailiwick, is rather small. Usually it covers the area immediately around his home, the place where he works and lives, and it embraces some 3,000 to maximally 4,000 voters. He can visit all the parts of his pocket personally, he is able to check the situation himself and he can do this frequently. The same holds for his visits to the local political clubs in his pocket. Again, contrary to the TD with his very large Dail pocket, the MCC does not have to divide his scarce time among a great number of clubs and areas. The population, on the other hand, can easily make a personal visit to their local MCC's home, for the distance is not great. Also, the people will find their MCC more often at home than their TD who has to attend Dail meetings in Dublin. In short, as a result of his centrality and the scale of his area, te MCC's communication problem is rather small. Consequently he needs no "social relays" for furthering messages. His political machine therefore is identical with the generic model described previously.

THE TD

For the TD the communication problem is serious. It is not unusual for a rural Dail representative to have a Dail pocket which covers an area of 400 to 600 square miles, and his electorate ranges from 6,000 to 8,000 voters though it may embrace 10,000. He is able to keep in close touch with the voters in his own home area, but it is practically impossible for him to have equally good and regular contacts with all the voters in his very extensive Dail pocket. Indeed, the TD's problems are even more serious if one considers that the bulk of the people's questions fall within the realm of local government, which is the MCC's domain. Consequently, in theory the TD's credit rating is low.

How does the TD solve these problems? A partial way out is to be MCC as well, and indeed, most TDs are also MCC.[17] This is, however, not enough, for this function does not yet entitle a TD to hear all the local government problems in this very large Dail pocket, let alone to solve them. He may only do so for that small area which is his own CEA pocket.

The best way to solve the problems is by establishing a small but strong circle of helpers scattered over the whole constituency. And this is exactly what many TDs do.[18] These helpers occupy durable and specialized positions in the TD's machine. They have a special name: they are called *hatchetmen* or sometimes *touts*.[19] Roughly a hatchetman's task consists of giving all the information about his own local area which might be of any importance to his boss, the TD. He is a social relay or link in the communication pattern between the TD and the population of his own small area. As hatchetman and tout are rather value loaded words I call this right-hand man broker's broker or local broker. These local brokers cause the TD's machine to differ structurally from that of the MCC. His machine, as illustrated in diagram II, is more complicated: it is hierarchical in its leadership segment. Structurally the local brokers, who are also bosses, occupy a lower rung on the leadership ladder than the main leader, the TD, because they deal in lower order resources.

Diagram II. The TD's Political Machine

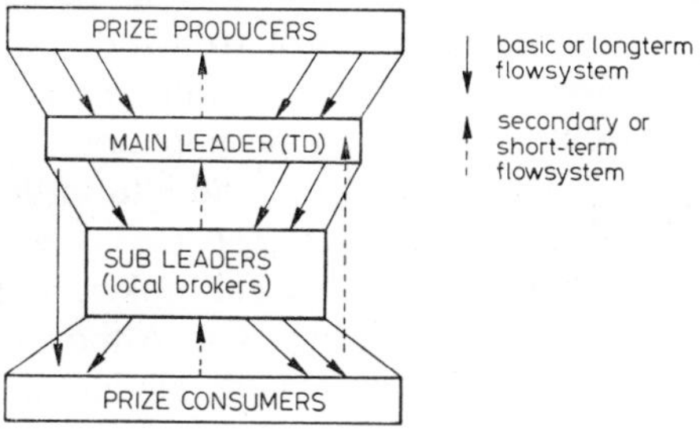

The basic differences between the machines of the MCC and the TD have now been described. The next section completes the picture by taking a closer look at the broker's broker. (A detailed description of a local broker's career is given in chapter five.)

IV. THE BROKER'S BROKER

Who are these local brokers and what are their tasks?

Tasks

A local broker has various tasks. A very important one consists of funneling all the personal and local problems to the TD, irrespective of their belonging to local or central government. He thus short-circuits the local MCC who in many cases is actually in charge of local government problems.

As a broker's broker is always well-informed of his own local situation, he can give his TD valuable information and advice on his strategy of producing prizes. He can decide better than his boss where the prizes will give maximal voting results. In the same vein, he can also protect his boss from making decisions or supporting cases which might well cost the latter local support. In all these situations a TD is very dependent upon the background information which his local broker can provide him.

Local brokers are also important for a TD during election canvassing. The official agreement made at constituency conventions dictates that each candidate shall only canvass his own pocket or bailiwick. Thus, a TD has no entry in other areas. Through his circle of local brokers, however, a TD can circumvent this rule and have other areas canvassed for him as well.

A circle of local brokers is also of vital importance for a TD in nomination matters. Representatives of the local political clubs, as observed, decide which candidates will be nominated. So primarily a TD is dependent upon the clubs for the continuation of his office. When an ambitious MCC tries to be nominated for the Dail elections, the TD must attempt to prevent this. The best way to do this is by inducing his local brokers, who invariably are active club officers, to have their clubs vote against this MCC. Thus, a circle of local brokers is a powerful weapon for the TD to keep his position and to minimize the opportunities for rivals of becoming TD. This is, however, his final weapon, so to speak, for a TD will do his best never to let it come that far. Long before the elections he will be constantly alert to rivals. And here again his local brokers play an important role: they must watch the actions of all politicians in their areas and inform their boss of all steps and manoeuvres. A rather spectacular case took place in the area where I lived. Through the information of his local broker, a TD was able to roll up part of the machine of a very ambitious MCC. Although this man did not belong to the TD's party, he was definitely undermining the latter's credit and popularity.

Liam Dowling, a young Fine Gael MCC, was busy working his way up. He hoped to be nominated and eventually elected as TD during the coming general election. Various local clubs in the area had promised to support him at the nominations, and now he was busy improving his position by being very alert to all the problems in his own home area. A friend of his, a local government official in temporary service and in charge of road repair, water and sewage matters, promised to help the MCC building up his "pull". Together they developed a very ingenious policy to do so. Whenever a politician from this MCC's area tried to solve problems relating to water, sewage or road matters, the friend would put these questions aside for some weeks. At the same time he would inform Dowling about the cases. The latter would then quasi-accidentally go to the people concerned, who of course would also ask him for help. Dowling could then guarantee the population that the matter would be arranged within a few days. Next, Dowling would inform his friend that he had "made his round" in the area, whereupon the local government official would immediately write a letter to the people concerned, stating that the problem would be solved shortly. This strategy would give the population the impression that other politicians had less "pull", and that, whenever you "pulled" Dowling you could be sure to have the problem solved.

Several problems arose in the area and things worked according to plan. One problem had to do with the repair of a council water pump for a row of cottages, another with resurfacing part of a road, and a third with the provision of water and sewage connections for a particular house. In all cases people went first to Tadgh O'Sullivan, a very popular local broker of a Fianna Fail TD Sean Dwane. O'Sullivan informed his boss who in turn brought the cases to the attention of the local government official. The people had to wait, however, very long and it seemed as if nothing would be done about their problems. In the mean time Dowling, the young Fine Gael MCC, arrived at the scenes and he had the matters fixed very quickly. O'Sullivan sensed that something was wrong and began to look for an explanation. Through various "backdoors" he discovered the ingenious set-up of Dowling and his friend in the county office. He informed his TD who had the matter investigated and pressed the county manager to replace the official. If the manager refused to do this the TD said he would bring the case to the notion of the minister for Local Government. The official was transferred to a bigger town and even obtained a better job with the help of Dowling, who had been responsible for the whole affair. Thus, through the information from his local broker, the TD was able to counter the machinations of an ambitious MCC.

Finally, a broker's broker functions as scapegoat or buffer for his TD. When problems are not solved or cannot be solved, it is important for a TD that he can blame someone for not having acted properly. The TD thus keeps his popularity and makes someone else responsible for the failure. In other cases a TD has to do things against the wishes of the government, the party or the population. He himself cannot always act openly without severe consequences but again, he can often use his local broker who then acts as a buffer.

Personnel

Who are these local brokers? Theoretically one might expect the MCCs to fulfill this role, for all the fellow party MCCs in his area should support the TD. Formally they must inform him of all problems related to central government and support him during Dail elections. Practically they are also suitable persons for the job: they are active in politics themselves, they know how to handle voters' problems, and they are well-informed about the area. In actual fact, however, they seldom belong to a TD's circle of local brokers. Often there exists a covert rivalry between TDs and MCCs. This does not mean to say that there is no cooperation at all between MCC and TD. Indeed, there is much: MCCs will deliver election speeches in their own and other areas for the TD, but this is in their own advantage as well, as these speeches form an opportunity to make themselves known to a wider public. Again, MCCs will often support their local TD at nomination conventions. The point here is, however, that a TD is *never sure* of the support of the MCCs in his Dail area. There are always reasons for a TD to be afraid of the MCCs in his pocket. He might expect them to have some secret deal with another TD in the constituency who attempts to have him outvoted at a convention. Again, a TD knows that the most of the MCCs are not interested in a strong local TD because such person is only a barrier to their own political aspirations.[20] Consequently MCCs will not automatically follow him. Finally, MCCs are too close upon a TD's heels, for they have already reached the first rung on the political ladder; and this is an almost necessary one at present for becoming TD. Thus, an MCC is usually not the right man for a position in the circle of local brokers: he is a potential rival.

Who then are these brokers? In principle and in fact many persons are considered for this role. It is hard to say who will joint the circle, and it is equally difficult to state from which side the initiative will be taken. As Bailey observes in his analysis of machine politics in India: . . . "the situation is there and the man with the right sense of opportunity must come along".[21] One should remember that this is not an official decision, formally agreed upon by both parties. It is often a process of trying and of making covert hints to each other, and later it is difficult to say exactly when the two came to terms.

Although it is difficult to answer the question on personnel, more information can be obtained if we approach the matter from the point of the tasks contained in this role. This is to say, only persons who comply with the requirements, as these come to the fore in the tasks, are considered for the job.

Broker's brokers actually do the same sort of work as official politicians; they are small replicas of their bosses, the TDs. Therefore, it will be no surprise that they share many characteristics with them, which I described in chapter three. Table III illustrates this on the point of occupations.[22]

Many of these occupations have high centrality in the rural communication network. Journalists, publicans, shopkeepers and roundsmen, all meet people frequently; some because the people come to their shops, others see the population on their rounds through the countryside. Moreover, all the

Table III. Occupations of Broker's Brokers in County Tallow (1969)

Occupation	Number	Percentage
Journalists	2 (plus 1)	5
Publicans	12	33
Shopkeepers	10	27
Farmers	6	16
Roundsmen (milk, bread, groceries)	3	8
Factory clerks	3	8
Shoemaker, electricity meter reader, journalist	1	3
Total	37	100

84

persons in the table increased their centrality by becoming active members of various sorts of voluntary associations, and they are all considered as "good mixers" and "real locals". Without exceptions they are also active in their local and regional party organizations. Again, most of them can carry out the time-consuming task of local broker while they work so that it does not bring them into conflict with their ordinary occupation. In short, they are all well qualified to act as local brokers: they have politics in their blood, so to speak, and they are fond of "messing around" and "intermeddling" in all cases they come across.

Prizes

Finally one may ask: What makes these individuals take up this brokerage role? Although the 37 brokers whom I interviewed gave different responses, their answers converged on two points. First, they justified their activities by explaining that they were indispensable for their parties. Second, they all stressed the point that their communities had obtained what they legally were entitled to. If they had not always "slept with one eye open" the area would continually have been put on the bottom of priority lists for public amenities. One informant put it very simply: "The basis for my activities is love your neighbour. My father told me so when he died."

Although I do not doubt the sincerety of these answers I also know that there are other reasons why individuals become local brokers. Their motives can be explained further in terms of prizes they gain through their role. there are all sorts of prizes and here again the general picuture is the same as sketched before for the politicians proper. Some people take on the brokerage role with a specific aim in mind. They have an eye on a particular prize: a piece of land or a better job.[23] But generally they do not seem to join the machine for a specific prize. As a rule they become local broker to make profit in general. An informant humorously, but in my mind correctly, compared local brokers to little ducklings. He said, "They dive into the water and they like the feeling of it; every moment having a dip. And once they get used to it they come back in a second time, and it's done naturally everytime more. After a dive they like drying in the sun".

The prizes range from local prestige, money, a better job, to a grant or benefit, or an increase in customers for the shop. Being a broker's broker gives one prestige in the eyes of the local population. It means that one has close connections with politicians and that one is often in the position to inform the people of a local improvementf rom the county council. The role can also be a good stepping stone for political office, but I deal with this aspect in more detail shortly.

After this description of the broker's broker and the reasons why a TD needs these helpers, one vital question must still be answered: If one of the main tasks of a local broker consists of undermining the MCC's position for his own boss, how then can an MCC ever expand his power and become TD?

It might be expected that an ambitious MCC would increase his number of voters for Dail elections by infiltrating fellow party MCCs' pockets. There one might presume him to subvert voters by rendering them services and thus create much credit that could be harvested during Dail elections. For that purpose, one might expect him to set up a circle of local brokers. However, this is not the usual strategy and even not a proper one. If his target is a seat in the Dail, he will concentrate his activities primarily on the various local clubs in part of the constituency. He will try to influence their voting behavior at nomination conventions, for *there* the basic decision is taken whether he will stand for Dail elections. To improve his chances there, an MCC will certainly try to render services to influential club members, who in their turn, might vote for him at the convention. But these rather short-term transactional relations can of course not be compared with the relations between a TD and his local broker.

Another reason can be mentioned why an ambitious MCC will not primarily focus on a large circle of electors. It is a lengthy process for an MCC to build up a bank of potential voters through "hearing confessions" and solving problems in areas that do not belong to his pocket. Indeed, it is dangerous because other MCCs and TDs might well hear about his machinations and form a temporary coalition to vote against him at the convention. In short, it is not worth the costs and the risks to build up voting support through rendering services straight to the voters from a large area or by means of local brokers. Thus, both under normal circumstances and when he wants to expand his influence to become TD, an MCC does not make use of a circle of local brokers.

V. CONCLUSIONS

In the preceding pages a model of the political machine has been developed and tested for the Irish situation. It appeared to be useful at MCC and TD level, and it explained the structural differences between the two types of machines.

The political machine is frequently described as a pyramid, with the big bosses at the top and the smaller ones below them, whereas I preferred the hour-glass form.[24] This is no mere playing with metaphors. For several reasons the hour-glass model provides a better picture of the machine. Firstly, it emphasizes the actual dependency of the leaders upon prize producers and presents these as an (analytically) separate category.

Secondly, it contains no notion of a hierarchically organized system. Indeed, why should leaders occupy a more important position than the prize producers or the consumers, and which criterion should be used? Let us take a closer look at the three types of "wheels" that I distinguished and see whether more can be said about a hierarchical nature. To begin with, the prize consumers cannot be considered as an internally hierarchically differentiated category. Of course, some voters may be locally more influential than others; they may be able to advise certain persons how to vote. But this does not give them a position in the long-term communication system which differs hierarchically from other voters.

The same holds for the prize producers. Once again, which criterion should be used: the frequency with which they provide prizes, or the weight of the prize? This is difficult to say, and from the previous description no rigid hierarchy can be deduced. Although the departmental secretary and the county manager are often the most powerfull persons, the TD will not automatically approach them. Generally he will go to that person in whose direct discretion the matter lies, and only when this man does not help will he go to a superior. When, for example, some big and influential farmer asks an MCC to have the road opposite his house tarred, the MCC will go to the foreman of a gang of road labourers who work in the vicinity. This man can make the decision directly. In such cases a politician will generally not go to the county manager or engineer despite the latter being the foreman's superiors. (The MCC, of course, wants to save his credit with the higher ups for other occasions). In short, the formal bureaucratic organization has a hierarchical structure but this structure should not be mixed up with the "informal" organization of the political machine. Anyway, for Ireland there seem to be no indications for differentiating the prize producers hierarchically.

The only category in the machine that may be hierarchically organized is that of the leaders, though even here it is not a necessary characteristic as has been demonstrated for the MCC's machine. The TD's machine presents a hierarchical pattern. The TD is the chief and the other leaders, second in rank, are the local brokers. Both are leaders because they attract support for political (and other) purposes but the TD is higher up than the local broker, for he is closer to the sources of prizes.

Thus, it seems that only the leaders' section of the machine may present a hierarchical organizational pattern, and an important reason for this pattern, as argued previously, is the size of the electorate. Indeed, it may be posited that the structural complexity of a machine is always a function of the size of the electorate, though this proposition must be tested cross-culturally.

Finally, it is frequently argued that the hierarchical organization is of a bureaucratic nature. That is, that tasks are divided among the leaders to the extent that each has his own specific and exclusive business. This is however not the case; each type of leader in the machine does the same work as all the others do. Therefore, the hierarchical organization can better be compared to a feudal system. Each local broker has a "fief" from his TD and works and lives like a small prince in his own domain; indeed, each local broker is a TD on a micro scale. The very fact, however, that the leader's section of the TD's machine is ranked according to feudal principles makes it susceptible to all sorts of detrimental influences and it may even cause the machine to break down. This is described in the next chapter.

CHAPTER FIVE

The Frailty of Political Machines:
Wheels within Wheels

I. INTERNAL AND EXTERNAL MANAGEMENT PROBLEMS

Every leader has problems of keeping his flock of supporters tied to him, that is, he has management problems. Management can be described as all those activities which are aimed at keeping a fair balance between costs and resources. This is a rather economic definition but it is equally applicable to political leaders. Each leader has certain costs which he must cover with his limited resources. He has to spend time, money and a number of other resources to keep his organization together and working. The leader of a machine in particular must cope with severe management problems. The ratio of costs to resources is unfavourable for him. Contrary to the leader of a movement, who can catch whole groupings with one blow, so to speak, the machine boss must bind supporters one by one, by giving or promising each of them a specific prize. This of course limits the size of his support severely. If he wants to expand his machine he must create more relationships with each potential follower separately; each new supporter forms an extra drain on his budget. This holds not only for attracting supporters but of course also for holding them durably. Put differently, the machine leader must do his utmost to keep his credit rating high.

In addition to these internal difficulties, the machine leader's management problems are also caused by external difficulties, from the fact that more politicians are seeking support in the area. These problems of course constitute two sides of the same coin, but it is well-worth distinguishing them to some extent, for they oblige a leader to fight on two fronts. He must keep his flock together and damp down or prevent internal conflicts, he must also fight other politicians and prevent his followers from deserting to the enemy. Put differently, part of the leader's resources are spent to his own supporters and another part is used for reducing or even destroying those of his opponents.

Thus, in a discussion of management problems of the TD and the MCC, and the ways in which each attempts to solve them, one must not only bear in mind that their machines are constructed differently, they are also differently positioned in the arena. Problems stemming from the nature of the cementing ties and the machine's composition I call *internal management problems;* those which are the result of the specific position in the arena are *external management problems.*

Internal problems

Although the MCC's problems are not so severe as those of the TD with his very large and complex machine, his are serious enough. He must attract 3,000 to 4,000 voters and he needs many prize producers for this purpose. Moreover, the members of his machine are not morally barred from withdrawal because in almost all CEAs there is more than one representative of the same party. They can thus make a shift from one politician to another without crossing the ideological line.

There are three ways for an MCC to reduce his costs and bind his support more durably. Firstly, he can cut down his costs by attracting voters not separately but as whole categories, though still on a transactional basis. Secondly, he can divide his work among a staff of sub-leaders. Thirdly, he can change the nature of the relationship by tieing people by more than one strand, on a moral basis. These solutions are treated separately but on various points they overlap and supplement each other.

Collective Prizes

Rendering services to whole groupings may reduce the politician's costs, and MCCs are eager to provide them with prizes. It is common practice with them to render all sorts of services to whole towns and villages: public lights, new houses, better roads, public conveniences, to mention but a few. These are amply publicized in the local newspapers, and each politician mentions them during his election speeches. Also, MCCs will give all possible help to various sorts of organizations, such as sporting clubs, religious confraternities, local development organizations, farmers and business organizations, and personnel of local government office. A good turn to them may be of help in the future. However, these collective prizes do not release the MCC from solving problems of individual voters. Indeed, they are less effective manoeuvres though the MCC is forced to do this for reasons that become clear shortly. From the point of view of an individual, a new pitch for his sporting club is a less important prize than the cottage that he obtained through the help of the politician. In this case the prize is personal and this will certainly have stronger consequences for the way this person votes. In discussing this point with an MCC, he explained that these collective prizes are in effect an extra burden. Some few years ago, he told, he provided a regional county office with central heating. The personnel was very grateful and sent him some bottles of whiskey. Some months later, the MCC needed the help of the county engineer for a constituent. The engineer was not prepared to help, and when the MCC reminded the official of the service that he had rendered him and his colleagues in the office, the engineer said: "Sure, Paddy, you've done a grand job. But that was to the whole crowd of us here. I hadn't asked for it".

Creating a Staff of Sub-Leaders

Creating a staff of mini-leaders is not a proper solution for the MCC to cope with his management problems. Contrary to the TD, he does not need a staff of local brokers; indeed, they would only be a threat to his position. These specialists could easily learn the tasks of the MCC and become his rivals. The MCC needs specialists only for short periods, such as canvassing and nominations, though they hardly deserve this name. And as a result of their temporary tasks these helpers are no threat to the MCC's position.

Creating Many Stranded Relations

The most effective solution is to link the supporters by more than one tie. This makes the relationship many stranded and brings more stability into the machine. Any MCC does his best to realize this, and he does so in various ways. Creating friendship is an important means. The politicians use to send Christmas cards and turkeys or some whiskey to local government officials. They also visit their prize producers on special occasions such as births, weddings, anniversaries, and burials. They stand them drinks in office or pub when they are off duty. I know from one politician that he married his two daughters to influential local government officials, and it is alleged that he has "big pull" because of this relationship.

Another way for creating many stranded relationships consists of joining many voluntary associations. This is not only a must for the Irish politician because it enables him to increase his centrality in the rural communication network, but it also enables him to resolve his management problems and to reduce his costs. The machine member is not only a follower now because he is going to get something from the MCC but also because he and the leader are members of the same group and share a common goal for which they strive. They feel united by moral ties as well, and such ties are less easily broken.

Kinship has the same function. Being bound by kinship to a person means that one has close connections and an obligation to mutual help. No wonder then that politicians are always at pains to trace kinship relations to as many people as possible. They mention them whenever they can, and before elections in their stencilled "personal letters" to the voters they invariably claim to be related to previous politicians and late freedom fighters.[1] However, blood is not always thicker than water, and self-interest may easily prevail.

A final means to reduce management problems consists of introducing an ideology. This in theory gives the MCC a moral hold over his followers. But

90

since the majority of the electorate votes along party lines, and competition is thus an intra-party affair, this is not a proper solution.

Thus, although many MCCs make use of various means to tie their following morally, it has become clear that the transactional relations remain predominant. In the last resort they appear to be more important. This was illustrated very clearly during the 1969 general elections in the town where I lived. Liam O'Driscoll, a rural Labour politician, had built up the support of about 30 voters in the town. He had always worked hard for his electors, and some people called him their father or patron saint. As a result of the revision of the constituency boundaries in 1968, Liam's constituency had been redeced by one seat. From a five member constituency it had become a "four seater". It was quite clear that O'Driscoll was going to be one of the losers, for he had always been at the bottom of the poll, and now the larger part of his pocket had gone to another constituency. What had been predicted happened: Liam lost his seat. Indeed, he lost more votes than those that went to the other constituency. Many people had realized that Liam's machine was desintegrating and voted for another candidate. In my town only nine or ten out of his former 30 supporters gave him their votes. When I asked an old man, whom Liam had provided with a cottage, whether he had voted for O'Driscoll, he answered tersely: "Yerrah, I did not! I'm not going to give me vote to a man whose pull will disappear from him. What's the use? What's the use for both of us?"

EXTERNAL PROBLEMS

An MCC has also external management problems, stemming from his position in the arena of the constituency. The MCC is in competition with a number of other politicians. His position is weakened by fellow-party MCCs, TDs, and local brokers. Each of these attempts to outdo the MCC by subverting his supporters, and they all try to prevent him from being nominated and from standing during elections.

A first step for the MCC to make his position more certain is to tie the club members in his area to him as tightly as possible, for they decide at the nomination convention who will stand as candidates. He will do this by urging friends and relatives to join local clubs and thus look after his interests. He can also bind club members transactionally by providing them with prizes. This is also a frequently used manoeuvre. If a person wants to improve his position, he must join a political club, for there are always occasions on which a politician needs his help.[2] Another way for an MCC to ensure his chances of staying in office is to make a deal with a colleague to support each other at the nomination conventions. This is, however, not a very safe manoevre, for his colleague may double-cross him.

One of the most dangerous enemies of the MCC is the local broker. MCCs still have some interests in common, but the local broker is only interested in the destruction of the MCC. The broker is operating right in the MCC's own domain, busy short-circuiting him and building up his own support. The MCC will try to get rid of him in various ways. He can make the local broker's life and that of his family difficult in the community. An MCC in a town not far from my residence succeeded several times in causing a local broker to lose his job. Sometimes an MCC attempts to buy a local broker out. This is however not always a successful manoeuvre: the MCC must be able to provide the man with a good prize and this is rather difficult, for the local broker obtains both prizes from his TD and from his own local people for his services. On the whole it is difficult and rather risky to obstruct a broker's broker. If an MCC tries too hard his efforts might well ensure that the TD will attempt to have him outvoted at the nominations.

In sum, there are a considerable number of persons with whom the MCC must compete outside the boundaries of his own machine, and his attempts to reduce the external management costs are only partially successful.

III. THE TD AND HIS MANAGEMENT PROBLEMS

EXTERNAL PROBLEMS

The TD's external management problems are structurally the same as those of the MCC, be it that he has to cope with more politicians, for his area is larger and thus contains more competitors. Also, the ways in which the TD attempts to cope with these problems are in many respects the same. There is however one very remarkable difference which justifies dealing with TDs separately from MCCs: a TD has local brokers at his disposal and they fulfil an important function in his coping with competitors. Local brokers form counter-weights to threatening MCCs. A broker's broker can keep an MCC generally weak by poaching on his preserve. And if an MCC is going so fast that he might become a threat to a TD's Dail seat, this TD may well be able to cause him to disappear from the local government scene and have him replaced by his local broker. This is an asset which an MCC totally lacks. Brokers are of course also effective for undermining the strengh of a fellow-TD. If a TD feels that a colleague expands his domain at the cost of that of himself, he will certainly try to create new brokers in the domain of his opponent, or attempt to take over a broker of the latter.

INTERNAL PROBLEMS

Like the MCC, the TD also attempts to cut down his internal management costs by provinding collective prizes and linking his supporters morally to him. For the TD, however, it is in principle more difficult to keep his supporters together because his machine is structurally more complex than that of the MCC: it contains a circle of local brokers. These local intermediaries may be compared with feudal lords who were *de jure* dependent on their king but actually led a rather independent life. They are small "kings"

92

themselves in their "fiefs", and they have the same sorts of power and functions as their "kings". Like their colleagues in the feudal society these brokers are capable of growth to a certain point where they can hive off and begin for themselves, that is, become MCC, or offer their own small machine to another TD.

A TD can cope with this serious problem in several ways. The very fact that he has not only one broker but a whole circle is of great importance. He can play one off against the other and keep them all weak. Indeed, generally one local broker does not allow the other to move faster. They knife one another wherever possible and their TD can sit down, so to speak, and watch them destroying each other. Again, the TD may give all his support to the MCC whose position is threatened by a local broker and thus reduce the chances of the broker replacing the MCC.

Such is the situation for the TD. By means of divide and rule tactics he can generally reduce his internal management problems and keep his machine running efficiently. Local brokers are small wheels within the larger system. A TD must constantly be alert to keep them running properly, for they can become "dysfunctional" or break away. This chapter concludes with a concrete example of the relationship between a TD and one of his local brokers.[3]

IV. THE LIFE HISTORY OF TADGH O'SULLIVAN, A LOCAL BROKER

Tadgh O'Sullivan, a bachelor of about 50, is a shoemaker, an electricity meter-reader, and a local journalist, living in Patricksville, a small town of about 900 inhabitants. His father had been a shoemaker in town and an active member of the local Fianna Fail club. Together with some other ex-IRA freedom fighters he had founded the club. Father O'Sullivan knew some of the old politicians and ministers very well: they had been comrades in arms during the fight for independence, and later in the civil war. Whenever these politicians came through the town they would drop in at the O'Sullivans and speak about the past and present. Tadgh received secondary education as his parents had big plans with him, but he had to drop out at school when his father died and take up the family trade. The boy had joined the local Fianna Fail club, and because of this education and inclination to work hard, he soon got the office of club secretary. As secretary Tadgh is automatically a delegate to the regional and constituency meetings of his party. It was here that he met many politicians and watched them manoeuvring. He widened his network of personal contacts in the party sphere. Later he became general secretary of the regional organization of the party, and since 1968 he has also been one of the secretaries of the constituency organization.

Young O'Sullivan for years has been a very active member of the local Gaelic Athletic Association, GAA for short. From local secretary he worked his way up to secretary of the regional board, and for some years he has occupied the same function in the county board. He still keeps these three functions as they are important for his political ambitions. Through these positions he is able to patronize the town because he can influence the decisions as to where the various matches will be played. Patricksville has a very good pitch for a small town, and Tadgh had used this argument often to have regional and county matches played in his town. Shopkeepers and publicans make good profit during and after those matches, which are generally attended by very many people. Even at an early stage of his career he was already able to make some profit out of his position: various shops and pubs give him either longer credit or commodities at reduced prices. Moreover, at the various GAA meetings he was able to develop "the gift of the gab" as he calls it, and widen his network of personal contacts.

Through his position locally in the GAA he became involved in a long lasting local conflict, and this brought him to the second stage in his career. In 1948, an organization was introduced in Patricksville parish called *Muintir na Tire*. This organization was intended to coordinate all sorts of activities of the parish, to introduce new ones, and to act as community development organization generally. Muintir na Tire was introduced by the parish priest who was in fact anti-GAA. The priest selected as committee or council members some farmers and other local notables: arch-enemies of the leading men of the local GAA, and not popular with many people in town due to specific historical und economic circumstances. Previous to Muintir's introduction in the parish, all the local manifestations and festivities, like fairs and carnivals, were organized by the GAA, and many times, I was told, officers made personal profit out of these feasts. A cleavage developed thus between the two organizations; it became a competition for local leadership between GAA and Muintir.

During this competition, in 1965, a Fianna Fail TD cum MCC, Sean Dwane, from a nearby bigger town entered the Patricksville scene. This rather young TD had reached his position with the help of an older one, who worked and lived in another part of the constituency, but who was threatened by a very enthousiastic newcomer, a senator who wanted to reach the top and become TD. Though Dwane was "wedged" in between two standing TDs, and he had a very small pocket he got the seat through the many second preference votes funneled to him by the older TD mentioned above. Dwane had to extend his pocket to be safe for the next general elections. It was quite natural that he set his sights upon Patricksville, for this town was very close to his own. Moreover, the Fianna Fail TD from that area did not attend his homework very well: he was often away from home with his children in England, and the Patricksville people had already begun to be disappointed with their local TD. Dwane thus was seeking for an opportunity to infiltrate the area. Young Tadgh O'Sullivan was most suitable: ambitious, a leader of many people, and because of his two "mobile" jobs he covered a vast territory, saw many people and could hear confessions in all secrecy and send them through to his boss. In order to tie O'Sullivan to him, Sean

Dwane helped him to become a regional journalist for the newspaper he was already working for. This provided a steady and pensionable job. The advantage for the TD, on the other hand, was that O'Sullivan could now travel over a far bigger area (at the newspaper's expense), and do more work for him.

At the same time Dwane displayed his "pull" openly to the people of Patricksville, and in two ways. Both as secretary of an agricultural organization, and as a relative of a top-official in a big factory in Streamtown he was able to provide many people in the area with jobs. O'Sullivan also began to work on his homefront. He agitated publicly at Muintir meetings and criticized the local TD for having failed to provide some amenities asked for. He suggested asking Dwane for his help. At a GAA meeting, shortly afterwards, he announced that the club could buy a plot of state land for enlarging the local pitch at a low price. At a Muintir meeting he had proclaimed it a scandal that the local school stil had a dry closet; he did not understand why the parish priest, who is the manager of the school, had called off the installation of a water closet. O'Sullivan said he would do his utmost to get it there by asking Dwane for help. Some weeks later the water closet was installed.

To many people it became clear that Dwane was *the* man for the area, and that O'Sullivan was his right-hand man. From then on people came to Tadgh for "confessions'. O'Sullivan had gained not only in local leadership and influence but in political credit as well. The basis of his power *vis-à-vis* the local people in this respect was that he could select and decide who would be helped and what matter should be given priority. The people realized this and he made use of it. In other words, he developed "pull" himself, but it was in fact still completely based on his communication channel to Dwane. With these assets he entered a following phase in his career.

At the 1967 local elections Tadgh O'Sullivan decided to stand for the county council. He had gained a solid basis of backing from his own local club, and various delegates from other clubs in the area had promised to support him at the convention. He also knew he would have the support of many of the local electorate. But when Dwane heard about Tadgh's plans he was afraid, because O'Sullivan might well take many of his votes, even from his own local area. Dwane was rather unknown in GAA circles, for he backed other sports, and this might well cost him the votes of many GAA supporters from within his own area. The TD went along to see many members of the clubs in the CEA and persuaded them by means of promises, small gifts of money, drinks and other prizes, not to vote for O'Sullivan at the convention. Moreover, as Dwane was well known in other corners of the area where O'Sullivan had hardly been heard of, he could attain what he wanted. And, of course, other MCCs and Dwane's other local brokers were only too glad to support Dwane in this case. In short, O'Sullivan was not nominated. As reaction he started canvassing for another man, and not for Dwane. The result was a breach in the relatonship, but as each needed the other and as there was no man more suitable for the job, the two got on again after some time.

After this show-down O'Sullivan started to work in a slightly different way: he had been taught a good lesson in tactics. He began to nurse particular people who were also members of Dwane's network – influential men in the various local clubs – by promising them help and giving them all sorts of small favours and priorities on his list. Thus he began to build up a very tiny though important circle of helpers for himself. He scored his first big victory by providing a small row of houses at the edge of Patricksville with sewerage connections. For some time he had been "pestering" the officers in charge to give the matter priority, which, at last, seems to have occurred. The residents were delighted; a delegation came to his home to show their gratitude and left £ 15 on the mantlepiece. O'Sullivan, of course, did not make a secret of his own independent activities and results. Again, he began to make speeches at regional meetings against Dwane's policies. At one meeting, for example, he attacked the farmers by argueing that the prices of milk were too high for the consumers. This, of course, aroused the animosity of the farmers (an important category of supporters in Dwane's home-area). But by showing and explaining his detailed calculations he gained sympathy with many non-farmers, the majority of the delegates.

O'Sullivan strengthened his position as local broker in another way by laying his hands on a most vital channel. One might say, as broker he converted part of his secondary resources of a lower grade into those of a higher grade. He got a position as a liaison officer between the party's National Executive and the constituency. It became his duty to inform this top-body about every month on the situation at the grass roots: he thus reports on all the clubs, the MCCs and the TDs in the constituency. He gets a travelling-allowance and some pocket money for meals. Through this "backdoor" he is now able to meet the top-men of the party: ministers and secretaries of the departments. This position, created for other purposes, is a unique channel for Tadgh; he uses it to short-circuit Dwane. "When Tadgh goes up to Dublin", as his travels are called, he can contact these top-men, ask for help, advice, favours, and intervention in various local government matters. The ministers and the others know that he is a valuable person as he is active and familiar with the constituency set-up, and they are inclined to help him. At home he now is the "big fella": he tells people about his contacts with the party's "brass", what they told him about various opportunities and plans for the area, and so on. In this way, and in many others, he has both increased the quality of his credit and he is able to make a more direct profit too, as the following example shows.

One night a businessman from a nearby town dropped in at the O'Sullivans. The man was in trouble: the importation of a shipment of commodities was delayed at the Customs. It was of vital importance for the man to have it next day. O'Sullivan was asked whether he could help. He promptly rang up one of the ministers living close to the harbour; he was in and told

Tadgh to bring the businessman down to his home. The two drove to the minister's house, the man explained his case and the minister told him he would do his best. Next evening the businessman was back at the O'Sullivans and he told him that he was delighted that the matter was fixed. He wanted to show his gratitude to Tadgh but the latter refused. However, he mentioned in passing that he had been looking for a motorized bike for some months but that the prices were too high. Some days later the businessman came back with a brand new bike for which O'Sullivan had to pay only half the price. And apart from this he told Tadgh he would help him, at election times and whenever and wherever he could.

Here I must stop my case, for it is at this point in the local broker's career that I had to leave the scene. This whole process of a local broker's rising by means of a TD's channels was once described to me in a very vivid metaphor: " . . . it is like ivy in a tree: it's a parasitic, collateral growth. It is not of the tree, not of the system, it is just attached to it, it sponges on it and is spawned out of it. At the same time it is too dangerous a thing to shed. It is too deeply embedded in the edges. You cannot cut it off, for you might injure the main trunk of the tree".

V. CONCLUSIONS

In the previous pages it has been argued that the strength of a machine leader and the stability of his organization depend not only upon his place vis-à-vis his supporters, but also on his position in the arena. A leader's actual strength is the result of the way he has solved his internal and external management problems. Internally the TD has more problems than the MCC because the former's machine is not only larger but also contains a number of sub-leaders. Externally the MCC is in a less favourable position because he has to cope with many rivals with none of whom he can ally himself durably. The TD in this respect is better off. His local brokers, who are small wheels that weaken his machine internally, are however very effective weapons against ambitious MCCs and fellow-TDs. Also, local brokers keep each other weak.

Bailey has argued that this strategy of divide and rule tactics has its risks, for it may lead to a coalition of the weaker leaders who then dominate the stronger one.[4] It must be noted, however, that such a coalition will be formed only when the weaker leaders have some interests in common, and believe that they can overthrow the stronger one by combining their forces. For Ireland it seems evident that these counter coalitions do not take place, just because the weaker leaders have no common interests. A local broker and an MCC will not coalesce because none of them gains from this combination. Indeed, for an MCC these tactics would weaken his position. Again, local brokers will not combine forces because this does not strengthen their position or increase their chances for a seat in the county council.

The conclusion is therefore that the benefits of the TD's divide and rule tactics outweigh his internal management problems and thus keep him superior on all fronts. Consequently, the actual competition in the arena of the constituency is dominated by TDs. They fight each other and handle MCCs and local brokers as "passive" chess-pawns, so to speak, in subverting supporters. This game is described in the next chapter.

CHAPTER SIX

Machines as Processes:
Setting and Background *

I. INTRODUCTION

Up to this point I have been primarily concerned with the structural form of political machines. It is time to take a more dynamic approach. This chapter serves two connected purposed. First, it gives a description of machines in competition. It presents thus a picture of machine politics. Second, it deals with machines as processes. This second purpose can be subdivided into two: I will not only give a description of a particular machine and how it expanded and/or contracted through time. I also want to describe how and why this machine came into being. The general conclusion as to how and why it originated is that it resulted from an earlier competition between other machines within the same field of the constituency. Therefore, I must first deal with that competition in this field, the machines it contained, their relationships, strengths, and positions. This makes up the setting and background which I call Part One. Part Two then is a detailed description and analysis of the weal and woe of Sean Dwane's political machine. Part One passes almost automatically and inperceptably into Part Two. In the second part I actually change my position and focus on a relatively new machine though in roughly the same political field. To follow the argument better a map (Map II, page 110) is added.

II. MACHINES IN COMPETITION

1950-1961: POSITIONS, RELATIONS, AND STRENGTHS IN THE CONSTITUENCY OF TALLOW NORTH AND TALLOW EAST

Prior to the boundary revisions of 1961, the main parts of what is at present North-East Tallow constituency belonged to two constituencies, namely Tallow North and Tallow East. Each returned three members to the Dail.

Con Doherty

Tallow North was predominantly Fine Gael; it returned only one Fianna Fail member. The Fianna Fail politician, Con Doherty, lived on the fringe of the constituency, near Clonferry.

Doherty, or Fatty as he is popularly called because of his stout build, is a farmer with a family of 14 children. When one comes to talk about the size of his family, Doherty jokes that "the country up there is very fertile". Con Dohery began his political career as local broker for Sean Pearse, a Fianna Fail TD from Streamtown, and later he became MCC. However, Doherty was anxious to become TD. He had twice been nominated for the Dail elections as the running mate of the sitting TD, Sean Pearse, but he lost. When the very popular Pearse, a former hero of the war of independence, became minister, Doherty saw his chance to realize his dreams. As a minister, Pearse had to live in Dublin and in the enthousiasm for his work he neglected his voters and came back to his home town only sporadically. This gave Fatty the chances to expand his influence in a larger area. Streamtown was very attractive for him. It is a town of about 9,000 inhabitants and roughly 50 per cent vote for Fianna Fail. Doherty bought a pub in Streamtown and put his cousin behind the counter. He also began to bribe the secretary of the local Fianna Fail club. Both men started working for him. This caused many rows in Streamtown, and one of the results was a split of the local club: each formed an independent Fianna Fail club.

When Pearse came down to Streamtown, he felt that his popularity was declining. During the following Dail elections, both Pearse and Doherty were nominated again. It became a neck-and-neck race, with Doherty being elected, be it with a very small majority. About 18 months later, Pearse died of a heart-attack. The intrigues, together with the passing of Pearse, made Doherty unpopular with those Streamtown voters who stayed behind Pearse. This unpopularity was an important reason for Doherty losing his seat during the 1961 elections. The Pearseites gave their votes to a new-comer in this area, Steve Corbett, with whom I deal shortly.

The other part of what is now roughly North-East Tallow constituency, Tallow East, was also a three-member constituency. One seat belonged to Fine Gael, and the other two frequently to Fianna Fail.

Joe Miller

Joe Miller, the first Fianna Fail TD with whom we deal, lives in a corner of Tallow East, near Ballydown. Miller, also a farmer, is a tiny little man with a light stutter and nervously wandering eyes. Joe Miller had been TD before for some time, but he lost his seat to an old Labour MCC. It is alleged that one of the main reasons for his defeat was his lack of interest in his constituents. This seat, however, has always shifted between Fianna Fail and Labour. Miller married a farmer's widow when he came back from England, where he had been in the army during the second world war. Back in Ballydown he studied law for some years and got a B.A. degree. He went back to England and lectured at some college for about twelve months. When the Labour TD who had replaced Miller died, he came back to Ireland, was nominated in the by-elections, and won the seat. In normal elections, however, his position would be rather weak, because in this area Labour roughly equalled Fianna Fail in voting strength. Therefore, to make it stronger, Miller had to expand his territory. Due to his peripheral location he could not expand much to the East or the West. The only direction open for him was southward, but in the South was our second Fianna Fail TD, Steve Corbett.

Steve Corbett

Steve Corbett, TD cum MCC, lives in the southern part of Tallow East, near the small town of Cregg. Stevie, as the people call him, is a strong and rough character with a large moustache and a pipe which is always clenched between his teeth. It is alleged that his inseparable pipe twice set his sheets on fire. At present he is a well-to-do farmer though he himself does not do any work on the farm. Corbett has long been in politics. He was an officer in the IRA during the war of independence and later, in the civil war, he fought on the anti-Treaty side. When this troubled period came to an end he went into politics, first as MCC, and then in 1932 he became TD. His political career ended in 1969.

Various reasons can be mentioned to explain why he has been in politics for such a long time. An important factor is that he never became a victim of constituency revisions. His area remained the same during the changes which have caused serious troubles to many a politician. Most importantly however he was politically powerful because he was completely absorbed in politics. Strong as a bull and very shrewd, he was always working for the safety of his own position; politics was his life. He never stuck to the rule that each fellow-party politician should only work in his own pocket; he infiltrated others wherever and whenever he could. He always found an excuse to be present at places outside his pocket, where fellow-party members gathered. Wherever possible, he created small local brokers by bribing them or offering other items. Those persons then rallied support for him during election times. Moreover, he also approached the voters directly, he had small chats about the IRA times with the older people, many of whom had been active during the Troubles. The result of the tactics was always that he gathered votes from every corner in the constituency. When he lost some support in one part of his pocket because of lack of attention, he threw himself with more energy on some other area.

The following is an example (which I observed myself) of how he attracted voters in another politician's area. When the Patricksville Fianna Fail club met, Corbett dropped in. He said that he had been looking for his old friend Sean McDwyer at his home, but he was told that Sean was at the meeting. Next, he selected one of the old men and began to chat with him. Corbett said – and this is verbatim – : "I don't know who you are but I remember your face. God, it's a long time since I saw you in the old days. Weren't you in the (Streamtown) brigade"? (i.e. the IRA). The man said that he was in the brigade for a short time but his brother Joe belonged to the "brass" up there. Corbett: "Ah, yes, Jesus, he was a fine soldier, that old Joe. I remember him, shake hands to me here and have a drink. What old IRA fellers are round here and stayed alive"? The man gave the names and Corbett wrote them down. "Yerrah, I must certainly go and visit them". The old ties were strengthened again, and the next time, when the ballot boxes are opened, it is certain that Corbett has some twenty votes from Patricksville.

Steve Corbett improved his material position considerably during his political career. He was much involved in land speculation around the bigger towns of the county, and now he owns two farms, some racehorses, and a greyhound racing track.

Corbett built up a fairly strong circle of local brokers. Predominant among them was Ian Lynch, a farmer who lives on the northern flank of Corbett's pocket, near Bullaun. Lynch who is well-rooted in this area, was his main shield against intrusions from the North. Corbett had brought Lynch into his machine by offering him the formidable prize of a seat in the Seanad. This office carries a salary of £ 1,500 (1969) yearly. This kept Lynch dependent upon Corbett. Two other important local Brokers in Corbett's machine were Tom Kiernan from Drumsnagh, an Urban District Councillor, and Jim Spratt from Ardrahan, a small shopkeer who tried several times to become MCC.

It has always been Corbett's strategy to play off these three against each other. He promised to support them during local government elections and later, he hinted that they might succeed him in the Dail. This kept these three men very busy for him and at the same time made them fight each other like dogs, which kept them weak. When one of them "kicked over the traces" and expanded his influence too much, Corbett began to push, to flatter, and to make promises to the other two who then tried to run the third man down.

Corbett versus O'Broin

Corbett was never seriously affected by changes of the constituency boundaries and kept the forces in his machine balanced. A real danger began to develop on the easetern fringe of his pocket – be it that he did not realize it at the outset. Diarmud O'Broin, a poor barrister and lecturer in Irish in a Dublin college, launched himself into politics in the big town of Shanmore, which has about 7,000 inhabitants. The prime minister, a personal friend, had provided him a seat in the Seanad, and during the 1958 local government elections, he won a great victory in Shanmore and became MCC. This was O'Broin's first step. He was firmly determined however to push forward and become TD and eventually, because of his professional status, to reach ministerial level.

At first Corbett did not consider O'Broin a serious contender: he was a stranger in the Shanmore-area, and a man from the professions, who is as a rule at a disadvantage in Fianna Fail circles. Indeed, as O'Broin told me one night, Corbett supported in all secrecy O'Broin in the local elections to make the chances of his local brokers, Kiernan, Lynch, and Spratt, smaller and to keep them weak. The 1958 local elections demonstrated however that Corbett had underestimated O'Broin, for this politician came out of the battle very strongly. He almost equalled Corbett in voting strength. Corbett was now "hoist with the devil" and did not know how to get rid of him, though he had been able for a long time to prevent O'Broin from entering the dail.

O'Broin was firmly determined to move forward and become TD. He began to expand his domain. One of his first serious blows to Corbett was that he won Spratt, one of Corbett's local brokers, over to his own political machine. Spratt was rather easy prey because he had become soured on Corbett, from whom he had expected support at the nominations for the local elections. Spratt also thought that it would be easy to replace O'Broin in the county council after some time.

O'Broin's tactics against Corbett consisted for a long time of taking up those problems of constituents where Corbett failed. More importantly, however, O'Broin paid special attention to a number of local clubs in Corbett's area. The clubs, it will be remembered, are of basic importance for a person to be nominated. This led of course to confrontations and clashes between Corbett and O'Broin. Two of them were rather violent and are worth mentioning. Both were the result of Spratt's "floor crossing". When Corbett heard about this, he threatened Spratt and told him that he, Corbett, would make life very difficult for him. This did not help however. One night a gang of men entered Spratt's shop, kicked up a row and smashed part of his stock. Another night, when Spratt came back from a regional party meeting, his car was forced to stop by another car. Some men came out of the car, beat Spratt up, and told him that this is how they dealt with traitors. Spratt was outraged and went to his new boss, O'Broin, who promised to bring an action against Corbett. Later, Corbett was fined and had to pay for the damage. At the same time Spratt himself looked for revenge. One morning Corbett received a message that his greyhound track was damaged, and some weeks later, one of his own fine hounds was found poisoned. It is alleged that this was the work of Spratt's men.

Corbett felt that he was losing ground in the eastern part of his pocket and began to push northwards. He began systematically to infiltrate Joe Miller's Garvan-area, with Lynch as a front. Lynch was well-prepared to help Corbett get more votes in this area, for these votes would eventually be his, when Corbett stepped down. These activities led to many troubles, especially in the local Fianna Fail clubs around Garvan. Thus, instead of cooperating with Miller against new-comer O'Broin, Corbett adopted the tactics of expanding into Miller's area. This led automatically to a hostile relationship between him and Miller.

Such was the position of Fianna Fail in the constituencies of Tallow North and Tallow East up to 1960, when the 1961 Dail-elections drew near. In Tallow North, Con Doherty replaced the old minister, Sean Pearse from Streamtown, though he soured many people in the Streamtown area through his activities. In Tallow East, Joe Miller from Ballydown came in during a by-election, but he was not sure of being able to keep his position. The Dail seat from this area had always shifted between Fianna Fail and Labour as a considerable part of the electorate consisted of floating voters. Also in Tallow East, in the sourthern part, there was Steve Corbett, who had been safe for a long time but saw his position now threatened by O'Broin. These "forces" began to work upon each other in 1961, when the political field changed considerably due to the revision of the constituency boundaries.

The 1961 Encounter: Tallow North and Tallow East become one Constituency

Late in 1960, it was known in Fianna Fail circles roughly how the boundaries of the new constituencies had been drawn. These new constituencies would be the battle fields for the 1961 Dail elections which were to be held at the end of that year. The larger parts of Tallow North and Tallow East were put together and now became the North-East Tallow constituency, and returned five members.

Four Fianna Fail politicians were fighting for a seat: three sitting TDs, namely Doherty, Miller, and Corbett, and a very active new-comer, O'Broin. But on the basis of past electoral experience, it was predictable that two contenders must become losers.[1] In terms of losses of territory, Doherty and Miller had become weaker. The only sitting TD who was not hit by the changes was Steve Corbett.

Each of these four men prepared themselves for the elections and each followed three main lines in their strategies, be it that they gave individually different weights and priorities. First, all of them paid special attention to a strategy of enlarging the number of voters within and outside their pockets. This process goes slowly, however, and time was limited. Second, they all did their best to be nominated at the constituency convention, and canvassed members of local clubs to that end. Third, they were all engaged in bargaining with fellow-party politicians about exchanges of second preference votes, which they might need to become elected.

A detailed description of especially Corbett's activities is important, for these resulted in the birth of Sean Dwane's political machine. Corbett was troubled in his own pocket by O'Broin's intrigues. O'Broin began to attack Corbett on the western flank. He organized some six new local clubs in this area and, according to Corbett, bribed members from other clubs to vote for him at the nomination convention. (It is alleged that O'Broin could do this with a legacy of some £ 8,000 which his wife had recently inherited.)

To make up for these losses, Corbett began to operate over a long distance, in Streamtown. He began to play a masterful game here. It is here and at this time in fact, that the foundations were laid for Sean Dwane's career with which I deal in Part Two. Streamtown was a very attractive niche for Corbett, but it had been rather useless from a political point of view up to 1960: until that date Streamtown belonged to another constituency. Corbett is co-director of a big factory for processing agricultural products which is located in Streamtown. Moreover, he is chairman of an organization of cultivators of agricultural products, F.C.F. for short, and which also has its headquarters in Streamtown. Now that Streamtown belonged to his constituency, these two offices provided him with highly important political assets. As a result, Corbett had a vast network of personal relations in the Streamtown area, which he could use for rallying support. He was one of the few who commanded jobs in the factory and decided which farmers from the F.C.F. might provide the factory with agricultural products. These were very important means to attract voters.

Corbett was able to mobilize support not only on these transactional bases but also on a moral one. He had inside knowledge of the Fianna Fail split in Streamtown which was the result of Doherty's infiltrations there, and which in its turn had led to the defeat of the late minister Sean Pearse. It was rather easy for Corbett to bring the old Pearseites into his machine. They were against Doherty and since Corbett and Pearse had been old comrades-in-arms in the IRA and close friends, many Pearseites were well prepared to give their votes to Corbett.

This potential support, however, had to be organized and protected against intruders by a qualified person, willing to become local broker. Corbett selected Sean Dwane, the young secretary of the anti-Doherty club, who had been one of the initiators of the split. Corbett set his eyes upon Dwane because the latter was enthousiastic, well known in the area, and wanted to rise on the political ladder. Moreover, Dwane himself came from the Garvan area and has many relatives up there. These people might well give their votes to Corbett if Dwane put in a word for him.

Corbett got Sean Dwane committed by offering him a job as secretary of the F.C.F. which carries a salary of about £ 60 monthly. Dwane "took the bite" not only for financial reasons – he had a part-time job as local journalist – but also because it gave him an opportunity to build up credit for his own political career. This office provided him with opportunities. It made him the liaison between the F.C.F. producers (farmers), anxious to obtain a contract for delivering part of their produce to the factory, and the factory where Corbett was a man of weight.

In this way Corbett sought to make up for the potential losses in his own pocket, where O'Broin was undermining his position.

Such was the situation in the new political field of North-East Tallow close to the 1961 Dail elections.

About four months before polling day, Fianna Fail headquarters in Dublin ordered its constituency boards to organize nomination conventions. Headquarters advised the North-East Tallow board to nominate three candidates on the basis of past electoral experience. The nomination convention, however, voted for four candidates, namely Doherty, Miller, Corbett, and O'Broin. The weakest contender, O'Broin, was not outvoted because many clubs in Doherty's pocket voted for his nomination as a reaction against Corbett's intrusion into Streamtown, which was considered to belong to Doherty.

The general elections were a fierce battle. When the ballot boxes were opened and the first count finished, it appeared that none of the eleven candidates of the three parties obtained the quota. After the fourth count, no Fianna Fail candidate had yet obtained the quota. O'Broin was now at the bottom of the list and hence had to go. About 150 of his second preference votes went to Corbett, but far more were added to Miller's list. However, these 150 votes placed Corbett well over the quota. He was declared elected, and his surplus, some 120 votes, was redistributed. Miller obtained about 100 of them: he squeezed in and was declared elected. All five seats were filled. Doherty lost: he was more than 1,900 votes short of the quota.

Despite the losses in his own pocket, Corbett won through his infiltration into the Streamtown area. Miller won by backing two horses, as a right-hand man explained to me later, namely O'Broin and Corbett. O'Broin lost since his machine was not yet large enough. Finally, Doherty lost for two main reasons. First, his pocket had been reduced as a result of the constituency revisions. Second, he had not been able to make a deal with a candidate to the exchange of second preference votes.

III. AFTERMATH OF 1961 ELECTIONS, AND THE 1965 ENCOUNTER

Doherty and O'Broin lost the elections, but this did not imply that they disappeared from the political scene. Indeed, their activities were of considerable importance for the political game in North-East Tallow during the next four years. With no changes of constituency boundaries in the near future, each of the four politicians went back to work again. In the pages that follow we look at these machine leaders; how they worked out their strategies, and why, and how they put them to practice.

Diarmud O'Broin

It was of basic importance for O'Broin to expand his machine at the cost of Corbett and to consolidate the already existing ties with his own support. He began to activate a channel to Dublin: his senatorship gave him the opportunity to represent costfree his electorate at the various departmental offices. Moreover, he had become a member of the circle of top-men from the party, ministers, parliamentary secretaries, which he could approach rather easily. This was a unique asset for an MCC. It increased his status in the eyes of his supporters. Indeed, many of Corbett's followers began to realize that "strong Stevie" was not the only man with influence in the centre: O'Broin had "big pull up in Dublin" as well.

O'Broin continued to pay much attention to the areas around Templewater that he had taken over from Corbett. He often went to these areas, concentrated upon the club members, paid extra attention to their personal problems, and was able to solve some communal problems in a spectacular way.

O'Broin had more strings to his bow. He began to undermine Ian Lynch's faith in the sincerity and fidelity of his boss, Steve Corbett, with the ultimate aim of bringing Lynch into his own machine. (Corbett alleged that O'Broin had bribed Lynch with money from the former's wife though Lynch denied this. This is however quite well possible: Lynch is a heavy drinker and ran frequently into debts.) O'Broin had little chats with Lynch in the lounge of the county hall. He hinted that Corbett was rubbing shoulders with his young local broker from Streamtown, Sean Dwane. O'Broin suggested that Corbett might well cooperate with Dwane with the intention to obtain the two Fianna Fail seats for themselves. If this were true, Lynch's own chances for a TDship would be minimal, if not lost.

What O'Broin predicted became reality in Lynch's eyes, for Dwane became MCC in the 1962 county council elections, with much canvassing help from Corbett.

When Lynch obtained his "proof" that Corbett was no longer primarily interested in Lynch, it was easy for O'Broin to bring him into his own machine. Lynch, from his side, was well-prepared to work for O'Broin. It might enable him to make a deal for the exchange of second preferences during the 1965 Dail elections, when Lynch hoped to stand as a candidate.

Steve Corbett

Corbett, who heard about O'Broin's machinations with Lynch, began to put the latter and his relatives under severe pressure. He also explained that he would withdraw his support for Lynch's seat in the Seanad. Although the two came to terms again, Corbett was no longer certain of Lynch's active support. This and O'Broin's machination made Corbett begin to work in the Streamtown area with doubled energy. He began to "cultivate" an area below Streamtown which had never been worked upon much by any Fianna Fail politician, as it had always been in a corner of the successive constituencies. Together with Dwane he frequented the area as much as possible, went to all sorts of public manifestations, such as races and football matches. They founded more than ten local clubs, brought dormant ones to life again, and built up much credit through their important positions in the Streamtown factory and the F.C.F.

Joe Miller

Tiny little Joe Miller, the third man, also began to work following his narrow escape in the 1961 elections. He had been able to retain his Dail seat thanks chiefly to second preference votes from Corbett and O'Broin. He realized very well, however, that he had to expand his territory to become less dependent upon others. He thus began to operate westwards, into Doherty's area. He took over two local brokers from Doherty's machine, and built up some credit with the population. Miller concentrated however primarily on making himself known to this new territory. He got himself elected as chairman of a regional branch of a dairy suppliers' association. He revitalized old hurling relationships, and soon he was chairman of the regional GAA board.[2] Joe Miller made however one grave mistake. In 1963, he accepted an 18 months' job as lecturer in an English college where he had taught before. He thus had to leave his country. This became fatal: it gave Lynch the chance to infiltrate Miller's area. Moreover, many of Miller's supporters became disaffected with their absent TD.

Con Doherty

Finally, the fourth politician in the field, Fatty Doherty, was predominantly in the defence during the period 1961-65. Miller was infiltrating his pocket in the North-East, and Corbett, with Dwane's vigorous help, kept a large part of the Streamtown area closed. Indeed, those two brought some of Doherty's leading supporters of Streamtown into their own camp.

Nomination Negotiations

Early 1965, nominations were organized, and Fianna Fail intended to put up the two sitting TDs and two other candidates. A fierce battle was fought again, especially before the Fianna Fail convention was held. Hedquarters, in Dublin advised again to put up three candidates. Later, it appeared however that the convention was in favour of four, but the fight was determined by the issue of *who* were going to be nominated.

A period of negotiating, dealing, and secret double dealing began. Miller, back from England, realized that his position had been weakened. He supported Corbett for the nomination, provided that Corbett would do the same for him, and further providing that Corbett, as Lynch explained me sourly, prevented the latter from standing. Earlier, Corbett had been able to put the whip on Lynch who thus had not tried to be nominated. Miller told me once, after some glasses of whiskey, that he did not want to make a deal with O'Broin that time, for he was not certain about O'Broin's voting strength. O'Broin and Doherty had come to terms to support each other at the convention. When Corbett heard about this deal he became very afraid, for O'Broin had improved his position considerably since the previous elections. It was of basic importance for Corbett to prevent O'Broin from being nominated, or, if this appeared to be impossible, to have another strong supporter who could back him in the elections. He went to Dwane and asked whether he would stand as a candidate. Dwane, an ambitious politician, accepted the offer and made sure that Corbett would support him at the nominations. At the same time, Corbett advised Dwane to go to Miller and ask for his support at the convention. This was an attractive offer to Miller, who judged Dwane to be leader of a still small machine. Thus, if Dwane were nominated he would soon be eliminated in the elections, and his second preferences would go to the man next to him. Therefore, Miller accepted the offer, provided that he and Dwane would also exchange second preferences in the general elections. Corbett felt safe now, for Dwane was backed at the nomination by Miller and by himself. The clubs from Dwane's own area would naturally also support their local candidate. Thus, either O'Broin would be outvoted at the convention and thus be harmless to Corbett, or if he were nominated, Corbett would have much support from Dwane's area.[3]

Thus the nomination battle had been fought in fact before the constituency convention was held. It was a short but hectic meeting. Corbett, O'Broin, Miller and Dwane were nominated as candidates, and Doherty lost for the above mentioned reasons. O'Broin slipped in just before Doherty, for a number of local clubs in Miller's pocket, below Garvan where Lynch had worked for O'Broin, voted him in.

The Count

After a hectic period of canvassing, during which Steve Corbett wandered like an itinerant throughout the constituency rallying support wherever possible, polling day arrived, and it ended with the count. After several counts, no Fianna Fail candidate had yet been elected. Miller, however, began to see the writing on the wall. He had lost in strength as a result of his stay in England, and many supporters had given their number-one votes to the Labour candidate from the same area. Miller had expected to improve his position when Dwane was eliminated, but Dwane had more preferences than he. To his great astonishment and outrage he found himself at the bottom of the list, and hence was eliminated. Most of his second preferences went to Corbett, a smaller number to Dwane with whom he had made a deal and even fewer went to O'Broin. Through this redistribution Corbett, Dwane, and O'Broin improved their positions. For Corbett this was more than enough to obtain the quota, and he was elected. The redistribution of his surplus votes began. As there was still one seat and only two contenders, namely Dwane and O'Broin, the candidate with the most of Corbett's second preferences would win. It became a neck-and-neck race. In the end Dwane won with 37 votes more than O'Broin. This meant that Dwane was declared elected without having obtained the quota.

The power structure in the political field of North-East Tallow constituency had changed. Miller, one of the sitting TDs, had been defeated and lost his seat. Doherty, an old contender, had not been able to regain his power

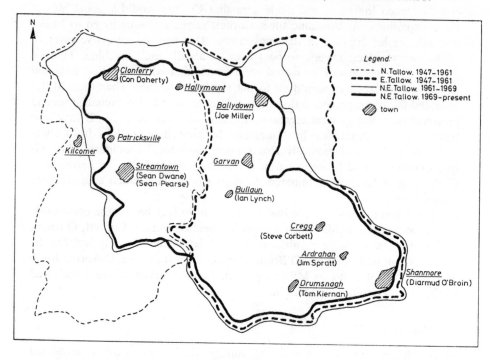

due to Corbett's infiltrations in the Streamtown area. Strong Corbett had once more been able to get rid of O'Broin, the formidable danger within his own pocket, and kept his seat. Finally, there is Sean Dwane, the new star on the political sky. His being launched into politics was the result of choices which an other TD, Steve Corbett, had to make when he met problems within his own territory.

Sean Dwane had thus become Fianna Fail's number-one man in the western area of the constituency. However, his position was not all that strong. He was wedged between two main contenders and owed his seat largely to Corbett's help. Doherty and Miller, who had been forced to make room for Dwane, were however firmly determined to regain their positions and push that "Johnny-come-lately" aside. It is worth-while therefore to look closely at the competition in this part of the constituency as it enfolds from 1965 onwards. This will be examined in the following chapter.

CHAPTER SEVEN

Machines as Processes (Continued):
Sean Dwane and his Political Machine

I. EXPANSION, IMPROVEMENT, AND CONSOLIDATION

Although Dwane had won over Miller and Doherty, he could not be sure of a re-election as he had not obtained the quota. Indeed, his election had been so marginal that he might well lose his seat to Miller, O'Broin, or even to Doherty, next time. His voting strength, at best some 4,500 votes, was confined to Streamtown, his home-town, and the surrounding areas. This number would not suffice for a safe seat, for the quota is always between 6,000 and 7,000 votes. This meant for Dwane continued dependence on and cooperation with Corbett. On the other hand, however, Dwane had to expand his own machine as well, for he could never completely rely on Corbett for several reasons. To begin with Corbett's power position was declining in his own territory due to O'Broin's machinations. This might well result in Corbett just getting enough votes to be elected at the next Dail elections. In that case there would be no second preferences for Dwane. Secondly, if Corbett's position was growing weaker, he might well pay more attention to the Streamtown area than during the 1965 elections. This would be at Dwane's expense, for Corbett had many personal contacts in the Streamtown area. If Corbett came in dire need of support, he could mobilize these persons *directly* and ask for their first preference votes. In other words, Dwane was not even sure of the first preferences of many of his own local voters. Another important reason why Dwane could not rely solely on Corbett's cooperation has again to do with the latter's declining power. There were no indications that O'Broin would stop infiltrating Corbett's area. Corbett therefore might well make a deal with Miller for the exchange of second preferences. In that case tiny little Miller could slip in and Dwane would lose his seat.

Thus, Dwane would have to concentrate his strategy on the following points. First, he would have to cooperate with Corbett for prizes (for the time being anyway). At the same time he must take over Corbett's support in the Streamtown area. Second, he needed to increase the number of prize producers in his own machine. Third, he must enlarge his territory. However, he could not infiltrate Corbett's pocket to do this: it would cause severe difficulties and might destroy their cooperation. Therefore, Dwane would have to concentrate his energies on Doherty and Miller. Dwane was the of-

111

ficial Fianna Fail representative now for the northern and western parts of the constituency. He was sure, however, to meet severe resistance when it came to visiting the local clubs in the areas which belonged in the past to Miller and Doherty. These ex-TDs were firmly determined to regain their positions, and they would not let Dwane enter their territories. Therefore, Dwane had to look for other ways to obtain support from their areas.

In the pages that follow we investigate how Sean Dwane, a Kennedy-like person with the same posture as the late John Kennedy whom he emulates in several respects, tried to improve and expand his machine.

Dwane and the Streamtown Area: Improvements and Consolidations

Although Dwane had important political assets in Streamtown, the entire town did not belong to him. Doherty maintained an important stronghold there in the person of local broker Joe Linehan, secretary and acutal leader of the second Fianna Fail club. Linehan had considerable "pull" with many people in the town and adjacent areas.

The first event to improve his position in Streamtown, and to damage Doherty's, was his marriage to Maire Sheehan.[1] Maire has a well-visited pub in the centre of the town. This had many advantages for Dwane: Maire brought in the money for the household. Thus aside from the time he spent as secretary of the F.C.F., Dwane could now spend most of his time on politics, Maire was centrally located in the local network of relations for reasons other than her pub. Her kinsfolk were well-rooted in town, especially in the business sector. This provided Dwane with other important assets, such as jobs for his voters, and potential financial and other help during his election campaigns. Moreover, some of Maire's relatives were important members of the pro-Doherty Fianna Fail club. As a result of his marriage and through various political manoeuvres, Dwane not only divided Doherty's stronghold but also brought these people close to, and eventually into his machine.

Dwane gave a final blow to Doherty's Streamtown stronghold when he took over the local broker, Joe Linehan. He had helped Linehan win a seat in the urban district council. Now time was ripe to use this credit. When Linehand ran into financial difficulties and lost his shop, Dwane offered him a good job. Dwane hinted however that the job was still in the palm of his hand.

Through these manoeuvres Sean Dwane was able to penetrate the heart of Doherty's stronghold. After about 12 months, the pro-Doherty club in Streamtown merged with the other club. This meant that Doherty was definitely defeated in the Streamtown area.

After this victory, Sean Dwane began to concentrate on undermining Corbett's strenth in the Streamtown area. Although Dwane was dependent upon Corbett's political capital, he was in a more advantageous position for frequent and regular contact with the voters than Corbett, who lives some

112

40 miles from Streamtown. Dwane frequented all the clubs in the area, "heard confessions", and was able to solve several problems. He went to every meeting and social happening to show his face. He made speeches. In short, he became well-known in the area, discovered how to maximize his potential voting strength and acted accordingly, with Corbett as the main channel to sources of prizes.

Although he improved his position through these activities, Dwane was still uncertain whom the Pearseites would support in the elections. Corbett had close connections with friends, relatives, and admirers of the late minister from Streamtown. This "clannish" circle might well give its first preference votes to Corbett. Dwane looked for ways to attach these people more closely to himself. He visited Pearseites and was in the front ranks when Pearse's anniversary was celebrated. His big chance however came when he got Pearse's son, Niall, a poor solicitor, on the hook. Niall is a spendthrift and a weak character, though held in high esteem among the Pearseites, and Dwane tried to take advantage of this. He had done a good turn to Niall in an earlier period, when he was "angling" for a directorship of a local bottle factory. A second chance turned up when the big agricultural factory in Streamtown needed a legal adviser. Again, Niall Pearse was highly interested in the job. When Corbett, the chairman of the board of directors, was too vague in his promise to Niall, he went to Dwane and asked to press the matter with Corbett. Dwane, as Corbett's chief adviser for the area, could persuade him to give the job to Pearse. After Niall's appointment, Dwane was certain of Pearse's support. Indeed, Pearse has been providing jobs for Dwane's voters ever-since.

Thus Dwane brought the leader of the Pearseites into his own machine and dealth therewith a severe blow to Corbett's position in Steamtown.

Although Sean Dwane increased his "pull" in several prize producing sectors, he was still rather dependent upon Corbett's contacts in the county offices. It must be said, however, that his experience there had increased during the three years that he was MCC. Here again Dwane determined to make his own way. It appeared that luck was with him. A very important channel was a barrister from Patricksville, who had much influence in the county offices. This barrister had no political ambitions, but wanted to climb in the legal world. And as the normal road to better legal jobs is via party affiliation, this barrister attached himself to Fianna Fail and was an active officer in several party organizations. Dwane and the barrister met frequently at party conventions and they became close friends. When the state solicitor from the county died and a close friend of Dwane was appointed, Sean Dwane saw his chance to activate his relationship with the barrister and translate it into political capital. Dwane was able to arrange with his friend, the new state solicitor, to give the legal cases to the barrister. This meant important additional income for the barrister. Since then he has done much for Dwane in the county offices. Sean Dwane in his turn introduced him in the party top in Dublin. The barrister, incidentally, was appointed district justice in 1971.

Thus, this first period of Sean Dwane's activities was characterized largely by entrenching himself firmly in the Streamtown area and by making himself more or less independent from Corbett. It can safely be said that by the end of 1967, the Fianna Fail part of the Streamtown area was solidly behind Dwane.

Towards Expansion of the Territory: Dwane's Strategy in the Garvan Area

A strengthened position in Streamtown was not enough. Dwane could rely maximally on some 4,500 to 5,000 voters which is still far below the quota. To increase the number of votes, therefore, he needed to cover a wider territory. As the elected Fianna Fail TD, he was entitled to cover the whole western side of the constituency. Miller and Doherty however barred him. They considered large parts of the constituency as their pockets, although they were no longer representatives to the Dail. Dwane tried various times to force his way into the club meetings in Miller's home-area but he met severe resistance. One time he came to this area, accompanied by some 20 supporters, with the intention of intimidating Miller. It came to a real fight and the Dwaneites were bloodied and forced back. Since that time Dwane has stayed away from Miller's home-area.

Sean Dwane began to concentrate on a more peripheral part of Miller's pocket, namely the Garvan area. This area had always been carved up by several Fianna Fail politicians. The clubs were either dead or dormant, springing to life only during nominations and elections. Infighting was then more the rule than the exception. Under normal circumstances the area was run by circles of local brokers. Miller ruled a large part now by means of several local brokers. An important supporter of Miller in this area was Liam MacDonagha, an old MCC from Garvan who was actually more interested in the revival of the gaelic culture than in politics. Ian Lynch, Corbett's right-hand man, had also some strongholds in the area, and even Corbett himself had some men there. This set up was favourable for Dwane. In such a fragmented area he could easily slip in without disturbing seriously any organized system.

But there were still other important reasons why Dwane considered the Garvan area attractive. He was born and bred there. He has many relatives and friends around Garvan, and his mother has a very centrally located and well frequented pub in town. Moreover, the old republican tradition is still very much alive in the area and Dwane is from real republican stock. His father and other elderly relatives had been active in the old IRA. The Dwanes are therefore held in high esteem. Finally, many farmers are members of the F.C.F. agricultural producers organization of which Dwane is secretary. Thus Sean Dwane was in an advantageous position in Garvan; his relationships had an extra "tone", so to say, and they might well be activated for political purposes.

Unobtrusively he began to poach in Miller's preserve. He made regular

114

visits to his mother's pub, chatted to many people, stood them rounds of drinks, he showed himself widely, and went to various meetings. In short, he began to tighten the old bonds and to forge new ones. Soon his mother's pub became a place for regular political meetings, where Dwane "heard confessions". Of course, Miller did not like this, and soon Dwane's mother became dramatically involved in the competition between her son and Miller. One night her pub burnt down. Dwane received indications proving that one of Miller's local brokers had had a hand in it. He put both men under severe pressure. Miller kept quiet from that date, and the broker has been a "loyal" member of Dwane's machine ever since.

Dwane went on digging in around Garvan. He expanded his circle of local brokers there. He created new ones, and brought some of Corbett's brokers into his machine.

Sean Dwane also started working on the formal political front of the Garvan area. He brought dead clubs to life again and established new ones in some villages and towns. He did this to be sure of well-organized cells for nomination conventions and elections.

Garvan was not the only area to which Dwane paid attention. He expanded also in another direction. The immediate cause, as he explained when we were discussing this period, was a small incident. A businessman from Hallymount came to Dwane and asked whether Dwane could obtain a state grant, for he wanted to establish a small factory in town. The case interested Dwane more politically than financially: it might be an opportunity to expand. Hallymount had formerly belonged to Doherty, but it had lately been taken over by Miller. This meant that the area was not yet well organized. Dwane promised the businessman to do his best in Dublin, and he himself came to Hallymount to establish a local industrial development association. The association met several times, and this provided Dwane with the opportunity of establishing a local broker. He had this broker organize a regional survey on the labour potential. Meanwhile, the broker was to mention in many houses that he could contract jobs in the new factory with Dwane's help. When Dwane received a positive letter from Dublin, he went to the businessman and made a deal: Dwane would have a say in the selection of labourers for the new factory. Soon Dwane was generally considered *the* man for jobs.

Thus Sean Dwane expanded and consolidated his machine. Streamtown was firmly behind him, and the Garvan part of his machine also ran fairly well. Two important members of Dwane's machine estimated his support late in 1968 to be 6,500 to 7,000. As they put it: "(Sean) was running on ball-bearings". This does not mean, however, that small wheels, that tended to run counter to the general direction, did not exist in Dwane's machine.

Internal Management Problems

Although Dwane's influence in the Garvan area had expanded considerably there was still a small stronghold of resistance. The local Fianna Fail MCC old Liam MacDonagha, and some of his adherents belonged still to Miller's machine. MacDonagha was not a serious threat to Dwane, but he had many contacts with old republicans. These contacts might well be used in a general election to the benefit of Miller, if MacDonagha put in a word for him. However, as we see shortly, Dwane brought the old MCC into his own machine for the very reason that Dwane met internal management problems.

These problems arose during the 1967 local government elections, when one of Dwane's local brokers, a man from Grenane, announced that he would stand as a candidate. The broker lived very close to Dwane's area; so close that he might even take many votes from Dwane's own area. Initially, the broker's activities did not bother Dwane. He could play him off against old MacDonagha. And if it were to come to a test, Dwane would support MacDonagha who was farther away from him. Sean Dwane's ideas changed however when Miller began to mix in the affair. Miller saw a chance to make a hole in Dwane's machine and to regain a stronghold. He contacted the ambitious Grenane broker, promised to support him at the nominations, and to canvass for him during the elections. Although this implied that he might lose MacDonagha, Miller would certainly be paid for his work: the young broker would be a much better wheel. When Dwane heard about this deal, he went to MacDonagha, explained what was afoot, and promised to support him. MacDonagha and Dwane, the two sitting MCCs, and the young Grenane broker were nominated. Dwane brought a large part of his machine into the field and canvassed vigorously both for himself and for Mac-Donagha. His local broker from Grenane got a severe show-down, and MacDonagha was re-elected though only on Dwane's turnovers.

Thus Dwane turned internal management problems into political capital. He brought MacDonagha, now dependent upon his second preference votes, into his machine, MacDonagha will support Dwane although he knows that Dwane poaches in his preserve; Dwane deals, via local brokers, with local government problems, which belong to MacDonagha's domain. Furthermore, Dwane taught his Grenane broker a lesson. The man understood that he cannot expand and turn his influence into office without Dwane's approval: he has been working for Sean Dwane since that date.

In Streamtown, the heart of his pocket, Dwane was also confronted with problems. Again they had to do with the 1967 local government elections. Two persons fought for a seat in the county council. Dwane however played them off against each other. This resulted in neither being nominated. Indeed, both candidates have been trying to build up credit with Dwane since that date, and hence keep each other weak.

Major Political Windfalls

The period between 1965 and 1968 was hectic for Dwane. He improved his position considerably in the Streamtown area, and he drew all possible ties tighter in Garvan. Yet he was not sure of the future. He did not feel easy about Corbett. If Corbett were to grow weaker in his own pocket, he might well become very active in the Streamtown area and try to obtain as many first preferences as possible.

Another problem had to do with Miller. Although Miller had grown weaker too, Dwane had still to be careful of "this little rat", as he once referred to Miller. If Corbett were in a difficult position, he might well make a deal with Miller for the exchange of second preferences. In that case Corbett and Miller might be elected, and Dwane would lose. In short, many important problems had still to be solved. However, the problems solved themselves without any effort of Dwane.

In 1968, the Fianna Fail government introduced an electoral amendment bill, providing for changes of constituencies. This bill became law early in 1969. As a result of the revisions, North-East Tallow became a four member constituency – and lost thus one seat – with an electorate of about 45,000, which is 10,000 less than in the 1965 general elections. Clearly, at least one of the five sitting TDs would lose his seat. And when the new boundaries became known (see Map II) it was evident that the Labour TD, whose party was the weakest in the constituency, would be the loser. His area lost about 6,000 voters. Indeed, the larger part of his home-town area went to another constituency. More important for Sean Dwane's position however was that two old contenders lost much territory through the boundary revision. "Fatty" Doherty became a victim. About 3,000 voters, of whom some 1,000 voted for Fianna Fail, were cut out of his pocket. This meant that Doherty would no longer be in the ring, and hence could not be a threat for Dwane. Joe Miller had also been severely hit. He lost a territory quite close to his home-town. This embraced about 2,000 voters, of whom approximately 1,200 belonged to his machine. This was an enormous windfall for Dwane. Miller's position, already below the margin in the 1965 elections, now crumbled so far that he would not have the slightest chance in the next elections. Dwane could safely conclude that Miller would not stand at the coming general elections, and consequently, Corbett could not make a deal with him. The positions of Corbett and O'Broin had not been affected, and this implied that the old feud between them would continue. Finally, Dwane himself had also been affected by the revision. Part of Doherty's area, which Dwane took over during 1967 and 1968, went to another constituency. This costed Dwane some 700 votes. However, when we consider the total result of the constituency revision, it is clear that Dwane's position had increased in strength. Doherty and Miller had gone, and Corbett could only affiliate with Dwane. Corbett might however do still some damage in Dwane's own Streamtown area.

Some months later, it appeared again that luck was with Dwane. In May 1969, Corbett announced that he would not stand for the next Dail elections. This came as a great surprise to many, including myself, for I was anxiously watching the developments of the coming elections. What had happened? Corbett had been involved in a corruption affair. It seems that he had provided a friend with a county contract for constructing a large public building. This friend, a contractor, had given Corbett some £ 2,000 for his help. I do not know exactly how the affair came into the open, but it is alleged that his mortal enemy, Diarmud O'Broin, had had a hand in it. It is true, however, that the party executive forced Corbett, under a threat of legal prosecution, to step down. Corbett made the best of a bad bargain and stepped down; and so avoided being fined and losing his TD pension. Obviously, this was an important political windfall for Dwane. It meant that he could now rely on a majority, if not all, of the Fianna Fail voters in the Streamtown area. Dwane felt now safe to face the general elections.

II. THE 1969 GENERAL ELECTIONS

Negotiations for the Nomination Convention

In May 1969, a message came from Fianna Fail headquarters that a nomination convention must be held within a few weeks. Headquarters advised North-East Tallow to nominate three candidates. Soon it became known however that five politicians wanted to be nominated: Dwane, the sitting TD, O'Broin, Ian Lynch, Tom Kiernan, and Jim Spratt. O'Broin could however persuade Spratt to withdraw, and thus four men remained. A hectic time for these four contenders began. They went along all the clubs in their areas, making promises and advising how to vote at the convention. They also attempted to bargain with fellow-contenders for support at the convention.

The various organizational segments of the party came also to life again. First, each local club held a meeting to decide whom they would support and in which order, and who would be their local representatives at the convention. Regional meetings, at which the clubs try to reach consensus about whom they would support, were organized next. Usually, each area meeting tries to attain an even spread of candidates over the constituency. On the other hand, every meeting attempts to make sure that its own candidate does not suffer from a colleague too nearby. North-East Tallow has four regional conventions: Streamtown, Ballydown, Shanmore, and Drumsnagh. The Streamtown area decided to support its local politician, Sean Dwane, first. O'Broin would be supported next, for he and Dwane would vote for each other at the convention. The third vote would be for Kiernan from Drumsnagh. Kiernan had been chosen because he was farther away from Dwane than Lynch. Moreover, Lynch had many contacts in Dwane's newly won Garvan area.

The Shanmore regional meeting supported O'Broin first. As a result of the deal with Dwane, it would give its second vote to him. For their third choice they had to make the best of a bad bargain. Both Lynch and Kiernan were members of Corbett's machine. The nomination of either politician might well cause O'Broin losing many votes. Finally, Shanmore decided to give its third vote to Lynch, for he was farther away from O'Broin.

In Drumsnagh the set up was as follows. Tom Kiernan was number one, and Dwane was to be second. Lynch was mentioned third because both Kiernan and Lynch were former members of Corbett's machine, and as such they could rely on Corbett's former supporters.

Finally, the regional meeting from Ballydown, Miller's domain, brought a great surprise: it voted for Dwane first. Miller, who bore an old grudge against Dwane and had kept his home-area closed for him, had changed his strategy. The cause of this abrupt change, which was confided to me by Dwane's main legal adviser who was one of my key-informants, was the following: Miller, who knew that he had no chance of regaining a seat in the Dail, had set his eyes upon another prize, namely the chairmanship of the regional health authority; a well-paid job with much prestige. Miller hoped to obtain this office with Dwane's help. He knew that Sean Dwane had much influence in the county council's appointments committee. So Miller realized that Dwane's support was of basic importance. He therefore promised to support Dwane. He would open his area, vote for Dwane at the convention, and provide him with his apparatus for the canvassing period. As counterprestation Dwane must help Miller to obtain the chairmanship of the health authority. Dwane accepted the offer, provided that the Ballydown area would vote in the same way as Dwane's own area. These proposals were accepted. Ballydown voted for O'Broin as number two, despite the resistance of representatives from some local clubs. Kiernan would be number three. Miller, incidentally, was well paid for his services; he was in fact appointed chairman of the regional health authority.

When the convention met, the situation seemed clear. Dwane would be supported by four regional meetings, O'Broin by three, and Lynch and Kiernan by two. Kiernan had naturally more chances, for he was supported by Streamtown and Ballydown, which have a large number of clubs. However, things turned out differently. The minister from Dublin who presided over the meeting made a grave mistake in the voting procedure. This resulted in Dwane, O'Broin, and Lynch (instead of Kiernan) being nominated. Before the candidates went their way they first had to agree about the division of the constituency into pockets; areas where only one candidate is entitled to canvass for votes. Despite several meetings however they could not come to an agreement. The constituency was therefore declared "open country", meaning that anyone could canvass anywhere.

Organizing the Harvest

The nomination over, another hectic period began. During this period, usually covering three to four weeks, strength and organizational qualities of each machine are put to the test. Each leader then urges as many voters as possible to go to the polling booth and vote for him. This is done by door-to-door canvassing, by asking people directly for their votes. Each candidate should ideally himself canvass all the voters in his pocket, for the Irish are slow in giving their votes to a candidate whom they do not know either personally or via some personal contact. However since some 10,000 voters must be canvassed, of whom the majority lives scattered over the countryside, it will be evident that this personal approach is impossible. The leader therefore divides this work among his machine members. For this purpose his local brokers will not suffice; he must also mobilize active members of every club in his area. Together with him, these persons make up the primary and the most fundamental action set for mobilizing the electorate.[2] To keep this action set – which actually consists of numerous sub-sets – running smoothly, the leader needs resources. He need cars to transport his canvassers, pocket money for each to pay phone calls, meals, and drinks. He needs mobile loudspeakers for public addresses, and rooms for meetings. These expedients are paid partly from his private election fund. He will however also try to get machine members to pay these costs, especially businessmen who are indebted to him or want to build up credit. They make up another action set. A third set consists of members who write scripts for the leader's addresses and/or deliver speeches themselves. Finally, a fourth action set can be delineated for which the previous three are activated, namely the voters who go to the polling booth and vote for their leader. These four action sets make up that part of the machine which is active during the election period.

So far in this section we have been dealing with the general organizational structure, stemming from a basic model of strategy. A strategy, it will be remembered, results from choices of a number of possibilities. Some possibilities are better than others because they are less expensive or promise more profit. Although this structure is the same for every machine leader, each follows a somewhat different strategy, makes different choices, and choses from different possibilities, because his circumstances differ from those of others. We now take up the thread again and see how Dwane organized the various parts of his machine.

Sean Dwane's first choice had to do with the scope of the territory which he would cover. In this respect he was not hampered by binding rules, for the constituency had been declared open country. However, Dwane had expanded his electorate within a well-delineated and rather compact territory. This counted some 10,000 Fianna Fail voters, enough for a safe seat. Consequently, Dwane decided not to organize "flying columns", as he put it, wandering throughout the constituency. He would give all his energy to areas around his bulwarks of Streamtown, Garvan, and Ballydown. For safety, however, he made a deal with O'Broin for an exchange of second preferences. (After the election, Dwane explained, sitting in his favourite rocking-chair, that he thought it safer to cooperate with O'Broin than with Lynch, for the latter has many contacts in Dwane's area).

Now that Dwane had decided which area he would cover with his machine, he had to determine where he himself would be the most active. Clearly, he could not pay equal attention to all his areas. Indeed, it would be unwise to do this, for his strength differed from area to area. He decided to leave his home-town area, Streamtown, to his local brokers and some other club members, who made up the core of his machine there. Dwane thought it necessary to pay more attention to the Garvan area, for Lynch had many contacts and some local brokers there. Moreover, Lynch would certainly ask Steve Corbett for help; Corbett might well persuade his former local brokers, who now belonged to Dwane, to work for Lynch. Dwane therefore decided to pay personal attention to the Garvan area. He would also add some relatives to the local canvassing teams. They could supervise the day-to-day activities. His presence was even more necessary in Ballydown, which Miller had recently thrown into his lap. Here he could make use of Miller's well-organized network of local clubs. He himself however had to do the bulk of the canvassing work, for the population hardly knew him. When Miller had introduced Dwane to the core of his personnel, Dwane decided to work here without Miller's personal help, two men was wasting capital. Dwane decided to station Miller in Streamtown, where he, together with Dwane's wife, could supervise and direct the canvassing teams. Owing to his experience as TD, Miller was valuable not only for this work, he was also a good speaker and could thus deliver speeches at meeting places in and around Streamtown.

Thus Dwane worked out a plan for his election campaign. He created three headquarters where the activities would be supervised and directed. Each was headed by two or three persons, one of whom had a closely, personal tie with him. He himself would stay the first week or ten days in Ballydown during the day, and at night in Garvan. The next week he would reverse the schedule, and the last few days he would be in his home-town area.

When Dwane had thus developed the main lines of his strategy, he started organizing his team and selecting the personnel for the action sets and sub-sets. Per area he invited one or two active members of all the local clubs for a meeting in the "snug" behind his pub. This little room, which I visited often during the election period, looked like the headquarters of a general at wartime. Constituency maps with lines and figures were pinned to the walls, posters and stickers piled upon the tables, and Dwane himself would walk from one map to another, meanwhile grab frequently for the telephone, and back again to his maps. He explained his men that there would be three headquarters this time, and he introduced them to those in charge of supervising the activities of their area. He divided his entire territory into three parts, and indicated which clubs belonged to which headquarters. Next, he appointed one man for each club and charged him with the local organization. This person must report daily to his headquarters about the local position. He must also form the canvass teams of two or three men, each in charge of canvassing a particular part of the local area.

Finally, Dwane told these local leaders about his deal with O'Broin. It was their task to induce the electors to give their second preference votes to O'Broin.

In the mean time, Sean Dwane contacted many businessmen, especially from Garvan and Streamtown. They provided him with motorcars, money, and meeting rooms. Dwane had some 35 cars for canvassing activities, and at polling day, more than 60 cars brought old, sick, and isolated voters to and from the polling booths. Moreover, five solicitors and barristers wrote scripts, and three delivered speeches on his behalf at church gates before and after Sunday-masses. Thus, in addition to some 10,000 voters, Dwane mobilized about 230 persons of whom some 140 were canvassers. ((See diagram III.)

Dwane's machine functioned properly on the whole. Apart from the usual small problems, such as illness of some men, defective motorcars, quarrels between canvassers, no serious difficulties turned up this time. Only once, early in the canvassing period, did a clash between Dwane and another candidate take place. One night, Lynch and some supporters entered Garvan and started canvassing a sector of the town. They thought that Dwane was not in town and that they could rally some support while he was absent. When Dwane heard that Lynch was poaching in his preserve, he selected some "bully boys" and a small fight developed. Lynch was soon driven out of the town. Late that night, Dwane told Lynch by phone to

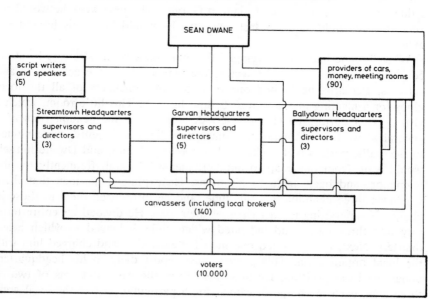

Diagram III. Personnel of Sean Dwane's political machine in action during 1969 general elections. (lines indicate communication paths)

keep off the grass, or else he would instruct his canvassers to advise the voters not to give a vote to Lynch. This kept Lynch quiet for the rest of the time. Apart from this, Dwane's machine "ran on ball-bearings". Each little canvassing team worked its own "strip of country". It followed the same routine. As I saw and heard it some 40 times during my stay in 1969, I give two verbatim examples here.

Canvass Talk

A small row of cottages had had to be canvassed. The leading canvasser – this is usually the man most familiar with the area – told me that some families here were "dagglers", meaning floating voters. One of the canvassers knocked at the first door. The woman of the house came out, and the leading canvasser said: "Good day to you, Mrs. Gould; God bless ye. Sorry for troubling you, but you know, we're out canvasssing for the general election. Will you support Sean Dwane? You know, he's our local man". Hands were shaken, and the leading canvasser went on: "It's a fine day. I see you've the laundry out early. It's a great blessing, thank God, these windy days. Here's some election stuff for you. Don't read it now, you can do that tonight". The canvassers gave the election literature, a stencilled "personal letter to the elector" from Dwane. Finally, they handed her a specimen ballot paper with the names of all the candidates of the constituency. Dwane's name was printed in thick capital letters, and opposite his name a 1.

Leading canvasser: "This is your man, Sean Dwane. Give him your vote and you'll be safe for the rest of your life".
"And for Limbo too", joked another canvasser.
Mrs. Gould, cleaning her hands on her apron, suddenly came to life and said: "Come in here to me. Ye are the very fellers I want to see. Look, my husband applied for a medical card three years ago. And he applied to Paddy Malone from Fine Gale, 'cause that man was in town. And we didn't hear from the medical card since. There's no pull in them feller. And there's no meaning at all now to that Mrs. O'Shea down the road. She can get a medical card, and why cannot we get a medical card? We understand that the health act is free, and that she can get the pills and bottles of medicine at the dispensary. And we have took along with a fair doctor, with a pound out of me pocket to pay him. And despite me fist and heel, he told me to go down the chemist".

Leading canvasser: "Jesus, that's a bad thing, Ma'am. God forgive me for cursing, but you should have told that to me. I'll write it down and discuss the matter with Dwane. He'll certainly help you out. I'm really sorry to hear that now. Yerrah, you know that Dwane is a great man for these things. Hasn't he fixed Patsy's pump? And don't you remember them splendid new water pipes that were laid down below New Street? It was all Dwane's work. He has big pull, I can tell you that, he has big pull up in the offices. So if you want big pull in the area, vote him in".

Mrs. Gould: "That's something anyway. But what to do with me other votes? What 'd you advise me? Let me see, who is more on that paper (the specimen ballot paper)? Ha, O'Broin. I don't know him. Ian Lynch? Isn't he a relative of Paddy from Main Street? Yerrah, Paddy is a nice and decent man. I think I'll give him a vote".

Leading canvasser: "Well, ma'am, it's of course your own vote, but since you ask me, I'll give you my upignion (i.e. opinion). Ian Lynch won't get it, as sure as I'm not the devil himself. Lynch is a drunkard. Yerrah, he drinks the cross of an ass, and do you want to be represented up in Tallow by that man? He won't even get enough votes in his own district. And d' you know why? Because them folks up there know damn' well that he's a drunkard. Ah, there's no pull in that man. I'll tell you something now. Sean Dwane and Diarmud O'Broin are going to work for the whole area. O'Broin is going to replace Corbett, you remember him and all about him in the newspaper. O'Broin is a great man. He'll certainly make it. So you'd better give him your second vote".

Mrs. Gould: "I didn't look at it that way at all. I'll think it over". The leading canvasser concluded the conversation: "That's oke, and you can make up your own mind now about what you do up the booth".

The second example comes from a farmer's household, consisting of two brothers and a sister; all unmarried. They were Fianna Fail supporters, but it was always hard to get them to the polling booth. They were old and near their seventies. After a knock at the door, the three came out and said: "God bless ye. Won't you come in?"

We sat down and the canvasser who belonged to this area and knew the people well, said: "We're out canvassing on behalf of Sean Dwane, the Fianna Fail man inside Streamtown".

"A good man, a good man", was the answer. "We tried him here around the district. A good man; we certainly support him at the election. We weren't off the place last time, for we did not bother going out".

"Tell me", said the old woman, "is it true that if this Labour party gets control now, that they will take all our money off us?"

"Where did you read that?"

"Ah, there came a man and he said like on television". The old woman referred to a broadcast where Labour promised to nationalize banks and industries. "And to tell the truth now", the old woman continued, "God souls, we have put together a little bit o' money, and it's for our old age, when we're worn and tired. And then it's them couple of shillings in our pocket to spend, and we don't want to lose it. We find it very hard to bring it to the bank. And when these jokers (Labour) come and take it from the bank, we're gone". "Yerrah, that's why you must go out this time and vote, 'cause if you don't, and many others don't, them Labour party wins", said the canvasser. "Ah, we're going out this time and vote, and no more about it", was the determined reaction. "But could you get us a car to bring us up the booth? We find it hard to walk the three miles up the road".

124

"Certainly, we will arrange that for you. At what time d' you want to go?"

"Well, I'd say about ten in the morning".

"Fair enough, we'll send the car down to your place".

"Well lads, we must go now. And we won't bother you any longer. God bless ye. Hope you make a good choice up the booth".

Counting the Votes

When polling day was over, all the ballot boxes from the constituency were brought to Streamtown, where the count was to begin next day. When the day arrived, many people gathered in the big counting hall. Whenever a box from a polling district was opened, the candidates with their "tallymen" gathered behind the counters – counting is done by hand – to study their position in each electoral district.[3] Soon it became clear that Dwane was "going very fast". Ostentatiously he left the hall and went to his pub. He did not come back to the count but was kept informed by messengers. Late that night the count was finished. Dwane won with a land-slide. He was about 1,000 over the quota, and his surplus was almost equally divided among O'Broin and Lynch. They went very close to each other through the subsequent counts. In the last count, however, when there were no candidates to eliminate, O'Broin won from Lynch and was declared elected without obtaining the quota.

Thus Dwane obtained a very strong position. This was the result both of his well-organized machine, of Miller's support, and of Corbett leaving the scene. Some weeks later, Dwane was paid for his work. The prime minister appointed him as secretary to a ministerial department, which carries a salary of £ 2,500. On top of this Dwane receives his normal income as TD, £ 2,500.

Part three: Politics at the Grass-Roots

Introduction

In the second part of this book the structural characteristics of a political field and the dynamics of its power process were analyzed. Part Three continues this enquiry but focuses on a very small segment of this field. That is, it describes machine politics at the grass-roots level, the parish, which is the basic social unit and the heart of Irish rural society.

The inclusion of this small local unit is not merely a matter of anthropological tradition. Up to this point only a partial picture of machine politics has been given. The attention was focused on the TD, and his local broker, the pre-eminent leader at the local level, was touched upon only in his relation with the TD. A broker's broker however, is more than a "passive" pawn on a TD's chess board. He is a micro-leader of his own small machine that he tries to expand and protect against subversive activities. Thus, an analysis of the parish, concentrated on the local broker, is necessary for a better understanding of machine politics.

The broker, however, is also involved in more parochial games. And although machine politics and parish politics are intricately intertwined at the village level, they form different types of games, and therefore must be treated separately. In Patricksville, the community under consideration, parish politics changed into machine politics when one local leader became broker for a particular TD. Although many purely parochial issues remained, there was a change from one type of game into another. New ways to win support, new prizes, issues, and external resources were added to the old game.

This process of transformation is described in the chapters that follow. The first one of part three, chapter eight, gives the local setting of the games. Chapter eight concludes with the structural characteristics of the parochial field, that is, it delineates the various actors, their power base, and their ideologies. Chapter nine describes the dynamics of the process which took place in this field, it deals with parish politics. It constitutes the background of the division and ultimately the cause of the development of competition in the machine political sphere which is described in chapter ten.

CHAPTER EIGHT

The Parish of Patricksville and its Inhabitants

I. A FIRST GLANCE AT THE PARISH

Patricksville is a parish of about 1,500 inhabitants. The town, with some 900 people, is the centre of the surrounding region that consists almost exclusively of scattered farms and a few villas. Together with a small hamlet called Ardea, which counts some 15 houses and 50 persons, town and rural surroundings make up the parish. The parish is the basic unit of the Catholic Church but it is also the organizational basis of many social, economic, and recreational activities for which the town is the institutional centre.

Patricksville is a typical Irish country town in its phycial structure. A long and straight main street with two-storey houses, harbouring many small shops and pubs, forms the centre. At both ends of this street are some small lanes with cottages. These lanes change gradually into country roads with still a cottage here and there, and at last a signpost "End of Town" explains that Patricksville is left behind and that one enters the rural part of the parish.

This rural area has a very scattered residence pattern and consists almost entirely of farms which look clean, white-washed, and prosperous. The northern, eastern, and western parts of the parish form a rather monotonous panorama. It is a gently undulating area with rich and fertile limestone soils covered with grass. This green surface consists of meadows and is intersected by small limestone walls, narrow country roads, brushwood, and groups of old and tall oaks, beeches, and chestnuts. One's eyes are sometimes caught by a big drive with tall trees. The entrance is flanked by massive pillars that sometimes support the remnants of an iron gate. These drives lead to nowhere, or at best to some remains of walls overgrown with ivy. These are the remnants of old country houses, once occupied by English and Anglo-Irish landlords, the ascendancy. After the Famine and during the war of independence, several of these impressive buildings were destroyed by the local IRA, and their inhabitants were killed or fled to Northern Ireland or England. Only some eight mansions are still intact. They are occupied by descendants of the old landlords who lead a rather isolated life.

The southern part of the parish stands in sharp contrast to the other areas. It is almost uninhabited and consists of an old eroded mountainridge with marshy boglands at its foot. The population fears this area for many reasons. It is treacherous because of the marshy bottom but it is also believed to be a favourite meeting place for spirits. Many people told me about their unpleasant experiences when they passed the spot late at night. It was also a hiding place for the soldiers of the IRA during the war of independence and the civil war. They had a drillground on the other side of the ridge, and this is still used by young enthousiast IRA-men from the area.

Patricksville is not an isolated community. It lies half-way between two cities, at a distance of some 40 miles from each, and a national road runs right throught the town. Some six miles southward is the big country town of Streamtown, and northward, at a distance of nine miles, lies Kilcomer. Both towns have some factories, supermarkets, and recreational facilities which attract many people from Patricksville. A bus stops at the town twice during daytime, and the train stops four times a day and carries one within an hour to the "big cities".

The town is not interesting for tourists as it has no old buildings worth visiting. On its fringe are the remnants of a Norman castle, referred to as "the castle", but it is a ruin used as a shelter for the sheep. A stone's throw behind the castle, and near a lime quarry, lies "the church", that is the Church of Ireland. This is the common term for the Irish form of the Anglican Church; the Catholic Church is invariably called "the chapel".[1] It is a dark-grey, unattractive building. Higher up in the main street are some remnants of the town wall, which dates back to the middle ages. Parts of it are used as back walls for houses. Opposite the street are the rests of a Norman tower that was used up to some years ago as a public convenience. In 1960, the county council built a proper urinal but the tower is still a convenient place for the many heavy drinking inhabitants. On the northern side of the town are the ruins of the English military barracks – Patricksville was a garrison town – which were destroyed by the IRA in the civil war. A row of derelict houses behind these ruins were once the "married quarters", the dwellings of the English soldiers and their families. At present they are inhabited by Irish labourers. What formerly was the drillground is now a well-kept local pitch of the GAA where hurling and gaelic football are played.

On the southern side of the town is a large green which is used for various public manifestations, such as the yearly fair and the gaelic dances. Once it was a meeting place for merchants and local buyers who had their goods checked and weighed in the weigh-house at the back of the green. This derelict building is at present used for indoor-sports and public meetings. It is called the parish hall or Muintir-hall.[2] Building, green and all the ground of the town belong to lord Welby, an English landlord who lives for some weeks of the year in a castle in an adjacent parish. The population of Patricksville must pay yearly groundrent to lord Welby. Adjacent to the parish hall is a tiny building which is used as a local police station.

The main street is the centre of the town. It consists predominantly of

131

pubs and small shops, especially groceries which sell also hardware, peat, kerosine, newspapers, and so forth. Apart form a few exceptions these shops and pubs have a precarious subsistence. Most houses are old and badly kept. The population tries to hide this situation behind a thin coat of paint. In very gay and sometimes remarkable colour combinations (deep blue with hard green, or pink combined with brown) these houses are painted before the annual Corpus Christi procession. In sharp contrast to this disrepair are the well-kept houses of the parish priest and his two curates, the Catholic church, the Convent of Mercy (a nunnery) with its large trees and rosariums, and the Munster & Leinster Bank. The small lanes of the town are lined with very bad and poor looking cottages. One lane forms an exception to this rule: the county council here built some 20 cottages about 15 years ago.

It strikes the outsider, when walking through the town, that almost all front doors are open throughout the day. What seems to be a sign of hospitality has in fact a more prosaic reason. They are kept open to drive the damp out of the houses, for the atmosphere is very damp and wet during the larger part of the year. (My typewriter rusted during its time in a Patricksville house.)

At present most of the houses in town have electricity and running water. The water system, however, is in poor condition and frequently defective. During my stay, Patricksville was on six occasions for several days without water. My Fiat functioned then as a water-carrier and brought the scarce liquid from a street pump to many a family.

There are television aerials on several roofs. People scrape the rent for the sets from their meagre incomes. Together with the many electricity wires which run via poles criss-cross through the town, these aerials give the impression that one walks through a mining village as painted by Van Gogh.

Patricksville is a quiet town during day-time, and life begins rather late in the morning. The men go to their work at nine o'clock, children leave their houses for school which begins at 9.30, and "women" go to "early" mass at ten o'clock. Shopkeepers open their doors at about ten and receive their early customers: farm hands who brought the milk to the creamery and now take a pint of beer, buy some cigarettes and the local newspaper. Around eleven o'clock the housewives do their shoppings and chat for a long time with other women at the corners of the streets, meanwhile smoking cigarettes. The local news is passed and gossiping takes place. The older men – but also many younger ones – begin to fill the corners of the streets, talk about the weather, the news, and the local sports, and play cards for a long time. These corner stickers, as they are popularly called, hang around for the larger part of the day.

Social life begins at night. Women and children crowd together in the kitchen, around the cosy range which burns summer and winter, and watch their beloved television. Men go to the pub where they drink, sing, play darts and fight, or they go to a meeting of the many local associations.

Thus life goes on from Monday until Saturday. Sunday is an exception; this is a very special day for the devout Catholic people. The church is then the centre of many activities. The twelve o'clock mass brings together people from all corners of the parish. They come walking, by bike, by pony and trap or by car at about eleven o'clock to the main street. The street is then crowded with people, all shops are open and one must wait long before one can buy newspaper and cigarettes. Many people take their purchases with them into the church which causes a curious noise during the frequent rising and kneeling which forms part of the ceremony. Women and children enter the church but men stand outside the gates and chat in small groups. When the bell rings, they hurry into the church and look for a seat. Men and women have their own separate places and they are seldom seen sitting together. The well-to-do people have their places in front of the church, the others sit behind them. The shopkeepers prefer to sit in the benches at the back; when mass is over they must hurry back again to their shops.

The church is more than a religious meeting place. After mass and outside the gates, politicians address the population during election times, and every local association puts up its table for annual or monthly contributions. When mass is over people go to the pub, have a few drinks, and go back home or visit some relatives. The commercial world closes its doors and Patricksville is quiet again until the evening. However, when a hurling or gaelic football match is played at the local pitch, the shops and pubs open, and Patricksville comes to life. Depending upon the importance of the game, more or less people fill the streets. They come by car or even in buses to the town. The air is full of cheering and singing. The streets become gradually covered with waste paper from sweets and ice creams, swirling around and into the open front doors, until the following Friday, when the dust lorry comes to collect it.

II. A DECAYING TOWN - A PROSPERING COUNTRYSIDE

Causes of Local Decay

Today, town and countryside form strongly contrasting elements in the parish of Patricksville. The rural part is clean and prosperous, whereas the town exhibits many features of social and economic decay, characteristic of the majority of today's Irish small towns.

This difference has not alway existed. Patricksville was once a flourishing centre of social and economic activities. Up to about 1920, it was an English garrison town. The "barracks", where some 1,000 to 3,000 men were stationed, provided the basic source of income for the majority of the 2,500 inhabitants. Early this century, it employed some 50 men for building and construction work, about 60 women earned a living by washing and ironing, horse dealers, carters, and numerous handy-men picked the fruits of the military's presence. Craft and trade prospered in those days, and more than 40 shopowners and publicans had a good income. An old man described the situation succinctly when he said: "We all drank the British soup those days. And it was a good soup, mind". A retired shopkeeper put it as follows: "The hardest thing to do in the morning was to open the doors . . . and the money poured in by buckets". Another important source of employment was the flour mill cum coal store, where some 40 men earned their daily bread. The railway company employed about 35 men, and some 260 farm labourers made up another considerable part of the working population.

This economic boom ended abruptly when the military left the town in 1921, shortly before the IRA destroyed the barracks. A period of depopulation, characteristic of rural Ireland since the famine, now began for Patricksville and has continued up to the present day. The population shrank to some 900 inhabitants in 1969. "This was our great famine", said an old man bitterly. Shops and pubs closed their doors, horse dealers, craftsmen and many more left the town. Scarcity of customers and lack of work characterized Patricksville.

The town received another severe blow in the early fifties, when the weekly market and monthly cattle fair disappeared. The local farmers' association had decided to merge with the Streamtown branch. This meant that shopkeepers and publicans lost their weekly and monthly trade; indeed, most of the farmers now do their shoppings in Streamtown. Some shopkeepers told me that as a result they now do 30 to even 50 per cent less business. Apart from a few, the nine pubs and 17 shops lead a marginal life now.

Continuing mechanization and extensivation in the agricultural sector has decreased the numbers of farm labourers. In previous times, each farm employed minimally a ploughman, a servant girl, and a boy. At present there are only 32 farm labourers in town.

Patricksville has become a victim of an increase in scale. The influence of the nearby big towns of Kilcomer and Streamtown with their supermarkets and other amenities is considerable. Many women go once or twice a week to these towns to buy the bulk of their purchases. My little Fiat was always full with hitchhiking women.

As a result of this decay, Patricksville has lost many functions. It has no longer its own local government. Politicians from a larger area represent the population's interests in the county council and the Dail. Only the police represents government authority in the town. Almost all public services are administered from a regional office in Streamtown. A dispensary, an unemployment and a home assistance office are still run locally, though the doctor comes from a nearby town and visits the dispensary only twice a week. The local creamery, once a flourishing enterprise, has become downgraded to a store; milk is processed in Streamtown. Bread and milk are distributed by roundsmen from another town.

134

As a result of the economic decay of the town, the employment opportunities have decreased. The occupation structure, set out in table IV, illustrates this. However, this picture is rather flattering: it suggests that only 73 persons are not gainfully occupied. From a survey that I conducted in 1969, it appeared however that from the service workers, the unskilled workers, and the farm labourers 96 persons (61 per cent) are unemployed during four to five months a year. Only a minority has a steady job in factories in nearby towns. Many building and quarrying labourers, for example, are only employed during a period when their employers have work for them. Seventy-six unskilled labourers work for the county council. However, they have a part-time job. The council adopts a policy of employing as many persons as possible for only part of the year. This is done for two reasons. First, it provides employment for a larger category. Second, it is a way of keeping the public expenses low, for people working longer than 12 months at a stretch for the council are entitled to a pension. Thus, the economic situation is far from satisfactory. The average income of an unskilled worker is (1969) about £ 10 a week, and when he is unemployed he receives even less.[4] The cost of living, on the other hand is high; it is higher than in England, the USA, and Holland.

The same precarious situation holds for most of the shopkeepers. Apart from three shops which have good business, almost all shopkeepers have changed their policy since the town's economic decrease. Each has now a great variety of commodities, ranging from peat, kerosine, sweets, vegetables, hardware, to newspapers and periodicals. They do this to bind their customers more closely to them. The result of this policy however is that each shopkeeper has only very limited stock. Their economy is almost similar to the old system of *Kundenwirtschaft*. Many shopkeepers explained that a reduction of shops with 50 per cent would be necessary to make this business sector healty. Publicans are also in a difficult position. They can hardly live from the £ 7 or £ 8 profit they make during the weekend, when the labourers receive their pay packets.

Table IV. Occupational Classes in Patricksville Town, 1966.[3]

Occupation	Total	Percentage
Professional (clerk, teacher, priest, solicitor barrister)	19	6
Commerce, Insurance, Finance	34	11
Service worker (soldier, policeman, driver)	21	7
Skilled worker (craftsman, technician, fitter)	23	8
Unskilled worker (industry, building, quarrying)	104	34
Farm worker	32	10
Not gainfully occupied	73	24
Total	306	100

To meet the expenses of the household, many people look for additional income, though the opportunities are limited. Especially housewives are involved in part-time work. Some 80 do knitting work at home for nearby industries, and another 36 are employed as maids at farms and with the wealthier local families. These are relatively well-off. The Tim Lehane family is an example. Tim is a farm labourer with a steady job and earns (1969) £ 10 6sh. weekly. He has three school going children "who eat the world of potatoes". His wife works as a maid at the local rectory of the Church of Ireland. When we came to live in the town, there was fierce competition about who would be our housekeeper. We selected Mrs. Lehane and paid her 10 sh. for one day per week which was above normal. She brings home £ 2 a week, which makes the total weekly budget to £ 12 6sh.

As a result of shortage of employment in the area, there is fierce competition for work. Steady jobs in factories are highly valued, but one needs connections to obtain work there. Locally the opportunities are very limited. A small construction business employs some men, the parish priest provides labour for the maintenance of his house, those of the curates, and the church. The convent patronizes some shopkeepers and craftsmen, and the few prosperous shops and pubs and the local creamery emply some people. So many persons compete for the small number of jobs that they are valued for more than they are worth, and this enables the employers to depress the wages. It is widely known that these jobs can only be obtained by currying favour with the employers. Small wonder then that these persons have powerful positions, as we shall see shortly. "The town cries for work, the government doesn't do anything about it, and it's always them same couple of men who get work from the local bastards", was an informant's bitter comment on the situation in Patricksville.

The situation in the rural part of the parish, the farming community (some 450 inhabitants), stands in sharp contrast to this decay. Contrary to the western and southern parts of the country, here the soil consists of rich and fertile limestone which is very suitable for grazing.[5] Milch cattle and dry cattle dominate the scene. The farms are rather large: out of the 119 farms, more than 45 per cent is in the category of 200-300 acres, and only six per cent is in the 50-100 acres bracket.[6] Although the farmers in this parish have never been poor, they have improved their positions considerably since the second world war. They pick the fruits of a protectionistic policy which is actually intended for the agricultural problem areas in the West and South. Farmers with fewer than 120 acres are free from income tax, and above this size they have other facilities. They can obtain all sorts of grants and they are protected by minimum prices for cattle and milk. They are the wealthiest category in the parish. Almost 80 per cent built new houses or repaired old ones with government grants. They are technically well-equipped, most of them have motorcars, and some even two. The townspeople envy them and they are sometimes referred to as the new ascendancy.

136

The town's decay is also reflected in its changing demographic structure. Table V sets out the differences between 1911 and 1966. A first remarkable characteristic is the great decrease of the population. In 55 years it fell by 1600 persons. The most important cause is emigration, though several fled or were killed during the Troubles. Many inhabitants left for England, Jersey, and the USA when they lost their jobs. Exact figures are not available because the statistics are not broken down at parish level, and people going to England are usually not registered as emigrants. However, it appeared from my survey that almost all grown-ups have children, brothers, and sisters abroad. They function as a first orientation point for the new-comers, for emigration continues. It is a normal feature of the town's processes, " . . . almost as normal as going to Dublin for some days", as an informant explained. Mrs. Twomy's family is an example. Her father was a farm labourer and had seven children. At the age of 16, the first child left for America where she was taken in by an uncle. She married and lives with her family in Detroit. Three sons tried their luck in Jersey. Twice they came back, but when they could not find proper and stable work at home, they went back again to Jersey and settled there. Two daughters went to England; one became a nurse, and the other married an Irish factory worker in Liverpool. Mrs. Twomy's own children continued the tradition. One is at home and looks after her parents, three went to England, and the youngest son went recently to his uncles in Jersey. Emigration is a "cure" for almost everything. It is the normal path to a decent living, sometimes leading to prosperity. It is also a mechanism for escaping local social control. I know that several people left for England to escape from the police, and it is also the normal route for pregnant girls. Most of the exiles, as the emigrants are usually called, leave Ireland definitively, though they come "home" at Christmas or during Summer holidays to visit their relatives.

Another characteristic of Patricksville's demographic structure is the strong representation of old people. About 25 per cent of its present popu-

Table V. Population of Patricksville Town Classified by Sex and Age Groups for 1911 and 1966.[7]

Age group	1911			1966		
	males	females	total	males	females	total
under 14 years	198	214	412	113	128	241
14-20 years	267	229	496	83	68	151
21-39 years	468	481	949	76	51	127
40-64 years	309	295	604	148	75	223
65 years and upwards	53	64	117	109	127	236
Total	1295	1283	2578	529	449	978

lation is in the category of 65 years and upwards, against only some five per cent in 1911. The town is old at present. Although the majority is retired, many do odd jobs to make the ends meet, for their pensions are low.

A very remarkable difference between the population in 1911 and 1966 is found in the categories of the working ages (21-39 and 40-64). In 1911 these counted for some 60 per cent of the population, whereas in 1966 about 35 per cent were in these brackets. "There is no belly in the town these days", said Tom Drane, aged about 45. When studying a picture of his 50 class mates in primary school, he came to the conclusion that all but some four or five had left the country.

The rural part of the parish also decined in population though the differences are not so great. It fell from slightly less than 1,000 to about 600 in 1966. Mainly farm labourers and other skilled and unskilled labourers left the countryside, but the farmers' community decreased also. In 1911 there were 147 farms against 119 in 1966. Although emigration is here also endemic, it did not lead to a situation as we observed for the town. Indeed, it is normal and healthy for the agricultural sector when only one or two children stay on the farm.

III. KINSHIP

Kinship forms an important cementing factor for both town and countryside. It brings many households together into a larger system of kin relations. This system, characteristic of all of Western Europe, is of the bilateral type. That is, kin relationships are reckoned equally through males and females. It does not lead to clearly delineated groups as in matrilineal and patrilineal societies. Here, each individual is at the centre of a vast network of cognatic and affinal relationships of which certain categories are more important than others.

Although Patricksville has no rule of local endogamy or exogamy, since 1881 more than 40 per cent of the marriages have been between people of the town. This implies that many inhabitants are related to each other in some way. It would be highly impracticable, however, for a person to recognize all these relationships. In fact, most people do not admit kinship beyond a certain degree though many are able to trace relationships far back. A person has effective kin ties with only a small category of people. It embraces his parents and their siblings, his own siblings, his children, grand children, grand parents, and first cousins. More distant relatives are usually referred to as "friends of ours", and often treated merely as fellow-townspeople.[8] This is illustrated in the following case. When a row between two men developed, one fighter's wife cried: "Beat him, he's not a relative", although the two were in fact second cousins. A person's most intimate circle consists of his parents, siblings, and children. These have rather clearly defined rights and obligations towards each other.

As a result of the tendency to local marriage, there are many Cahills, Linehans, Thornhills, and McDwyers in the town. For purposes of identification people use "string names" or nicknames. Both families and individuals have these special names. A person is usually addressed by his own nickname, and when referred to, that of his family is added. A family derives its nickname usually from the head of the household. This name gets into disuse when the father dies and his children have families of their own. Then the young father's personal nickname becomes the family name for his children, who also adopt personal nicknames. John Linehan, for example, was called Winger Hop. His two sons were Mousy and Count Hop. When they married and got children, their families' nicknames became Mousy and Count respectively, and the fathers are now referred to as Old Mousy and Old Count. Most of the nicknames are harmless and have been derived from incidents in a person's life. Many are borrowed from the locally very popular hurling sport.

The interconnectedness of kin which we observed for the townspeople exists also in the rural part of the parish. Indeed, only three farmers are strangers, the others are born and bred on the spot, and most of them married girls from the parish. This has led to a very intricate system of blood and affinal relationships. I traced kinship relations in detail for only a few farmers, but it appeared from those cases that they were related to some 18 per cent of the farms of the parish. Moreover, almost none of the farmers did not have some relatives there. These many cross-cutting kinship bonds reinforce the multiplex ties that are created by neighbourhood, common work and class, and bind the farmers together into a tightly united community. To illustrate this connectedness one farmer said: "When you blackguard one of us up here, the whole area will feel offended". Therefore his father had taught him "never open your mouth until you are eating". But he added quickly that they were "a fine crowd here". "Them town bastards call us a pack of in-breeders. But look at the results: aren't we well off?"

If kinship constitutes an important cementing element both in the town and for the rural part of the parish, one might expect it to form also a force uniting these two into one parish-wide system. Indeed, this is the familiar picture that one obtains from Arensberg and Kimball.[9] However, the opposite is true. The contrasts between town and countryside that we observed in other sections, is also found in the field of kinship. Apart from a few shotgun marriages, only four townsmen – the chemist, the two wealthiest shopkeepers, and the dispensary officer – married farmers' daughters from the parish. This lack of intermarriage has always existed as far as I could detect. The most important reason for it is the difference in status between farmers and townspeople. Contrary to the western part of the country where farms are small and often uneconomic, the farmers here have always been rather wealthy and look down upon the townspeople who are predominantly labourers. The institution of the dowry is an extra barrier. It means that property, given to a girl upon marriage, is distracted from the circulation of land in the farming community.[10] When I discussed this subject with a

139

farmer, he put it very straight: "We don't want to fatten them (i.e. the townspeople), for they don't return anything at all".

Kinship has lost many of its former functions. Today, the main function seems to be an instrument of introduction to new areas and sources of prizes. I dealt with that in detail in chapter three. Another important function, which is illustrated shortly, has to do with conflict alignments. Then kin groupings, only vaguely delineated in this bilateral system, have the noticeable function of faction alignment. It serves to delineate the boundaries of groups and coalesce individuals and families within kin based groups. Loyalties have rigidly established priorities: to family, *crowd*, town, parish, county, country, in that order.[11] Within each of these categories a dispute results ideally in a coalition of the group concerned, together with all those people and subdivisions composing it, against an equally unified opposition. The divisions reunite on the next higher level.

IV. VOLUNTARY ASSOCIATIONS AND RECREATION

So far we obtained a picture of a town which is decaying in many respects. A remarkable exception is the recreational sector, the sphere of the voluntary associations. In 1969, Patricksville counted 21 voluntary associations though some 10 led a shadowy life. Most of them are rather young, they were set up between 1950 and 1969. The oldest association, the GAA, was founded in 1889. This is a very nationalistic organization. It bans all non-Irish sports, and forbids its members to do other than gaelic dances.[12] It was also an important recruiting ground for IRA soldiers during the war of independence. Almost all the old GAA members in the town have been active IRA men, and today's core members have strong nationalistic feelings. Indeed, some are in the present-day IRA and were ready to fight when troubles flared up again in the North in 1969. Te GAA is the largest, the most active and influencial association in the town. Today it has some 250 members, but in previous times almost every family was involved in hurling. Apart from organizing hurling and gaelic football matches on its local pitch, one of the best in the county, the GAA started a drama group, a billiard club, a debating club, it runs a local bingo, and has its own brass band. Furthermore, a core group has been involved in founding a local branch of the Road Bowlers' League, a harriers club (fox hunting with dogs), and a local development association to bring work to the town. It also revitalized the local branch of the Gaelic League, and started *Comhaltas Ceoiltoire Eireann*, both organizations for promoting the Irish language, dances, music and literature.

Muintir na Tire, a community development organization which was set up in 1948, has also been of considerable importance for the town. It was intended to bring new life in the town. To that end Muintir organized a drama group, a music club, a billiard club, a football association, and started its own brass band. Several of these groups are dead now, only a few lead a dormant life.

There are still other associations, such as the National Farmers' Associations with its youth branch *Macra na Feirme,* and the Irish Creamery Milk Suppliers' Association. There are also the Field Club which gives lectures on Irish history, the Language Freedom Movement, aiming at bringing down to "normal" proportions the place of Irish in education, and the Tidy Towns' Committee. The Catholic Church started the Sodality of Our Lady (Children of Mary), and the Confraternity of the Sacred Heart which has separate guilds for men and women.

Apart from performing its specific function, all these associations organize recreational activities, such as annual dinner dances, excursions, and fund raising tombolas. Even the farming associations have their own debating evenings and small drama groups. This fascinating picture of overlapping functions, and in several cases of complete duplication, is largely the result of local factionalism, to be considered shortly. Indeed, several associations have been set up as strategic manoeuvres in parish politics.

Of all recreational activities, the annual carnival is the most outstanding. For some ten days in June, the whole town is one whirl of excitement. Carnival is concentrated around the day of the horse fair. When Patricksville was still a garrison town, the fair was more important though it is still an impressive event. Horse dealers and itinerants come from far and near to the town, often sleep in the open air, and do their business in Main Street, which is then packed with hundreds of horses, making regular traffic virtually impossible. Buyers come from all places in Ireland, but German, French, Dutch and American are also heard in the street and the pubs. It is a very lucrative day for the local buninessmen who sell then not only drinks but also serve meals. Many other activities are organized during the carnival days, such as raffles, a ballad session, a pageant, Irish dancing competitions; a tramps parade, and an important hurling march. During all these days a fun fair is held in the green opposite the Muintir hall, and every night old and young go dancing in what formerly was the local cinema. Carnival is not only a lucrative affair for shops and pubs, it is also source of income for the organizers. Small wonder then that it was an important issue in parish politics as we shall see shortly. In 1969, the GAA organized the carnival week and made some £ 400 profit.

V. RELIGION

As the field of recreational activities flourishes, so does the religious sector. Almost all parishioners are members of the Catholic Church. Only four families belong to the Church of Ireland, but these people play only a marginal role in the community. It is thus safe to conclude that religion does not function as a divisive factor in local affairs.

The Church plays a highly important role in the lives of the population.

It is a basic institution for the socialization of the population. It teaches both families and individuals how to perform correctly the various roles, and sanctions it teaching in several ways. The Church also regulates people's daily, monthly and yearly activities. The church bell rings the major divisions of the day: first the Paternoster, then the Angelus at noon, and again at eight o'clock in the evening. When the bell rings, people stop their work or conversation and kneel for a short prayer. Most inhabitants go regularly to mass and do their Friday confessions. Sunday mass is always visited and the same holds for the many other feast days of the Church's calendar. Outstanding among these are the holidays of obligation: Circumcision, St. Patrick (Ireland's national patron saint), Ascension, Corpus Christi, Assumption, All Saints, Immaculate Conception, and Nativity. On these days, the people abstain from work and do not conduct business; only the shops and pubs are open for some hours. Women generally are more pious then men; many attend mass daily though both will never pass the church, a sacred well or some other special religious place without making the sign of the cross.

Of particular importance are the May Procession, dedicated to the Blessed Virgin and held in the convent gardens, and the Corpus Christi procession. Especially the latter is of great importance for the population. Long before the date, people begin to clean and pain their houses. When the day arrives, they put flowers, pictures of saints, and candles in their front doors. There is a mild competition for the best performance; when the procession passes the houses, meanwhile singing and praying at special places, the people jealously compare the decorations of friends, enemies, and relatives.

The Church plays also a major role in education. The local convent runs a primary girls' school, and the parish priest is the manager of the primary boys' school. He is in charge of appointing and firing teachers, and he must keep the building in good condition and look after repairs and improvements. He also decides to a great extent what is taught. Although the priest has a main say in these matters, his powers are restricted by the government's Department of Education. Finally, the parish priest and his curates are charged with religious instruction in the small secondary school which is run by a teacher and his wife.

The local clergy are also involved in the organization of several voluntary associations. They run the Sodality of Our Lady, the Confraternity of the Sacred Heart, and the Pioneers Total Abstinence Association. Furthermore, until recently, they were chairmen or presidents of many other associations. Although the clergy are no longer active in politics with a capital P, they are much involved in local factionalism, and not a few coalitions are formed around them on local issues.

VI. PRESTIGE, STATUS, AND LEADERSHIP

In spite of the small size and its rural character, the parish of Patricksville presents clear differences in prestige and status. The inhabitants are very class and prestige conscious, and they can quickly provide the outsider with a status scale. They have also special names, often with negative connotations, for various social categories and groupings. The main factors and qualities affecting status are wealth (money, land, and other property), occupation, education, rank, and family. They determine a person's position on the class ladder. There is a close correlation between status and prestige: those on the highest rung of the class ladder have the most prestige. However, other more subtle but also important factors determining prestige have to be mentioned. Office in the town's various associations carries prestige, and so do contacts with influential persons such as politicians and bishops. Much prestige is obtained through membership of old and new IRA, and through being related to these members. Being a good hurler or gaelic footballer also provides prestige, and it is also gained through having a close relative become a priest or nun. "A pump in the yard, a bull in the field, and a priest in the family", expresses both comfort and prestige. Being "a real local and a good mixer" gives also prestige. "Good stock" is used for somebody whose family has produced hard working persons. A "decent man" does not depend for his position on his family background; he is a person who is straight-dealing, honest, and always prepared to help others. The "clever man" has also prestige, but it is slightly dubious. He is ambitious and not over-scrupulous about methods for achieving his aim. Usually he obtains his position from the necessity of others to keep on good terms with him. These qualities and factors are, of course, not of equal importance; a person's social standing is determined first by his class position and second by the sum total of the other factors mentioned.

Differences in prestige and status are clearly reflected in the stratification pattern which runs roughly parallel to the community's "socializing circles" or cliques. These differences cut the parish into two parts. The rural area is generally considered the best, the wealthiest and healthiest. It is predominantly the domain of the farmers who are seen as the backbone of Irish society. It has since long been an area of prosperity and independence, and those who can afford it will take up residence in the countryside.[13] The town, on the other hand, is associated with decay, poverty and lack of employment. It is an area that one should like to escape; it is unhealthy as a result of the smoke of the many open hearths, the dirt in the streets, and the traffic noise.

These two categories must be further differentiated, for they are not homogeneous. The population first distinguishes for the rural area between the remnants of the old ascendancy class and the farmers. The few who are left of the former class occupy the highest rung on the ladder though they are not always the richest. They include the landed aristocracy which does not work on the land, and retired English army officers. The ascendancy form a separate circle and are hardly involved in local activities. They only meet in the local Protestant church, but they send their children to Protestant primary schools elsewhere, and later to boarding school. Although few in numbers and scattered over the country, they have close connections with each other. They intermarry, see one another at the Dublin horse show, are members of the Royal Dublin Society, they have their own hunting societies, golf clubs, balls, and garden parties.

The second and largest part of the rural category, ranking next, is composed of farmers. Today, most of them are not involved in local activities, though there has been a time when many farmers were active in Muintir. I come to that in the next chapter. Farmers are usually differentiated according to their involvement in agricultural activities. Those who do not work on the land, the gentlemen farmers who "live on top of the land", have more prestige than equally big "honest to God and hard working" farmers. Although they are a class apart, especially the gentlemen farmers socialize with the ascendancy and try to penetrate their circle. Several are members of the same societies, and go to the same balls. Yet they are not completely accepted: they are not invited to marriages and other family occasions of the ascendancy, and they are not invited at the garden and tea parties.

The top of the town consists of the two vets, the chemist, the barrister, the solicitor, the clergy, and the bank manager. They are usually referred to as the "local brass". They have had a good education, earn more money than the majority, and have many connections far beyond the town. Their standards and way of life are determined by groups outside and largely unknown to the local people. Although education is certainly an important determinant of status, it is definitely less than wealth, for the farmers occupy a higher rung on the class ladder than the "brass". Both farmers and townspeople often explained that a famer has land which makes him less dependent upon other persons than a vet or a barrister, and therefore has a higher position. Apart from the cerlgy, the "brass" is not town-oriented and does not engage in local activities. Together with the farmers, they form a separate circle. They occupy the best places in the church, have their own local hunts, a tennis club, a golf club, and they frequently organize cocktail parties which have given them the widely accepted name of the "sherry clique".

Another circle, standing closer to the ordinary local people, is the "bastard aristocracy". It includes the bank clerk, the creamery manager, some local government clerks, the three big shopkeepers, the teachers, the midwife, the home-assistance officer cum interim registrar, and a local ex-army officer. Although almost all are of local stock, they feel a cut above the rest through their better education, work, and income. They occupy a hybrid position in the community and are not popular with the local folk. On the one hand, they are community-oriented and active in many voluntary associations. On the other hand, they try to socialize with the "sherry clique", go to its hunting dances and other socials, but they are never invited to the cocktail parties. A local man described their position vividly when he said: "This circle has its toes in both camps but a foot in none".

The rest of the local population is not clearly divided into circles with big differences in status. They are commonly referred to as "Joe Soaps". This is not to say however that differences lack altogether, or that everyone has equal contacts with others. It merely implies that more subtle prestige determinants play a more important rol for differentiation. Shopkeepers and tradesmen are slightly higher than the other local folk, for they once constituted the backbone of the town. Also, the three big shopkeepers are always mentioned separately; they run good businesses, and several persons depend upon them for work and credit. Skilled and unskilled labourers are usually taken together. More important however are offices in voluntary associations. These provide prestige, and the active members, of course, have frequent contacts. The same is true of neighbours and close relatives; they meet more often than others. Old men, especially old IRA members, have informal meetings, and fireside chats in the kitchen bring together circles of friends and relatives.

Finally, the lowest rung on the ladder is occupied by itinerants, commonly called tinkers. Especially the poor tinkers – and the majority is poor – form a despised and at the same time feared category. In their waggons they wander through the country, living from begging and small trade, and causing many inconveniences to the population. As a result of their being ambulant, they form in fact only a marginal category in the community.

From this description it has become clear that persons occupying the highest rungs of the class ladder do not function as leaders of the community. Indeed, the ascendancy and the brass have never been involved in community affairs. The farmers, once active in Muintir, have also turned their backs to the town. However, there is one notable exception, namely the parish priest. In the absence of a formal system of local government, the priest runs much of the town's affairs. He derives his authority of course from his religious office. He is the spiritual leader of the community, but he is also a man of great importance in the many voluntary associations. This does not mean however that his word is always law. People will accept his spiritual teaching, but in secular matters they consider him as any other man with high status. His status as a man is high and his advice will be accepted if he is on good terms with all classes, and impartial in his decisions. However, if the priest is biased, favours one class, or dictates how things should be done, people will not hesitate to oppose him openly and form a coalition against him.

In addition to the parish priest, certain other persons wield considerable influence, which appears from their leading positions in the local associations. The qualities for these positions were summed up to me as follows: A good leader has "the guts to come out against God, the priest and all men", he has "the gift of the gab", and is a "good mixer", and he is "well up in the grapevine". These qualities need some explanation. The first implies that a man must have an independent mind and the courage to fight for a cause, even against superiors. The gift of the gab means that one must be a good speaker, able to put one's case in well-chosen words. The leader must also be a good mixer. This implies that he should not feel a cut above the rest, but that he socializes with everybody. To be well up in the grapevine has two meanings. First, it means that one is well-informed of what is going on in the area. Second, it implies that one has many friends and relatives upon whom one can rely under all circumstances. These qualities are of course ideal ones but on this basis we can distinguish between two types of leaders. Indeed, the people themselves distinguish between "real local men", and "clever men". The clever man belongs to the bastard aristocracy. His education enables him to put his case clear, and his employment and income make him rather independent so that he can take a firm stand in conflicts. He does not really socialize with the people and therefore he is not well-informed of what is going on in the community. Above all, he is impopular, for many people are tied to him on a transactional basis. The home-assistance officer is an example. He has considerable autonomy in deciding how much will be paid to the sick, the poor, and the temporarily unemployed. He uses this power to improve his positon and to become stronger in the local associations. The same is true of the bank clerk, the local government clerks, and the three big shopkeepers.

The other type of leader, the real local man, belongs to the ordinary Joe Soaps. He socializes with everybody and is well-informed of the local news. He is also a rather independent man, but he has no material assets to attract support. His leadership is primarily based on qualities which the ordinary people value high, such as good at sport, active for the improvement of his community, and related to the old IRA. Pat Noolan, the local barber, is an example. Through his job and his many relatives and friends, he is always aware of what is afoot in the parish. His job makes him independent of the bastard aristocracy. In his younger days, he was a good hurler; he played in the all-Ireland team with a leading minister, and won six medals. He was also a soldier in the old IRA. This gives him much prestige, but it does not make him feel a cut above the rest. He socializes with everyone, and he is always ready to help others. He is active in the local GAA club where he takes a clear stand in all important matters.

VI. PARTY POLITICAL AFFILIATION

The contrasts between town and countryside which we observed in previous sections are also found in the sphere of party political affiliation. The countryside is almost exclusively Fine Gael whereas Fianna Fail dominates in the town. This division is the result of a slow but often very rough process of polarization which started long before the two parties came into existence. It is important to have a closer look at this process, for the outcome has bedevilled parochial life up to the present day. Indeed, it is one of the basic factors for the formation of coalitions and for a person's stand in parish politics and machine politics.

Long before the war with England (1916-22) broke out, town and countryside were already divided over the nationalistic issue. The town which consisted predominantly of labourers, was a regional centre of the republican movement. The leading members of the local GAA club were also the leaders of the regional branch of the Irish Republican Brotherhood, later the IRA. The farmers, on the other hand, were pro-England and thus against republicanism. England was the main importer of their products, and thus good relations with that country were of vital importance.

The first serious clashes between these two camps occurred during the war of independence. The local IRA was involved in intelligence work and raided ammunition from the local barracks. Several farmers, still mentioned by name, informed English officers about the names and addresses of leading IRA members, who were caught and imprisoned. As a retaliation other IRA members destroyed some farms and set fire to property. On their turn. the English soldiers again caught some IRA men, and prohibited the GAA, which was considered a cover organization, to meet or to play games. (From that time the farmers withdrew from the GAA and have never joined it again). When the war ended in 1922 with the ratification of the Treaty, the farmers chose the Treaty side. It meant a continuation of good economic relations with Britain. The majority of the townspeople chose the anti-Treaty side. They wanted to fight on until Ireland was completely independent of England.

Antagonism flared high up during the civil war (1922-23). The new Free State government, the pro-Treaty element, stationed a small army near Patricksville which was in charge of maintaining law and order. The local IRA ambushed and attacked these soldiers several times after which they fled back again to their hiding places in the mountains. Some farmers, however, informed the army of these places, whereupon many IRA men were killed. The IRA took revenge on these farmers, shot some of them and burnt their property. Soon large parts of the population became involved in the war. The local farmers set up a paramilitary organization to protect their property, and they joined forces with the soldiers on their search for IRA men. Together they raided houses of IRA men and of their relatives, and they tortured the inhabitants until these mentioned the hiding places. In reprisal the IRA suspected farmers, shot their cattle, and destroyed their farms. During the two years that this civil war lasted, more than 20 farmers were killed and 24 townspeople.

When the war came to an end and new political parties were set up, the larger part of the town, of course, voted for Fianna Fail, the republican party. Only a small minority joined Cumann na nGaedheal, later called Fine Gael. This minority consisted of some local notables and businessmen who were related to the farming community or had obtained from the pro-Treaty government important jobs in the police and the administration of local government. They and their descendants constitute the members of the bastard aristocracy. The farmers of course joined Cumann na nGaedheal.

147

Although the war belonged to the past, the parish did not yet settle down to tranquil, constitutional politics. Especially during elections the old enmities flared up again. Small gangs of "bully boys" then protected their party speakers and candidates on their tours through the area, and tried to break up their opponents' meetings. Farmers boycotted the shops of leading Fianna Fail members, tarred the fronts of their houses, and smashed windows. Local men, on the other hand, drove cattle of the hated farmers miles down the road, ambushed farm hands on their way to the creamery, and destroyed the water supply of that building.

After 1932, a new wave of violence spread over the community. In that year, Fianna Fail came to office and its leader, De Valera, withheld the land annuities which had to be paid to England as a compensation of the loss of revenue from the land. Britain, in turn, closed its boundaries for Irish agricultural products. This caused fierce reactions from the exporting farmers; the more since the annuities still had to be paid, be it now to the Irish government. They obstructed the government by not paying annuities and rates. To form a united front, they organized a local branch of the Blueshirt movement which was originally intended to protect Cumann na Gaedheal politicians against gangs of Fianna Fail and IRA members. Behind barricades and provided with guns, the Blueshirts protected themselves against the "seizure waggons" of the government which came along to collect the rates in the form of cattle. The local Fianna Fail core, former IRA leaders, joined forces with these "waggon men", fought against the farmers and drove their cattle away at night. This period of violence ended in 1935 when the government confiscated the arms.

The protectionistic policy that the Fianna Fail government adopted brought much good to the population of the town. It caused the labourers to vote for Fianna Fail, and many shopkeepers who had not yet taken a clear stand since they were dependent upon both farmers and townspeople, now opted for the republican party. The smaller part of the bastard aristocracy also followed Fianna Fail: they were dependent upon the protection of that party for the continuation of their jobs. The farmers, on the other hand, have remained Fine Gael followers. Indeed, new factors caused them to stick to that party. During the second world war, the Fianna Fail government ordered the farmers to till a certain part of their land with wheat for the nation's bread. The farmers in the parish of Patricksville who were not used to tillage, obstructed the government and tried to circumvent compulsory tillage. Several townspeople however informed the authorities of the farmers' obstructions, whereupon the government stationed some inspectors in the town who had to look after the correct execution of the tillage programme. The farmers took revenge upon the local informers; they thwarted them wherever possible, damaged their property and tarred their houses. Today, one old woman shopkeeper keeps a small part of her front-wall tarred in commemoration of those "black days".

Thus we have seen how the population of the parish has become strongly divided on the point of political affiliation. Successive outbreaks of violence divided the community into two clear-cut camps which have antagonistic and often hostile feelings towards one another. "Everyone here has a needle in from somebody: his father's brother's, mother's, or sister's. And these needles will be passed on from them to their children. They will never get out: you can be sure of that", was the bitter comment of an informant.

VIII. CONCLUSIONS

In the preceding pages we have obtained a picture of a community composed of the strongly contrasting elements of town and countryside. These elements differ in almost every respect; indeed, they constitute antagonistic and often hostile camps. The virtual absence of cross-cutting ties, as we have seen in the sections on kinship and socializing circles, emphasizes the separateness of each. The differences in wealth, status, prestige, demographic composition, and party political affiliation are the outcome of national processes acting upon specifically local circumstances. These two elements of the community have been further differentiated into separate social classes. The countryside includes ascendancy and farmers, and the town is composed of representatives of the professions, the bastard aristocracy, and the ordinary people.

On the basis of this description we can now summarize the structural characteristics of the political field of the parish. That is, we delineate the various actors, their relationships with each ohter, their power base, and their ideologies. Since ascendancy and professionals (apart from the clergy) have never been active in the community, only three categories constitute the personnel of the field, namely the farmers, the bastard aristocracy, and the Joe Soaps. The farmers form numerically a large category, and their power is considerable, though previously it was more important. These days, some 30 townspeople earn their living as farm labourers, and they can of course be fired. The farmers also patronize the three big shopkeepers in town, though increasingly they run their errands in the larger towns nearby. Furthermore, the farmers form an ideologically closely connected group; they are all Fine Gael voters. This ties them together and makes it possible to close ranks and form a strong coalition.

The bastard aristocracy, though numerically weak, have a very strong power base. Many local people are dependent upon them for work or other prizes. Another factor that strengthens their position in local affairs is their close relationship with the farmers. Almost all of them are of farming background, born and bred in the parish, and eight out of a total of twelve share party affiliations with the farmers. The remaining four joined Fianna Fail to protect and continue their jobs. The local population however does not regard them as "true Gaels" (real republicans) and therefore looks down upon them. Despite this division however the bastard aristocracy form a

149

fairly coherent group and will constitute a united front against the ordinary local people.

Finally the ordinary Joe Soaps. Their power base is very limited; indeed, many are dependent upon farmers and bastard aristocrats. Yet for three reasons they constitute a potentially strong grouping. First, their strength lies in their numbers, for they outnumber farmers and bastard aristocracy even if these join forces. Second, they are tightly connected by a common ideology. Almost all are Fianna Fail voters, and their parents or they themselves were active in the IRA. Third, a high degree of interaction exists between them. They meet in the pubs and the streets, they are members of the GAA, and as the poorest category of the community they are tied by relations of mutual help and assistance. These factors bind them together into a tightly united group, and provided that personal interests are not damaged, they will join forces against their common enemies of the farmers and the bastard aristocracy. The next chapter describes how these three categories were brought together into a clearly delineated area, that is, it deals with the dynamics of the power process which enfolded in parish politics.

CHAPTER NINE

Muintir na Tire:
A Plan for Parochial Government that Failed

I. PRELUDE

During the second world war, in 1941, a local government act introduced the idea of "approved local councils". These parish councils, as they came to be known, were intended to take over part of the county council's work when an emergency period would arise.

In 1943, parish priest canon O'Toole, born and bred in the parish, of farming stock and from a leading Blueshirt family, took the initiative to set up a council for Patricksville. To that end he selected six persons who would constitute the council; four were farmers and the other two were townspeople. The farmers were related to him, and the townspeople, the home assistance officer and a big shopkeeper, were of farming background. Although the ordinary townspeople were not content with this highly unproportional representation, they took no steps to change the composition.

The first task of the parish council consisted of providing the community with fuel since coal could no longer be imported from England. It bought some turf banks where every parishioner was allowed to cut a certain amount of turf at a low price. For the same purpose the council rent some woodland from local farmers. Every family could buy some trees and chop them when they wanted.

Although the intentions were good, the schemes were a failure since the council itself was charged with the execution and supervision. Nepotism and bribery flourished, and the old enmities between townspeople and farmers came again to the surface. Indeed, organized violence broke out between the two camps. "It was like in the old days", and old man said. "We had to fight for a bit of peat. Look at me thumb (it was dislocated); them bastards (the farmers) caught me one night".

WHO IS GOING TO GOVERN THE PARISH?

When the war was over and a parish council no longer needed, canon O'Toole decided to transform it into a local branch of Muintir na Tire. This movement, founded in 1937, is a national organization for community development. It aims at restoring a spirit of cooperation and self-help in the rapidly depopulating countryside. The organizational basis of the movement is the parish. Membership is open to all parishioners who together constitute a parish guild. The guild members select a community council which is constituted of an equal number of representatives of the various sections of the community.[1] This council acts as the management committee of the guild, but all its plans must be ratified by a majority of the guild members.

In 1948, canon O'Toole announced from the pulpit that he wanted to found a local branch of Muintir. He invited the population for a general meeting where he would explain the intentions and purposes of Muintir.

At the meeting he told his flock that the movement was intended to coordinate the community's activities and to create new ones. Patricksville had long been divided by hostilities; this was a splendid opportunity to get rid of them and cooperate to the benefit of the whole parish. From now on, all activities in the parish should be coordinated and organized under the supervision of Muintir. He told also that he had formed a council for one year. After that year, the full guild must vote for its own council. The managing body appeared to be an enlarged version of the old war-council. Other members of the bastard aristocracy and the farming community, arch-enemies of the ordinary townspeople, plus the two curates had been added to this old body. Chairman canon O'Toole finally announced that the council was making arrangements for new communal activities which would be proposed to the guild shortly.

Many townspeople did not like the composition of the council as it included no "real locals". On the other hand, however, several agreed with the parish priest that it was time to get rid of the old cleavage in the community. Therefore, they were prepared to support Muintir loyally. The GAA core, however, was violently against this new association. The only communal activity of any significance was the carnival, and this had always been organized by the GAA. So if Muintir took over this feast, the GAA leaders would be downgraded. They would lose a lucrative position, for they had always obtained personal profit from the carnival week. Indeed, they would be dethroned as the town's traditional leaders. The implications of this confrontation were quite clear to them. The issue at stake was: Who is going to govern the community? The GAA core decided to oppose Muintir's plans and to obstruct the council wherever possible.

The competition that developed between these two parties was largely determined by the structural characteristics of each, and by their positions in the arena in general. We must therefore examine these first.

COMPOSITION OF THE ARENA

The arena of Muintir included two opposing camps, namely the council and the core members of the local GAA club. The council, advocating the integration of the community under their leadership, was the largest camp. It

152

counted 14 members. Moreover, it was a strong and fairly coherent grouping, for many members were related to each other in more than one respect. They were tied by bonds of kinship, neighbourhood, common class and occupation. Furthermore, they shared a past in which they had fought against a common enemy, namely the local IRA and Fianna Fail leaders. Finally, they were relatively rich, independent, and better educated than the ordinary townspeople. Therefore, they thought it their right and duty to run the affairs of the parish.

This fairly coherent camp contained, however, a weak element which made it vulnerable to attacks from the opponent. Two councillors, the local bank clerk who is related to the parish priest, and the home-assistance officer cum interim registrar, were members of Fianna Fail. They had joined this party for the protection of their jobs and the improvement of their positions. They were also officers of the local GAA and Fianna Fail clubs where their opponents dominated. These cross-cutting ties made them vulnerable for undermining activities from the GAA camp.

The opposing camp, the GAA core, defending its traditional leadership of the town, was smaller. It comprised only six members. Moreover, none was represented to the council of Muintir. It was, however, a tightly united party. All its members belonged to the same class, and some were related by kin ties. They had also cooperated in the IRA and in the preparation of the carnival week, which had resulted in their having much organizational skill. Furthermore, they shared an aversion to farmers and bastard aristocrats as a result of the turbulent past. They were, of course, also stronger motivated than the other camp, for the prize at stake was not only the leadership of communal activities, but also personal financial gain. This latter fact was for them, of course, of more weight than for their opponents, who were relatively well off. Finally and very importantly, no member of this camp depended for his livelihood on personnel of the council. Some were retired and had an ex-IRA state pension, two worked in a factory in Streamtown, and one was a local shoemaker cum electricity meter reader. This independence gave them considerabele freedom of manoeuvring and therefore made them formidable opponents.

In addition to council and GAA camp, the arena of Muintir contained still a "third party", namely the members of the guild. Their role was of vital importance, for they had the power to vote for or against the council's plans. In other words, they constituted the support for which both camps had to compete in order to form the dominant coalition. For a proper understanding of this competition it is necessary to examine the composition of this third party and the positions of its members *vis-à-vis* the two camps.

As we have seen in the previous chapter, only three sections of the population were community-oriented, namely the farmers, the bastard aristocracy, and the ordinary townspeople. These sections formed the potential of a third party, from which the camps must draw support. On the basis of traditional alignments, farmers and bastard aristocracy would support the council. Together they constituted a united front against the GAA. The third section, the ordinary townspeople, made up the largest part of the guild. Indeed, they outnumbered the other two, and therewith held the balance of power. These townspeople, however, were related to both camps, and this caused the alignment pattern to be very intricate and difficult to predict. To begin with, the majority felt morally connected with the GAA and shared its aversion against the traditional enemy, the farmers. On the other hand, a considerable number were dependent upon farmers for their livelihood. They were employed as farmlabourers and housekeepers. They would support the GAA camp only in the dark and as long as their jobs were not at stake. The same held for the shopkeepers and publicans; they were dependent upon both farmers and townspeople. Another section depended upon the bastard aristocracy for jobs, credit, and help in bureaucratic procedures. Furthermore, almost every parishioner was slow to go against the wishes of the parish priest, the initiator of Muintir. He could use natural and even supernatural sanctions to push his cases. Moreover, several businessmen and craftsmen supplied goods and services to the convent, the church, and the three housholds of the clergy. Clearly, they did not want to risk this patronage by supporting the GAA camp. Finally, another segment of the townspeople agreed with the parish priest that the traditional enmities between town and countryside should disappear. Although they did not agree with the present composition of the council, they would likely support its projects.

The composition of the arena and the positions of the personnel of the third party towards the two camps have now been described. In the pages that follow we examine the power proces between the two camps as this developed during a period of six years. We study this process from the angle of the GAA as this camp was on the offensive.

II. GAA: FROM MINORITY TO DOMINANT COALITION

STRATEGY

The GAA camp attempted to achieve two related goals. First, it wanted to obstruct the council's proposals and therewith make Muintir unmanageable. Second, by means of these pressures it wanted to change the representation on the council, and eventually dominate that body. To that end the GAA had to bring the townspeople into its own camp. However, it could not offer this potential support better prizes than its opponents, for it did not command any such prizes. It could adopt only a strategy of levelling its opponent's power and therewith clear the road for a coalition with the townspeople. Levelling consists of " ... actions of field participants to "pull down" a social climber who, having gained more access to resources than they themselves enjoy, threatens to disturb the status quo".[2] The GAA pur-

154

sued three lines in its strategy. First, it activated the aversion against farmers and members of the bastard aristocracy, which it shared with many townspeople. Second, it created aversion against the clergy. Third, it demonstrated that the power of farmers, clergy, and bastard aristocracy were not as considerable as the townspeople believed. This levelling strategy manifested itself in a series of action sets through which the GAA attempted to achieve its goal. Most conflicts took place outside the arena of Muintir, but their consequences for the power process in that arena will systematically be investigated.

LEVELLING THE CLERGY

The Closure of the Churchyard

Patricksville's cemetery, which is located around the Catholic church, had become crowded with bodies. Moreover, it looked rather dirty and unkept. Canon O'Toole decided to do something about it. In order to tidy up the place and to make some more room, he ordered his sexton to pull down a number of the oldest and most broken tombstones and fences. He sold the material and gave the money to the foreign mission. This caused, of course, indignity towards the canon, but these feelings turned into open hostility when the parish priest decided to have the churchyard closed. He wrote a letter to the Tallow Health Authority to that end, in which he exposed the unhealthy situation, and asked for a new cemetery outside the town. This news transpired when a friend of the barber, who works in the Authority's office, visited the town. The whole parish was up in arms at once. The population considered this a serious attack on their rights. It was *their* yard, the place where their parents were buried, and where they wanted to rest.

Tadgh O'Sullivan, the local shoemaker cum electricity meter reader, and barber Noolan, both leading GAA members, took the initiative to bring the plans of the priest to a halt and to give him a severe showdown. They went to a retired local solicitor who had also given air to his indignation because he had already prepared a beautiful grave in the old yard. Together they decided to organize a protest meeting in the parish hall. Several posters were put up in the town, and the barber and O'Sullivan used their widely ramified networks of contacts to have the news spread. At the night of the meeting, the parish priest refused to open the doors of the hall. Therefore, the meeting was held in the open air. O'Sullivan delivered a flaming speech and explained that they would defend what was theirs "by right". He urged the meeting to sign a petition which should be sent to the Health Authority. About 500 people signed.

After some weeks, the canon received a letter from the Health Authority stating that an inspector from Dublin would come down to investigate the matter. From the pulpit the parish priest informed his flock about the inspector, and invited everyone to come to the meeting. At the meeting, the

155

canon mentioned his arguments. He was seconded by his curates and some farmers of whom it is alleged that they wanted to sell land for the new cemetery. The barber, O'Sullivan, and some other townspeople defended their rights, and asked for a vote on the case. The parish priest however thought that there was no use in voting, but when the inspector agreed, he gave in. An overwhelming majority was against the plans of the priest. (O'Sullivan told me that they wanted a vote in order to check their strength.) The inspector promised to send some men to check the situation in the yard. Later he would inform the priest about his decision. Up to 1969, the case has been undecided though a new cemetery has been built by the county council outside the town. It is however hardly used; the people continue burying their relatives in the old yard.

The Closure of Shops and Pubs on Sundays

One Sunday the parish priest fulminated from the pulpit about the lack of devotion before and during the mass. He thought it blasphemous that his parishioners entered the church packed with purchases that they had hurriedly gathered from the shops. He asked his flock to drop this bad habit, and he hoped that the shopkeepers and publicans would close their premises "for the rest of their souls". He urged the businessmen also privately, during his daily visits around the town, to bring this habit to an end.

Both population and shopkeepers were rather confused. They had always done business on Sundays, and before canon O'Toole no priest had ever condemned it. The matter was widely discussed in the parish and many people felt uneasy about it. Barber Noolan wrote a letter to his brother who is a priest in the USA, and asked him for advice. The priest answered that it was not forbidden by the Irish Catholic hierarchy, and that it was certainly not a sin. He thought it pure "blackguardism" of the canon. This news was spread to the shopkeepers and the general public, who felt relieved but also angry with the canon.

Canon O'Toole decided to take a tougher measure against his opponents. From the pulpit he mentioned by name those shopkeepers and publicans who had defied his will, and he asked them "in the name of Christ" to drop this bad habit. When this did not help, he brought the matter to a fireside chat of Muintir. A discussion failed however; only two members of the GAA camp opposed him openly. Despite this public discussion and many private intimidations by the clergy, the shops and pubs have remained open up to the present day.

The Christmas Fair

The previous parish priest had introduced a Christmas fair that consisted of a jumble sale and a dance in the parish hall. The proceeds were used for the sick and the poor in the parish. For some years this fair had not been held.

At a Muintir meeting, a member of the GAA camp asked whether a fair would be held this year. Canon O'Toole said that he had no intention to do so. These days, the sisters of the local convent looked after the poor and the sick, and the state supported the poor with a proper allowance through the local home-assistance officer. So there were no more real poor in the community. This aroused the anger of some parishioners, for there were still many people in the town who were not properly provided for. O'Sullivan told this to the canon and said that he himself would take the initiative if the priest would not organize a fair.

During the following weeks, the GAA camp met and made arrangements for a fair. It collected clothes and shoes, and several shopkeepers gave some presents. Sale and dance would be held in the parish hall. To make sure that the parish priest would not oppose them, some members of the GAA camp went to the estate agent of lord Welby, the owner of the hall, and explained their case. Apparently, the estate agent was able to persuade the canon, for the sexton informed the initiators that they could collect the key of the hall on the day of the fair. Sale and dance were a success and have been organized by the GAA ever-since.

The results of the conflicts described above are clear. The clergy had been given a severe showdown by their opponents. The GAA activated an aversion against the clergy; indeed, it created distrust and hostility among certain segments of the population towards the priests. Moreover, it had been clearly illustrated that the religious leaders were not so mighty, and that they certainly could not ignore the wishes and interests of the population.

The canon took revenge, but this turned out to be new grist on the GAA's mill. The repair and maintenance of the church and the houses of the clergy had always circulated among the local craftsmen. Now the canon gave this patronage to a few men who had been loyal in the conflicts, and he excluded the others definitively. These soured victims were, of course, easy prey for the GAA camp.

TUG OF WAR FOR THE CARNIVAL

Late in February 1949, a general Muintir meeting was to be held. The main issue was the organization of the carnival. The council had worked out its plans and would defend them. It would be a very important meeting for both camps, for now it would become clear who governed the parish: the council or the GAA camp. Although the GAA had improved its position by undermining the power and prestige of the clergy, it still constituted a weak council or the GAA camp. Although the GAA had improved its position by proposals, and look for other ways to influence the decision.

At the night of the general meeting, each camp had mobilized as much support as possible. The canon, as the chairman of the council, unfolded the plans for the carnival. After his speech the barber asked permission to

157

speak. In a long address he remined his audience of the many fine carnivals that the community had had. He thought it a good idea to have this feast organized by a parish-wide organization. However, it would be wasting manpower and experience to exclude those who had always organized the carnival. Therefore, he proposed the meeting that Muintir would be in charge of the general management of the feast, and that the GAA would cooperate. This proposal was received with an enthousiastic applause. Canon O'Toole agreed; he sincerely wanted to reunite his parish, and this provided him also an opportunity to win back some support from the townspeople.

The preparations for the carnival turned out to be a flat failure. Two traditionally hostile camps had to work together, and this gave rise to many conflicts. No party accepted directives from the other, they could not agree about the division of the profits, and various times members of both parties withdrew, or blackguarded each other in their private lives. The result was that some manifestations had to be cancelled, while others were not properly prepared. In short, the 1949 carnival was no success.

After this debacle, the GAA camp decided to go its own way and organize an independent carnival next year. To achieve this goal, however, and to constitute a united front, it must get rid of enemies inside its own homebase, the GAA club. These enemies were two powerful club officers, influential members of the bastard aristocracy, who also served on the Muintir council. The pages that follow recount how the GAA camp went about running these persons down. They thus describe a second series of levelling activities.

LEVELLING THE BASTARD ARISTOCRACY

McOwen put under Restraint

Con McOwen is an influential person. He is the local home-assistance officer, and for many years he has been the parish's registrar ad interim. He is also a public relations officer in the local GAA club, and a member of the council of Muintir. Especially the first position gives him much power, for it is his task to provide the temporarily unemployed, the sick, and the poor with financial support. Although there are some basic directives, he actually decides how much a person will obtain, for he checks the personal circumstances. This implies, among other things, that he can reduce someone's benefit if that person improves his position by obtaining some work. Many unemployed and poor did some odd jobs and in most cases McOwen had condoned this. However, after some conflicts between the council and the GAA camp he changed his attitude and threatened some people with a reduction of their benefits if they did not loyally support the council's plans. Hannah Riordan, an old sister of a member of the GAA camp, was the first victim. Hannah is a poor spinster who obtained a weekly benefit of £ 2/10.

158

To make the ends meet, she nurses the mentally retarded little daughter of a shopkeeper for which she obtains some pocket money and a few meals. One day, when she came to McOwen's office to collect her benefit, she received only £ 2. McOwen explained that he had reduced her benefit because she had some extra income from nursing Linehan's child. When her brother Joe heard about this, he was outraged and brooded on revenge. He went to Tadgh O'Sullivan and discussed what to do. As secretary of the local Fianna Fail club, O'Sullivan put the case before their TD, Sean Pearse from Streamtown. Pearse wrote a letter to McOwen and asked for an explanation, but it appeared that he could do nothing about the case. However, when some ten other cases were brought to his attention, Pearse decided to have a private talk with McOwen. When he discovered that McOwen's activities were in fact retaliations against persons involved in a local conflict, he asked McOwen to bring back the benefits to their original levels. The home-assistance officer gave in, for he was afraid of Pearse taking steps to have him fired as interim registrar. Since that time, McOwen keeps quiet.

The results of this conflict are clear. The GAA camp had won "a great victory" over one of its strongest enemies. By means of its political contacts, it had illustrated the townspeople that the home-assistance officer was not so powerful as they believed. Therewith the GAA had cleared the road for more local support.

Shaughnessy and McOwen are Banned

After its meeting in February 1949, Muintir's council had not stayed idle. It had developed several schemes for the expansion of local recreational facilities. Some of these schemes had already been put to practice. A billiard club had been started and a small brass band was set up, and now the council planned to expand the local sporting facilites. At a general meeting of Muintir, in October 1949, the parish priest unfolded the council's plans to set up a local football association. He told the meeting that many people in the parish had been interviewed about the issue and that it had been met with great enthousiasm. The need was especially felt among the youth of the farming community, who were forced to go to Streamtown to practice their favourite sport. A committee was appointed to make the necessary arrangements. It consisted of the council members McOwen, Kevin Shaughnessy, another GAA officer, who is a bank clerk and a relative of the parish priest, one of the curates, a farmer, and a schoolteacher.

The GAA camp was, of course, up in arms, but it had not been able to prevent the proposal from being accepted. However, it decided not to fight the committee openly but to undermine it indirectly. Shaughnessy and McOwen had trespassed one of the basic rules of the GAA, which states that every member, involved in other than gaelic games, will be banned from the association. The GAA camp decided to make use of this weapon in order to get rid of the enemy inside their own home-base. Tadgh O'Sullivan, the club secretary, wrote a letter to the GAA headquarters and explained what was afoot. He was informed that a member of the national board would come down to investigate the case at a special meeting which the secretary must convene. Both parties began to rally support, but since Shaughnessy and McOwen realized that they would lose, they took steps to make a general meeting impossible. They rented the town's two meeting places for false purposes (for the two farmers' associations). The GAA camp however had more strings to its bow and announced that the local club would meet in the cinema of a nearby town. The meeting appeared to be very quiet. No objections were raised since none of the opponents was present. The inspector from Dublin heard the complaints and said that he would put the case to the national board. At that moment however, a gang of some 20 man forced their way into the building. They were supporters of Shaughnessy and McOwen who intended to break up the meeting. But when they discovered that they were too late, they soon disappeared. Some weeks later, O'Sullivan received a letter stating that Kevin Shaughnessy and Con McOwen had been banned from the GAA.

Thus, the GAA camp had won another victory. It had pulled down two leading members of the bastard aristocracy and therewith cleared away the main obstacles to a united GAA front. Soon, however, it turned out that differences of opinion divided the GAA camp. These differences would determine its strategy towards the council for the next four years. In 1950, Muintir would hold its annual general meeting where a new council had to be elected. Some members of the GAA camp thought that time was ripe for a coup. After the showdowns of the clergy and the bastard aristocracy, they thought that they could mobilize enough townspeople to take over the governing body of Muintir. Other members, however, did not share this opinion. They thought that too many factors were still against them. To begin with, the business section would not support them because these people were dependent upon both camps. Most probably they would stay away from the meeting. Secondly, the GAA camp was not sure of the support of many friends and relatives. These persons were dependent upon farmers, clergy and members of the bastard aristocracy. They would certainly not turn up. Thirdly, the second largest section of the third party, the farmers, would of course support the council. So it was highly unlikely that the GAA camp would win the Muintir elections.

On the basis of these considerations the GAA camp decided to avoid an open confrontation with the council. It would go on levelling their opponents whenever an opportunity turned up. It decided also to organize its own carnival and present the population with other recreational facilities.

The years that followed were characterized by many activities on both sides. Each camp ran a carnival, and the GAA started its own billiard club, a drama group, and a brass band. In short, it was a tug of war time for public between the GAA and the council. Gradually, however, the balance began to tilt in favour of the GAA. Two events caused the council to lose the support of the farmers, by now the largest, most powerful and loyal segment of its coalition. These events are recounted in the following pages. They constitute the third and final series of levelling activities.

LEVELLING THE FARMERS

The Loss of Market and Fair

Early 1951, rumours were flying that the local farmers' association intended to abolish their weekly market and monthly cattle fair. Several farmers had been going to Streamtown lately, because the facilities there were better. Now the association wanted to merge with that of Streamtown. The town was upset; especially the shopkeepers and publicans resented the plan because it implied that they would lose a considerable part of their trade. They held a meeting and discussed what they could do to prevent the plan. Shoemaker O'Sullivan was also present. He suggested that the meeting form a deputation to discuss the matter with the farmers. He thought Tony O'Neill and Liam Linehan, the biggest shopkeepers in town, the most suitable representatives, since they were related to some leading members of the farming community. Herewith O'Sullivan had manoeuvred these members of the bastard aristocracy into a most awkward position. They would certainly be victims of a merger with Streamtown because the fair meant business for them, but they did not like a row with their friends and relatives. They did their best to get rid of the task, but finally the meeting decided to delegate Linehan and O'Neill.

When it appeared some weeks later, that the delegation had failed, O'Sullivan did a second move. He proposed to discuss the case with the minister of agriculture whom he knew personally. Together with some shopkeepers he went up to Dublin, but it transpired that the minister could do nothing about it. In May 1951, the farmers' association of Patricksville merged with the Streamtown branch, and weekly market and cattle fair disappeared therewith definitively from the town.

Although market and fair had not been saved, this conflict improved the GAA's position in the arena of Muintir in several respects. To begin with, the first cracks appeared in the so far united front of the council. Linehan and O'Neill would no longer cooperate with their fellow-council members because they felt betrayed by the farmers. Despite pressures from the parish priest and from other members of the bastard aristocracy, they stayed away from the meetings, and eventually gave up their seats. Secondly, this conflict added more fuel to the traditional aversion of many businessmen towards the farmers. This implied that the GAA could now mobilize more easily this segment of the third party. In short, the GAA camp was on its way to form the dominant coalition.

In 1951, the Streamtown Creamery Ltd. started a purchase cooperative. Its members could order here all sorts of commodities. Tractors, milking-machines, coal, fertilizers, radios, TV sets, and even furniture were sold at strongly reduced prices.

Early 1952, the Patricksville creamery, which is a branch of the Stream-town body, decided to follow suit. When this became known, the shopkeepers were outraged. This would be the death-blow to their trade, and therefore they had to oppose it with all possible means. At an emergency meeting, O'Sullivan and Noolan the barber, proposed to boycott any farmer who came to their shops. They also suggested holding a protest march to the Muintir meeting that was to be held shortly. Since other, more effective plans were not brought up, the meeting agreed with the two proposals. Noolan and O'Sullivan made some 40 protest-posters for the shop windows of the local businessmen. Together with some other GAA members, they also went about the parish one night, and painted protest-phrases on farmers' sheds and houses. However, these confrontations turned out to be no success. Indeed, they accelerated a process which had begun some years ago; more farmers began to shop in Streamtown.

The leading members of the GAA camp were however firmly determined to fight to the bitter end. They worked hard to make the protest-march a success. At their club meetings they called up every member to join the march, and they went about the town for the same purpose.

At the night of the Muintir meeting, some 150 persons turned up and marched with banners into the Muintir green. O'Sullivan had even been able to persuade the local Fianna Fail TD, Sean Pearse, to join in. During the civil war, Pearse had fought in the parish against the farmers, and he still bore a grudge against them. When the protesting crowd entered the parish hall, only a few members of the council and some farmers, officers of the local creamery board, were present. The rest of the farming community had not turned up. Sean Pearse asked chairman canon O'Toole permission to speak. He said that he had been informed of the intentions of the farmers to set up a purchase cooperative in this parish. Nobody, of course, could prevent them, but since the economy of a large part of the parish was at stake, the case should be discussed by the entiry community. Patricksville had its own guild and parish council; that was the proper body to take a decision. The chairman admitted that this was a serious matter which concerned them all. However, a decision should not be taken overnight. He urged the members of the creamery board to think the matter over again. He promised also that the council would discuss the matter with both parties. He asked farmers and shopkeepers to constitute delegations to that end. Within a month another Muintir meeting would be held at which the issue would be voted on.

Several weeks went by but no Muintir meeting was held. The parish priest tried to persuade the farmers to discuss the matter, but they were not prepared to meet the local businessmen. They thought it their right to pursue their own interests, and they were determined to set up a local purchase cooperative. However, when a bomb destroyed the water-pump of the creamery and more actions were announced, the farmers gave up their plan. These activities, however, did not prevent them from turning their backs to the town: they joined the Streamtown purchase cooperative.

The results of this conflict were of basic importance for the power position of the GAA camp. To begin with, the council lost its strongest coalition partner, the farmers. Indeed, several farmers started withdrawing from the council, and by the end of 1952, only some 20 per cent of the farming community still attended Muintir meetings. With the disappearance of so many farmers the council also lost its grip on shopkeepers, farm labourers and housekeepers. So far these persons had either stayed away or voted for the council. Now they could be mobilized by the GAA camp, which constituted therewith the dominant coalition. The final pages dexcribe how this camp set about dominating Muintir.

THE GAA IN THE SADDLE

Preparations for a Coup

So far, the GAA camp had taken no direct steps to change the composition of the council of Muintir. Almost all its confrontations with the opposition had been confined to situations outside this body. Now however it considered the time ripe for an outright attack on the seats of the council. At one of its informal meetings O'Sullivan observed that he had studied Muintir's constitution. It had struck him that this pamphlet was not clear about the rules of the recruitment of councillors. " . . . various sections of the community" could be interpreted in more than one way. It might give them a lead to attack their opponent. He suggested discussing this matter with a member of Muintir's headquarters. After that they could see whether this was a possibility to fight their opponent in a constituational way. Jack Riordan appeared to be related to an instruction officer of Muintir and proposed to contact this man.

Some days later, O'Sullivan, barber Noolan, and Riordan went to the instruction officer and explained their problem. It appeared that the phrase about the representation could bear more than one construction. This had been done to give each parish the opportunity to constitute a council based on its own specific local peculiarities. Up to now, two lines of interpretation had been followed. A council was constituted either of an equal number (usually two) of representatives from the urban and rural segments, or from the social classes of the parish. Only very recently some parishes selected their councillors from their voluntary associations. When the instruction officer heard about the failures of the Muintir guild in Patricksville, he ad-

163

vised to press for a representation based on social classes. He promised to attend the annual general meeting and advise the parish priest accordingly.

Back at home, the GAA core concluded that a representation based on classes served their purpose very well. In their opinion the parish consisted of five classes, namely farmers, professionals, businessmen, craftsmen, and labourers. They could successfully mobilize the latter three, and since the professionals were not community-oriented, their only opponents would be the farmers. Thus, things looked favourable for the GAA camp and its members started preparing for a coup at the annual general meeting which was to be held in January 1953. They selected from each class two representatives, who were either members of the GAA camp or loyal supporters. Next, they canvassed every supporter in the town and asked them to vote for their candidates. This took them some weeks because it had to be done secretly. But after that period it appeared that they could rely upon a strong support.

Meanwhile, canon O'Toole had been informed of the machinations of this opponents. He had also received a letter from Muintir's headquarters stating that an instruction officer would attend the meeting. The canon, realizing that his power was declining, planned to oppose any proposal to a representation based on classes.

Towards a Landslide Victory

When the night of the annual meeting arrived, some 100 persons, mainly townspeople, turned up and gathered around the remnants of Muintir's council. After a speech of the instruction officer, emphasizing the necessity of cooperating, the great moment arrived. Chairman canon O'Toole announced the election of a new council and mentioned the persons whom the council proposed. The candidates appeared to be loyal supporters. Now O'Sullivan arose and told the chairman that the community was dissatisfied with the way in which Muintir was run. The general feeling was that not all sections of the parish were equally represented in the council, and that therefore loyal support was lacking. His proposal, which was seconded by ohter persons, was to constitute a council based on the classes of the community.

The chairman admitted that things were not as they ought to be. However, he found it difficult to say what exactly constituted a "class" in this parish. Was it a "socializing circle", was it based on differences in income, or should occupation be the criterion? He asked O'Sullivan for advice. This was exactly the corner from where the canon wanted to attack his opponent. He agreed, and asked the people to group themselves in the hall according to what they thought to be occupational classes. Next, each class must select two representatives.

The canon's counter-move was very effective, for much disagreement arose about who belonged to which class. The mid-wife, the home-assistance officer, the teachers, and the county clerks considered themselves, together with the clergy, professionals. This was not accepted by O'Sullivan. If these persons, who in his opinion were no real professionals, put themselves there, he would also step into that quarter, for he was a local journalist. Some mechanics considered themselves a cut above the labourers and did not want to be grouped with them. A former craftsman, now a factory labourer, was not accepted in the corner where he should be in his opinion. In short, this regrouping was a complete failure, and it divided the canon's opponents against themselves. Canon O'Toole made a second countermove and proposed to constitute a council based on representatives from the local voluntary associations. If this plan was accepted, he had won again, for two out of the three associations, namely the Irish Countrywomen's Association and Macra na Feirme, were dominated by farmers.[3] The two representatives of the GAA could easily be outvoted. The disunity and the late hour were in the canon's favour, and his proposal was accepted.

Canon O'Toole had successfully sustained the GAA's attack; he had formed a "working majority". However, with the introduction of this new and clear representation criterion, he had in fact dug his own grave. During 1953, the GAA camp founded four new voluntary associations which were represented to the council of Muintir in January of the next year. After six years of fighting its opponents on every front, the GAA camp had finally won. Supported by the majority of the ordinary townspeople, and with ten representatives against four of the old council, it could go its own way and run the affairs of the town as it had done before the introduction of Muintir.

III. CONCLUSIONS

Parochial politics have now been described. Two questions about this process must finally be answered. The first is: Why did the GAA win? Three factors are responsible, namely the more coherent composition of the GAA camp, its more favourable position *vis-à-vis* the third party in the battle, the Joe Soaps, and the process of increase of scale that acted upon the parish. I deal with them in that order.

Although predominantly moral ties connected the members of each camp, and therefore made them rather strong and stable, it appeared that the GAA camp was more coherent. Unlike the council, in which farmers and big shop keepers would no longer cooperate, the GAA camp was never divided by opposing sectional interests because its members belonged to the same social class. It could therefore devote all its attention to fighting the opponent.

The GAA was also in a potentially more favourable position *vis-à-vis* the third party than its opponent, for it had strongly moral connections with the largest section, namely the ordinary townspeople. Initially these ties were of little use, but when the council began to lose its grip on many townspeople, the GAA was bound to win.

165

The process of increase of scale, accelerated by local conflicts, caused not only disunity in the council but resulted also in the farmers turning their backs to parochial activities. It did not affect the GAA camp; indeed, this process cleared the road for a strong coalition with the ordinary towns-people, through which the GAA eventually won the game.

Finally, why did Muintir fail as a system for parochial government? Basically this is because it has never obtained any constitutional powers. To function as such Muintir should have been given the powers to organize part of its own affairs, based on a local taxation system. But this was never done; the county council runs most of the affairs of the parish, and Muintir's finances are almost completely derived from local charity. As a result of this and the lack of cooperation of the parishioners, Muintir had almost become "just another association" and "just another local debating floor".[4]

166

CHAPTER TEN

The Fight for a Seat in the County Council

I. THE EMERGENCE OF MACHINE POLITICS

For several years the GAA camp ran the affairs of the parish supported by the largest section of the townspeople. It was, however, incapable of braking the power of its opponent completely. To begin with, it could not destroy the influence of the parish priest. Through his widely ramified network of influential contacts, the canon had been able to mobilize enough support for his election as president of Muintir. During the years that he occupied this office, he was a formidable opponent, skilfully manoeuvring for his own benefit. Secondly, the rules for recruiting councillors prevented the GAA from obtaining all the seats in the council of Muintir. Four were continuously occupied by members of the Irish Countrywomen's Association and Macra na Feirme, who loyally supported the parish priest. Thirdly, certain segments of the third party did not want to or could not support the GAA camp. These comprised the members of the bastard aristocracy, those farmers who had remained in the guild, and a number of townspeople who were employed by or in some other way dependent upon opponents of the GAA camp. Despite some vicious attacks from the opposition, however, the GAA remained in the saddle.

This period of GAA domination came to an end after 1957. In that year, Kevin Shaughnessy, a leading member of the anti-GAA camp, obtained an important asset that was to change the balance of power. During the 1957 general elections, Con Doherty from Clonferry, obtained a seat in the Dail. Doherty, as will be remembered, took advantage of the declining power of Sean Pearse from Streamtown, and replaced this Fianna Fail politician in the Dail.[1] However, Doherty had to expand his support and consolidate his power, for not much had been heard of him in several areas. To show his "pull" in the area of Patricksville, he selected his nephew Kevin Shaughnessy and asked to inform him of everything that turned up and might improve his position there. For Shaughnessy this was a unique opportunity for strengthening his own position in the local power struggle. Through his connections with his uncle he could bring many prizes into the community and therewith attract supporters.

With the introduction of this new role into the community, parochial pol-

167

itics changed. New ways to win support, an new external resources were added to this game and turned it eventually into machine politics. The power process that took place in this new situation is recounted in the pages that follow. We study this process from the point of view of the old council because this camp was on the offensive. Since Kevin Shaughnessy was the main initiator of new attacks on the GAA camp we focus the description on his activities.

THE OLD COUNCIL ON THE OFFENSIVE; KEVIN SHAUGHNESSY BUILDS UP A CLIENTELE

Strategy

Shaughnessy's strategy can be understood only against the background of his position in the power structure of the community. Therefore, a brief review of his position must be given first. Kevin Shaughnessy is a bachelor of 47 years (1969), and lives with an old aunt in Main Street opposite the Munster & Leinster Bank. His parents were farmers in the parish. When his father died, Kevin did not want to succeed him and left the work to his younger brother. He felt unfit for the hard work on the farm and preferred to "knock around" with women of the town. It is alleged that he fled to England because a local girl expected a baby from him. He stayed for some five years in that country where he was in a college. There he acquired "that nice bit of English" as many people derisively told me. After having failed in college, he came back to Patricksville where his uncle, Con Doherty, provided him with a job as a bank clerk. Since that time he has been actively involved in many local activities.

In terms of private resources Shaughnessy was a poor leader: he was only a bank clerk. His network of personal contacts however, contained many locally influential persons. To begin with, he was a relative of the parish priest who in addition to wielding much spiritual influence, also patronized several local craftsmen and shopkeepers. Secondly, he was related to several members of the farming community. These persons, as will be remembered, employed a number of local farm labourers. He was also connected with many young farmers and farmers' sons through his chairmanship of Macra na Feirme. He was their representative on the council of Muintir. Thirdly, as a member of the bastard aristocracy he was on good terms with the school teachers, the two big businessmen, and the home-assistance officer, persons with considerable influence in the parish. By means of these contacts and with prizes from his uncle, Shaughnessy could attack his opponent. He aimed at the ordinary townspeople and the pro-GAA representatives on the council of Muintir. If these supporters of the GAA could be placed on half-pay, the old council camp would regain its former power position.

168

We now examine the main moves through which Kevin Shaughnessy attempted to achieve his goal.

McOwen's Power Restored

With the help of Sean Pearse, the Fianna Fail TD from Streamtown, the GAA had been able to put home-assistance officer McOwen under restraint. McOwen, as will be remembered, had reduced the allowances of several persons as a retaliation against their supporting the GAA camp. When Con Doherty replaced Pearse in the Dail, the cause of this restraint disappeared. Shaughnessy considered this new situation splendid for subverting the support of the GAA. With his close friend McOwen he discussed how to take the most advantage of this regained asset. McOwen, however, was afraid of using this weapon again. He disliked a confrontation with the new Fianna Fail representative upon whose support he was dependent for the continuation of his position as interim registrar. Shaughnessy, however, assured McOwen that there was no need to be afraid. He would explain the situation to his uncle, and make sure that McOwen would retain his office, whereupon the latter gave in. Together they worked out the following strategy which McOwen willingly trusted to me in 1969 because Shaughnessy had betrayed him later. McOwen would reduce the allowances under the guise of a general retrenchment policy of the county council. This would be the explanation given to the "victims". At the same time, however, McOwen would suggest them to contact their TD who might find ways for circumventing this new rule. This would, of course, almost automatically result in the population going to Con Doherty's nephew, Kevin Shaughnessy.

The results of this plan were remarkable. Within a few months, Shaughnessy "heard confessions" of the majority of the poorest section in the community. He promised to put in a word for them at Con Doherty's. After some time, several allowances were brought back again at normal level. Soon it was widely held that Shaughnessy was *the* man for "good pull", and persons with other problems also visited him.

The first effects of this new channel to prizes became soon visible in the balance of power in Muintir. Many townspeople who had loyally supported the GAA camp up to this point, now shunned the Muintir meetings. They were afraid of retaliations from Shaughnessy, but on the other hand, they would not show their disloyalty towards the GAA camp and vote against its proposals.

The Construction of St. Breandan's Place

Early 1959, Kevin Shaughnessy informed a general meeting of Muintir that he had received splendid news from Con Doherty. Their TD had told him that the county council had ratified a plan for the construction of 20 new cottages in Patricksville. This was indeed good news for the community. It meant not only new housing facilities for many, but also work for local craftsmen and labourers, since the county council selects usually a tender from a contractor of the area concerned. For Shaughnessy this scheme was a unique opportunity to subvert the GAA camp. Indeed, it might enable him to restore the power of the old council camp. In order to obtain maximal results he traced out a very shrewd course of action, which is now known widely and called a public scandal. First, he went to the local builder cum contractor and told this man that he, Shaughnessy, might be able to obtain the contract on certain terms. The two made a deal. Shaughnessy would do his best to obtain the contract, and if he succeeded he was entitled to select the craftsmen and labourers for the work. Moreover, our local broker would also receive £ 100 for "services rendered". Shaughnessy's next step consisted of a chat with his uncle. He explained the TD that the builder was anxious to obtain the contract, and which terms Shaughnessy had stated. He said that this was *the* opportunity for Doherty to increase his "pull" in Patricksville. Doherty found it an attractive plan and promised to see what he could do in the county offices.

Two months later, Shaughnessy was informed that the builder's tender had been accepted by the county council. Now he could take a third and most effective step. At a fireside chat of Muintir he told that their local contractor had been selected by the county council for building the cottages. This would provide work for the community. To give each applicant a fair chance, however, the builder had asked Shaughnessy to constitute a small selection committee. This consisted of the builder, himself, and McOwen, the home-assistance officer. Shaughnessy invited those who were interested in a job to register at one of the three, whereafter the committee would decide.

During the weeks that followed, the committee members were besieged with candidates. Shaughnessy, however, had figured out who had to be selected, and he made sure that his proposals were accepted. Eventually, more than 40 persons were selected: electricians, carpenters, plumbers, and a number of skilled and unskilled labourers.

THE RESULTS

The results of Shaughnessy's manoeuvring for the balance of power in Muintir were impressive. In 1960, a large part of the ordinary townspeople were in one way or another dependent upon the construction works. Since they knew that the continuation of their work, or that of their close relatives, was in the hands of Shaughnessy, they dared not go against his wishes in Muintir. Some stayed away from the meetings, while others joined him openly to curry favour with him. The GAA camp saw its support thus crumble to a few. "We were utterly bewildered, we felt spoofed, and we did not know how to hit back", a member of the GAA camp told me. Moreover, four pro-GAA representatives on the council of Muintir were forced to renounce their allegiance to that camp because they were patronized by Shaughnessy. In short, by the end of 1960, the old council camp and its moral supporters had won back their power position and ruled Muintir again.

II. MACHINE POLITICS IN FULL SWING

Early 1961, the game that has been described so far took an abrupt turn. This was the result of the death of the Labour MCC from a near-by small town who had shot himself. Although his seat was filled by coopting his former running mate, a vacuum in the regional balance of power remained. The successor was weak and rather unknown, whereas his predecessor had always attracted many personal votes, even from Patricksville which is predominantly Fianna Fail. During the years that the old Labour MCC represented the area, Patricksville had not attempted to nominate a local Fianna Fail candidate. His chances would have been too small with a powerful Labourman on the doorstep. In this new situation, however, and with local government elections in the near future (1962), a popular and/or influential inhabitant might well have a chance.

Kevin Shaughnessy was the first one to discern the implications of the recent events. He thought them highly favourable for converting his local credit into political office. He had built up a considerable clientele in the community, and he felt sure that many persons would give him a vote.

A series of new actions and events, triggered off by the death of the Labour MCC, rang in a new era in the local power struggle. The already changed game turned now into full-fledged machine politics. Although many purely parochial issues remained important, the basic issue became now: who will be the Fianna Fail representative in the county council? and the ultimate prize: a seat in that body. With these changes the main point of the fight shifted from Muintir to the local Fianna Fail club. In the following pages we examine therefore the power process in that club. For a better understanding of that process we first review the composition of the new arena.

The New Arena and its Composition

Up to 1961, the Fianna Fail club was numerically small, it counted only ten members. Despite this small size, it has since long been divided into two wings, a left and a right one. The right wing, counting six members, is the largest and oldest. It consists of old IRA members, the founders of the club, and some of their sons. They are the hard core of the club, and consider themselves as the guardians of the old republican and gaelic tradition. Since they are the same persons as those who were described for the arena of Muintir as the GAA camp, I continue denoting them in that way. The other,

171

smaller, wing is composed of new-comers, who joined the club for pragmatic reasons. It consists of Shaughnessy, his brother Johnjoe who had obtained a job as a clerk in the local creamery, McOwen, the home-assistance
officer, and a small shopkeeper.

Although both wings usually cooperated during elections, tensions have
always existed between them. Each looked down upon the other. The GAA
camp considered the others floor-crossers who had joined the party for
their own benefit, whereas the new-comers looked upon the GAA camp as
naive, narrow-minded, and old-fashioned. These tensions had increased
during the fight in Muintir in which the members of each wing had taken a
clear and opposite position. And now that Patricksville made a good
chance of nominating a candidate for the 1962 local government elections,
the two wings became outright enemies. Each thought it its right to nominate its own favourite candidate. The GAA camp considered Tadh O'Sullivan, the secretary of the club the most suitable man for the office. He was
the son of the late IRA leader, and had exposed his superior qualities in other fields of activity. The others thought that local broker Shaughnessy was
the proper man. Each watched the manoeuvring of the other carefully and
attempted to achieve its goal.

THE NOMINATION BATTLE: PREPARATIONS FOR THE ENCOUNTER

Shaughnessy on the Offensive

In order to be nominated, and eventually elected, a person needs the support of three parties. First, he must make sure that his own local political
club will support him. Second, he needs the votes of a number of other local clubs in the County Electoral Area. Third, he needs the votes of many
electors. Kevin Shaughnessy was in a favourable position only towards the
third party. As local broker, he had developed much influence in the town,
and he was on good terms with the farming community whose members
might well give him a personal vote. In the local political club, however, the
first obstacle to be taken in the nomination race, his position was rather
weak. True, he could rely on the support of three other members, but the
majority was against him. Shaughnessy's contacts in the regional party body
were also minimal because he did not occupy an office in the local club
which enabled him to attend the regional meetings. All the offices were occupied by members of the GAA camp. Thus, if Shaughnessy wanted to be
nominated he had to improve his position both on the local and the regional political front.

In the following months, he spent all his energy to these goals. His first
move was aimed at disturbing the power balance in the local political club
by increasing the number of members. The big prize through which he got
four persons "on the hook" was his promise to have them put high on the
priority list for renting a newly built county council cottage. Until the de-

finitive allotments, Shaughnessy could rely on their support. These new club members brought the number of his supporters to seven; a very small majority but enough for an effective next move.

Rumours had been flying recently that Joe Riordan, the treasurer of the Fianna Fail club, had embezzled money from the GAA club of which he was also treasurer. This was a splendid opportunity for weakening the GAA camp. Shaughnessy brought the matter up at a meeting of the political club. Although it had not been proved yet that Riordan was guilty, in Shaughnessy's opinion there was sufficient ground for a vote of censure. His camp outvoted the other on the issue, Riordan's office terminated, and Shaughnessy came in his place.

This office provided our local broker the important link to the regional party body. Now he was entitled to attend its meetings where he could display his qualities and rally support for his nomination. Soon, however, it appeared that he had over-estimated the importance of this office. It became clear to him that this office alone would bring him not far along the road to nomination. The meaning of the often quoted saying *feiche bliain ag fàs* (twenty years of growing) became very clear to him.[2] He was only an unknown new-comer in the regional body, and it would take a long time before he would be accepted as a potential candidate by the other club representatives. In short, Shaughnessy had to look for a better way to gain influence among the delegates to the nomination convention.

After some months, this way turned up when the chairman of the club, barber Noolan, a man of weight in the GAA camp, crossed the floor and openly supported Shaughnessy. Noolan had since long been a member of the club and knew many members of other clubs in the area. He was also a well-known person in GAA circles, for he was chairman of the county board. This widely ramified network of personal contacts fell in Shaughnessy's lap, so to speak, when Noolan joined his forces. The reason of this sudden floor-crossing was that Noolan had run into debts towards Shaughnessy. For, what had happened? When the farmers turned their backs to the town, Noolan lost many customers, and when the local postmaster took up his former trade (haircutting) as a sideline, Noolan's clientele decreased even more. In order to keep his head above water, he mortgaged his house to the bank, but his position remained precarious. A part-time job as a clerk at the local creamery which fell vacant, attracted Noolan's attention and he started angling for it. When Shaughnessy heard about this, he went to Noolan and explained him that he could lay his hand on the job. Shaughnessy was prepared to give it to Noolan provided that the latter would canvass for him in the political clubs of the area. This was a very difficult situation for Noolan, but since charity begins at home, he gave in. When his fellow-camp members got the air of his secret activities, they were infuriated and ostracized him. Noolan tried to explain that he had no alternative, but when this did not help, he turned his back to his former friends and supported Shaughnessy openly out of pure spite.

Thus, Kevin Shaughnessy strengthened his position on several political fronts. He improved his nomination chances in the party's regional body, and expanded his support in the local club. By 1962, the number of club-members had more than doubled, mainly through Shaughnessy's activities. The support of this leader was, however, far from stable. Whenever a person had obtained what he wanted, or felt that he would never achieve his goal, he left the explosive scene.

The GAA Camp: Harping on the Republican Theme

While Kevin Shaughnessy was rapidly expanding his support by bringing new members into the local club, the GAA camp enrolled only a few members. This was, of course, the result of differences in access to resources. Shaughnessy commanded highly effective political connections through Con Doherty, whereas the GAA camp had to do without such vital assets. Shaughnessy's position *vis-à-vis* the townspeople was also stronger than that of the GAA camp. His political connections and his ties with many locally influential persons prevented the townspeople from joining the GAA camp in any overt attack on his strength. In one respect, however, the GAA camp remained stronger than its opponent. This was its basically moral bond with the townspeople. Shaughnessy was generally considered the "clever man" with "good pull", but the members of the GAA camp were the "real local" leaders of the town.

With no other, more effective ways left for attacking Shaughnessy, his opponents decided to undermine his power by tightening the ideological bonds with the townspeople. Although this did not increase their chances of nominating Tadgh O'Sullivan, their own favourite candidate, it might well result in many townspeople abstaining from voting for Shaughnessy. If they succeeded in preventing Shaughnessy's election, they had anyway kept the path free for O'Sullivan taking a chance another time. Headed by O'Sullivan, the GAA camp undertook various steps to that end. They revitalized the activities of the Gaelic League by organizing lectures on Irish and competitions in public gaelic dances. They obtained the government's permission for adding Irish signposts and name-boards of streets to the English ones. A festal procession, headed by the GAA brass band, hung up these new items. O'Sullivan had more strings to his bow. When he heard that every citizen was entitled to have his name registered in Irish, he urged many people to do so. This caused much extra work for McOwen, the local registrar. The GAA camp organized also a fund raising fair for a monument for the local IRA men who had died during the Troubles. At all these public manifestations O'Sullivan delivered speeches about their glorious past and their gaelic tradition which was undermined by "certain new elements" in the community.

By the end of 1961, when these ideological confrontations were still in full swing, new ways for attacking Shaughnessy turned up. These were the result of changes in the regional balance of power. During the 1961 general elections, Con Doherty lost his seat in the Dail. A main reason for his defeat was the revision of the constituencies through which he lost a large number of voters. His Streamtown bulwark fell into the hands of Corbett from Cregg who infiltrated there with Dwane's active help.[3] When it became known that Corbett's local broker, Sean Dwane, intended to stand for the county council elections, and that Corbett would support him, O'Sullivan saw his chance to "blow gunpowder into that bastard's (Shaughnessy's) arse", as he put it crudely. He informed Corbett and Dwane of Shaughnessy's machinations in the regional party body and the local clubs of the area. Both Dwane and Corbett wanted, of course, no competitor in the field. If Shaughnessy was elected, Doherty improved his position in the area, which Corbett did not want. And Dwane did not like a rival on his doorstep. Supported by O'Sullivan, Dwane and Corbett went round many members of local clubs and canvassed for Dwane's nomination. Especially Corbett's widely ramified network of personal contacts caused these activities to be very effective as we shall see shortly.

1962: Shaughnessy Defeated though not Destroyed

The last few weeks before the nomination convention were hectic for the two camps in Patricksville. Both leaders were active on various fronts. Shaughnessy, sure of his supremacy in the local club, concentrated on canvassing the local electorate and the members of other clubs in the area. Doherty and barber Noolan assisted him in this task. O'Sullivan and his mates did their best to enroll new club members in order to have the balance of power tilt in their favour. They spent most of their time and energy, however, on canvassing the members of other clubs.

At the night of the local nomination meeting, some 35 persons were present, of which the majority consisted of newly enrolled members. When it was about to begin, Con Doherty and some men burst into the meeting. Shaughnessy had asked Doherty to attend the meeting in order to be completely sure of his local nomination. A short fight developed which cost some chairs, as the owner of the premises told me. When O'Sullivan, however, shouted that this was against the standing orders, and that he would phone the party headquarters, Doherty and his gang disappeared. This was, however, the only score that the GAA camp could make that night. Shaughnessy's support was far larger and thus he was nominated by the Patricksville club.

The next step in the race was more difficult for Shaughnessy. At the regional nomination convention, he had to fight four other candidates. Only two of these could eventually obtain a seat in the county council. The board of the regional party body had therefore decided to nominate three candidates. At the night of the convention, one candidate withdrew because he saw that he had no chance. Moreover, the news was spread that the sitting

MCC, Sean Dwane, and another new-comer would support each other. When Shaughnessy heard about this set up, he decided to withdraw. This was a great triumph for the GAA camp; they had adopted effective tactics against their opponent. Although they had been defeated in their own local club, they had demonstrated their superior position in the regional arena. Enthousiastically they canvassed for Dwane, and saw their candidate win a seat.

III. COMPETITION BETWEEN LOCAL BROKERS

The Descending Star of Kevin Shaughnessy

With Dwane's election in 1962 as the Fianna Fail MCC for the area, machine politics entered a new and for my description the final stage. Although major encounters between the two camps did not take place during the next few years, the balance of power began to change. This was the result of Shaughnessy losing much power. The star of this local broker was descending for a combination of reasons. To begin with, when his boss, Con Doherty, lost his seat in the Dail, Shaughnessy's prestige received a serious setback. Indeed, it was decreased even further by O'Sullivan and his friends who told the population that Doherty was no longer interested in Patricksville. Doherty, now an ordinary MCC, would only work for the people of his own pocket which was far away from Patricksville. Shaughnessy did his utmost to prove the opposite.[4] But since Doherty spent most of his time on other areas, it seemed as if O'Sullivan was right. Thus, fewer prizes were given to Patricksville with the result that Shaughnessy's credit decreased.

Another reason for Shaughnessy's declining influence was the election of Sean Dwane. Dwane, now the official representative for the area, regularly visited Patricksville. About once a month he came to the town to "hear confessions". This made Shaughnessy's role of local broker almost redundant and decreased his "pull".

These changes in the local balance of power took place almost without any purposive actions of the GAA camp. As O'Sullivan put it: "Things simply straightened out for themselves". After 1965, however, regional political changes brought the GAA camp new opportunities for more effective attacks. In that year, Sean Dwane was elected as the Fianna Fail TD for the western part of the constituency. His improved position on the political ladder, however, created communication problems. Dwane had to live in Dublin for some days of the week, and his pocket had now become very large. These two factors made it impossible for him to make regular and frequent tours along all his local clubs. During his absence somebody had to look after his interests which might be harmed by Doherty or his broker Shaughnessy. He selected Tadgh O'Sullivan for this job because Tadgh was an influential member of the local club and a leader of many in the community.

O'Sullivan accepted the job enthousiastically, for it provided a splendid means for attacking Shaughnessy. Indeed, it might even enable him to make a bid for a seat in the county council, as his opponent had done. The period that followed was thus characterized as a competition between local brokers for supporters. My neighbour, a small shopkeeper, described those years very vividly. His phrase illustrates also clearly who was the strong man, and why. He said: "It was like them saints in the chapel. You prayed to saint Tadgh for the grub, but you promised saint Kevin a candle when he helped you out". With the experience that he had acquired in previous situations, O'Sullivan started attacking Shaughnessy and his supporters wherever possible. The final pages of this chapter recount how O'Sullivan went about running down Shaughnessy, and how he bid for a seat in the county council.

Tadgh O'Sullivan on the Offensive

To undermine Shaughnessy's position O'Sullivan had to attack his opponent in two respects. First, he must pull down Shaughnessy's image of effective "string puller"; second, he had to expand his own support in the Fianna Fail club. O'Sullivan was in an advantageous position for achieving the first goal. His channels to prizes were of a better quality than those of his opponent. Moreover, his boss, Sean Dwane, paid much attention to the problems of Patricksville because Doherty's strength had not yet been broken there. Dwane could handle these problems also quicker and obtain higher prizes owning to his connections with his former boss, Steve Corbett, who was a man of weight in many offices. Furthermore, O'Sullivan was also better equiped for the function of local broker. As a regional journalist and electricity meter reader he made regular tours along all the houses, meanwhile "hearing confessions". Finally, O'Sullivan's ties with the ordinary townspeople were better than those of Shaughnessy. The latter was considered the "clever man" whereas he, O'Sullivan, was a "real local".

O'Sullivan's first attacks took place in the arena of Muintir. He agitated publicly and criticized Doherty for having failed to provide some local amenites aked for. "If there was pull in that man", O'Sullivan proclaimed, "he should come out and show it". To illustrate that there was real "pull" in the area, O'Sullivan would take up the matters with Dwane, and see that the amenities would come. A month later, he produced a letter from the county offices stating that the amenities would come shortly. Another time, when O'Sullivan was again attacking his opponents, he referred to the work that Dwane had done for the GAA club. Without the help of their TD they could never have obtained their splendid pitch. Again, at a fireside chat of Muintir, he proclaimed it a scandal that the local boys' school still had a dry closet. He did not understand why the parish priest, the manager of the school, had called of the installation of a water closet. O'Sullivan challenged the canon and said he would do his utmost to get it there with Dwane's help. Some weeks later, the water closet was installed.

To many people it became clear that Dwane was *the* politician for the area, and that O'Sullivan was his right-hand man. Thus Tadgh bult up his political credit. But his star rose very quickly when he announced that a long desired industry would be established in the town. His boss, Sean Dwane, had obtained a grant from the government for establishing a knitting industry which would provide full-time employment for some 25 persons. This was, of course, splendid news for the community. More importantly, however, it strengthened the basis of O'Sullivan's power *vis-à-vis* the local people, for *he* in fact could select who would obtain a job. The population realized this, and O'Sullivan made use of it. From that date, our local broker has been hearing many "confessions".

The results of O'Sullivan's activities for the balance of power in the local Fianna Fail club were remarkable. Before he had started his actions described above, the balance had already tilted in his favour as a result of Doherty's defeat. But when he began to establish his name as local broker this process accelerated. Many members who had supported Shaughnessy, now disappeared whereas others simply crossed the floor and followed O'Sullivan, who therewith led the largest coalition.

The 1967 Local Elections: O'Sullivan's Coup and its Aftermath

By 1967, Tadgh O'Sullivan decided to stand for the county council elections of that year. He had gained a solid backing from his own local club, and various delegates from other clubs in the area had promised to support him at the convention. Moreover, he knew that he would have the support of many local voters. "I had a good chance, but that bastard (i.e. Shaughnessy) spoofed me, and (Dwane) queered the pitch" he told me one night when we discussed this episode. What had happened? It is alleged that Shaughnessy informed Dwane of O'Sullivan's machinations. When Dwane heard about Tadgh's plans, he was afraid because O'Sullivan might well take many of his votes, even from his own local area. Dwane was rather unknown in regional GAA circles, for he backed other sports, and this might well cost him the votes of many GAA supporters from within his own area. In short, Dwane considered it necessary to prevent O'Sullivan from standing for the elections. Supported by Shaughnessy and barber Noolan, Dwane went along to see many club officers and other influential persons in the area. He persuaded them by means of promises, small gifts of money, drinks, and other prizes, not to vote for O'Sullivan at the convention. Since Dwane was well known in other corners of the electoral area where O'Sullivan had hardly been heard of, he could attain what he wanted. Tadgh O'Sullivan was not nominated at the convention, though his own local club had proposed him and voted for his candidature. These complications caused O'Sullivan and his supporters to canvass for another MCC, whereas Shaughnessy and the remnants of his camp worked for Dwane.

The consequences of this clash for the power balance in Patricksville were soon felt. O'Sullivan had suffered a serious blow in the show-down. He had been taught a good lesson in tactics. Indeed, the relationship between Dwane and his local broker chilled. Dwane would no longer work in the town through O'Sullivan but selected Shaughnessy in his place. This meant that the latter could increase his "pull" again at the cost of that of O'Sullivan. After a short time, however, one of Dwane's advisers, a barrister from Patricksville, explained to him that he had made a tactical mistake. Rather than replacing one local broker by another, Dwane should have accepted both of them, so that the two would fight each other and keep one another weak. Dwane changed his strategy accordingly, which resulted in both Shaughnessy and O'Sullivan working for him like ants. Early 1968 however, Dwane changed his strategy again. At a club meeting in Patricksville, he declared openly that he would no longer deal with questions that came to him through Shaughnessy because the latter had betrayed and defrauded him. Although these allegations may be true, according to both the barrister and O'Sullivan, political reasons must have been more important for Dwane sacking Shaughnessy. The fact was that Dwane had heard about the intentions of Joe Miller from Ballydown and Con Doherty from Clonferry to stand for the next Dail-elections. These ex-TDs were still dangerous for his own position, and therefore had to be opposed on every front. By means of Shaughnessy, his (former) local broker and nephew, Con Doherty might try to cash in on the credit that Dwane had built up in Patricksville. To prevent Doherty from making an easy come back to the town, Dwane dismissed Shaughnessy. With this open sacking Dwane declared in fact to the voters of Patricksville that Shaughnessy had gone bankrupt, politically speaking, and that he therefore should no longer be listened to during the elections.

Since that time, O'Sullivan's position has never again been challenged by Shaughnessy. Indeed, the latter lost the last segments of his power basis when Con Doherty disappeared definitively from North-East Tallow in 1969, due to the constituency revisions. Since that year, Patricksville has been integrated into Dwane's machine, with Tadgh O'Sullivan steering the local wheel.

IV. CONCLUSIONS

In this chapter and the previous one a power process has been described which took place in Patricksville and covered a period of some 25 years. This process was the outcome of national en regional factors acting upon specifically local circumstances.

Looking back at this power process some concluding remarks can be made. Firstly, it has become clear that the widely accepted notion of structural balance makes no sense in this process. The camps were not evenly matched, and they had no view in common about the rules that should have to keep the game within reasonable limits.[5] Indeed, several times the games "went wild". Moreover, the camps and their coalition partners were always in motion. They shifted from a position of establishment to that of opposition and vice versa. But at last, one may argue, peace has come back to the parish, the GAA had restored its old power position, and thus nothing has changed. This argument brings us to my second point, for important changes *did* take place in the 25 years that I covered. They have to do with the changes in the nature of the camps, their structural composition, and way of fighting. The camps that competed each other in Muintir differed from those in the local Fianna Fail club in the ways in which the members were related to one another. In the first arena predominantly moral connections tied the members of each camp together, whereas transactional bonds dominated or were added in the Fianna Fail club. This change of what may be called moral camps into more transactional ones was the outcome of changes in the larger, regional, power balance. With the introduction into the community of the role of local broker the basis was laid for an "exchange-circuit", that is a " . . . system of paths through which goods and services circulate . . .".[6] Together with these changes in the basis for alignments a more pronounced differentiation between leaders and support took place. Those who led the camps in Muintir were actually the first among equals. The leaders in the Fianna Fail arena, however, were powerful superiors because they controlled the "flow-system" of prizes upon which the supporters were dependent.[7] In short, the camps in the Fianna Fail club were clearly leader-centered interaction systems whereas those in Muintir were not. Changes took also place in the nature of the interaction between the camps. Levelling was the characteristic strategy of the GAA camp in parish politics. Subversive activities dominated in the machine political game. Both Shaughnessy and O'Sullivan tried to win by publicly exposing the strength of their "pull", and by carefully subverting personnel from each other's camps. These changes in strategy were of course the result of differences in resources that were available in the field. In parish politics the GAA camp lacked the resources for attacking its opponent openly. Consequently it pursued a strategy of levelling. The council's opportunities for outright attacks diminished and became almost nil when many of its members and supporters left the arena. In the new situation, however, the increasing external resources enabled both camp leaders to subvert each other directly.

The main conclusion so far is that the transactional element in the political relations in Patricksville has been increasing. Is this conclusion correct? Is it not the consequence of a too narrow historical horizon? Put differently, are we dealing with a linear process or is it circular? The only way to answer this question is to look back. Political machines were, so to speak, no new phenomena for the community because the electors have always voted for particular politicians. They were thus members of machines. Machine politics, however, in the sense of clearly locally organized antagonistic interaction with a strong transactional element was new for Patricksville. This appears from the fact that a local broker had never existed in the parish before Shaughnessy adopted this role. Prior to this, politicians came to the town to "hear confessions", and the club secretary acted as intermediary by writing letters to the politician. A local actor, however, who deliberately and systematically exploited this function for increasing his own position was a new phenomenon in the parish. Another indicator that affirms my main conclusion is the view of the townspeople themselves. According to many people the present "troubles" had started after the defeat of Sean Pearse, the Fianna Fail TD from Streamtown. When he disappeared, Patricksville came into the turmoil of subversive activities of politicians who were rather unknown and had to expand their areas. At that moment, local brokerage developed in the town and has existed ever since. One old man summarized the change very vividly when he said: "After his death (i.e. Sean Pearse), things changed. We voted for him because he was a fine man. He fought on our side in the Troubles. And when you had a problem he would help you out. But after his death, this bloody whole place became rotten with politics. Today everybody looks for strings to get more grub. They know goddam' well where their bread can be buttered better".

CHAPTER ELEVEN

Epilogue

In the preceding pages I have given a description of politics within the boundaries of the constituency. I was mainly concerned with competition within one party, namely the Fianna Fail party. I treated in detail the ways in which different types of politicians, TDs, MCCs, and local brokers, compete with each other for scarce resources. Each of them tries to build up support, that is, attempts to organize a machine, by subverting voters from the others.

In my description of politics in rural Ireland I have pursued two lines of enquiry. Firstly, I have given what may be called a "static" analysis of political machines, that is, I have mapped out a chart of roles and statuses for a particular structure. Secondly, after this mainly static analysis, I have given a dynamic description of machine politics. In this description I have not much abstracted from time, in the sense of historical time, because this is a factor that determines the processes and social forms.[1] Thus I attempted to get away from the usual analysis of circular or repetitive processes. Any analysis that leaves out time is incomplete and unsatisfactory for two reasons. First, it deals with social phenomena as things that have no beginning and no end but are just there. Second, it is incapable of describing the nature and direction of change which is inherent of all social phenomena. Thus by treating historical time as an analytical element more could be described than a process of fission and fusion, of changing alignments between persons and groupings. By systematically treating factors in the environment of the parochial field of Patricksville, for example, and the historical processes that are at work in the society at large, I could explain how and why machine segments came into being and disappeared. Moreover, I could also explain why the transactional element in the interpersonal relationship had grown considerably in importance.

This final chapter continues this second line of enquiry, but the task I set myself is more extensive. I attempt to explain how the phenomenon of machine politics (political machines) in Ireland in general is the outcome of factors and processes which are and/or have been at work in the society at large.

Before endeavouring this some general remarks. To begin with, I have no intention of systematically comparing machine politics in Ireland with those in other countries such as India or the USA. Therefore, no elaborate statements about the development of machines in general can be expected. Secondly, although I pursue a diachronic approach, and treat machines as processes in historical time, no exact moment of origin can be indicated. It must be borne in mind that complex social forms, like political machines, do not come into being overnight. They are the result of principles and long-term processes which are at work in the society. In their wake, so to speak, parts of the phenomenon come slowly over the horizon, and only after some time one can discern such things as political machines. More directly, I cannot indicate a zero-point. My description begins when the first traces are visible, and I explain these traces by putting them in the context of society at that time. We then follow the development of political machines and machine politics to the present day.

I. IRISH MACHINE-STYLE POLITICS IN WIDER HISTORICAL PERSPECTIVE

In an article on corruption in developing countries, Scott mentions several factors that foster machine politics.[2] Outstanding among them are: 1) poverty, 2) fragmentation of power, 3) strong parochialism and widespread particularism in the relations in all sectors of social life.[3] This socio-cultural context is characteristic of Ireland to-day. Since it has been described in detail in various chapters of this book, a short review will suffice here.

1) Poverty or, more precisely, lack of secure and steady employment, is endemic in Ireland. Agriculture and the processing of agricultural products are the basis of the country's economy. The government, as the main promoter of economic development, tries to attract industries from abroad in order to expand employment opportunities. Despite its advertising campaigns and the favourable conditions it offers, the government is unable to bring enough employment into the country. The main factors for this failure are the lack of skilled labour, the dispersed settlement pattern, and the country's peripheral location.

2) Although Ireland's governmental system is no longer as fragmented as it was in the previous century, it is still far from integrated. With the introduction of the central government's Department of Local Government, the county council's power has been restricted, but in many respects it is still master in its own house.

3) Parochialism and particularism are characteristic of the relations in all sectors of social life in Ireland, and go hand in hand with a personalization of these relations. Comparing the present with the past, Chubb observes: " ... olicharchic rule, underemployment, and poverty all led most Irish people to view government, even though it was alien, as a potential source of help, jobs or favours, provided one knew how to tap it. By most people public authorities were thought to be best approached via some intermediary or notable. Forty years' experience of independence notwithstanding, authority is to some extent still thought of in these terms, a potential source of benefits or grants, still to be viewed with some suspicion, and still need-

183

ing the intervention or good offices of a man "in the know" or a person of affairs".[4]

This parochialism and perceiving relations in particularistic terms are reflected in the often quoted saying: "It's not what you know, it's who you know". An Irishman sees his world around him as a vast network of personal relations. It is through this network, and those of others, that he knows much about the world. He does not primarily know and consider England or America as we know them from newspaper, atlas, and geography books; for him each is a country where a brother, a sister, aunt or uncle lives and who writes and tells him about life there. He perceives persons not primarily in their formal roles, as bureaucrats, lawyers, company directors, but in the first place as friends, friends of friends, relatives of friends: persons who owe him or a close connection of his some favour. In other words, in his view each person is, morally or otherwise, indebted to a number of other persons.

The basis for this socio-cultural context that fosters machine politics was laid during the centuries that Ireland was dominated by England. Until the last quarter of the nineteenth century, Ireland was characterized by a rigid social dichotomy. A small upper stratum of English and Anglo-Irish landlords, mainly Protestant, formed the political, administrative, and economic elite. The largest part of the population, predominantly poor Catholic peasants, rented small plots of land from this elite. The Ireland of those days was politically segmented. The country's political centre – after 1800 this became Westminster – was established strongly but interfered only incidentally with the lives of the predominantly rural population. Because of an only rudimentarily developed bureaucratic apparatus, the centre communicated mainly with its periphery through the landlord-politicians and some officials in charge of the maintenance of law and order. The influence of the various regional bodies, however, was greater. Grand Juries were the main legal bodies functioning at county level, and within their territories a number of Boards were in charge of public works and the care for the poor and the sick. Their members belonged mainly to the landowning class. In many respects Juries and Boards were formally dependent upon the country's political centre, but in fact they were their own masters.[5] The horizon of most of the population was limited and usually hardly reached farther than the parish. When contact with the central or regional authorities was needed the peasant would frequently go to his patron, the landlord, or the latter's agent. More often, however, he went to the parish priest, who then contacted one of the persons mentioned.

Although machinelike phenomena existed in those days, they were small and relatively unimportant compared with those of to-day.[6] Indeed, machine politics could not develop beyond a certain point because of the specific political setting. Scott mentions three minimal requirements of a political context for machine politics to develop. They are: the selection of political leaders through elections, mass (usually universal) adult suffrage, and a

184

relatively high degree of electoral competition over time.[7] These requirements were not then present in Ireland. Only a limited number of persons
were allowed to vote. Moreover, only a few, such as priests, proprietors of
farms and land-agents had bargaining power. The majority of the voters
however were locked, so to speak, to a single patron who was thus not compelled to compete much for voters. The political ties were largely determined by traditional patterns of deference to the established powerholders,
the landlords. The leader of the machine, the landlord, competed with colleagues only for a small number of "free" voters. As a patron he himself
commanded prizes because he owned the land. Again, he was not dependent upon a large category of prize producers (bureaucrats) since policy
making and administration were to a great extent in his hands. In short, the
leaders then were more patrons than brokers.

The above mentioned requirements for the development of machine-style
politics were not present before the end of the previous century. The agrarian revolution which came to an end at the turn of the century, resulted in
the creation of a population of peasant-proprietors. The already weakened
class of landlords disappeared almost completely from the scene during the
political revolution which ended in 1923. A number were eliminated, and
many left the country and went to Northern Ireland or England. Thus, early
this century, a "free" population was created which obtained the right to
vote for leaders of their own choice.

In addition to the three minimal requirements described by Scott, another factor, typical for Ireland, must be mentioned. Indeed, this factor constitutes the specific framework for the Irish form of political machines. It is
the electoral system. Chapter two gave a detailed description of the mechanics of the system. Therefore, it will suffice here to repeat that this system,
combined with the political climate, form an ideal soil for the emergence of
competing political machines *within* parties.

The socio-cultural context fostering machine-style politics and the characteristics of the political setting have been described. In the pages that
follow we examine a period of some 60 years. For this period I attempt to
analyse the factors and processes determining the specific structure of machines and the increasing intensity of machine politics in Ireland.

The Revolutionary Political Elite

During the war of independence (1916-22), the last representatives of the
landed aristocracy disappeared from the Irish scene and were replaced by
a new elite. Almost all the new leaders were born and bred in the country
and of middle and lower middle class background.[8] Most of them were
"true gaels"; they participated actively in the war against England, the civil
war, and in other nationalistic organizations such as the Gaelic League and
the GAA. They are popularly referred to as the freedom fighters.

This change of political elite had two closely connected implications for

185

the development of machine politics. Firstly, it increased the approachability of the leaders for the voters. In a country where the personal approach is quite natural, and where government is viewed as a main source of help for jobs and other favours, it makes a great difference whether basically alien leaders or ordinary rural men are at the top. The new leaders, who were also bearers of the same particularistic culture as the ordinary population and who had suffered from the same injuries, were more easily approached than the previous political elite. This difference in approachability was illustrated to me by a very old man in Patricksville. He said: "In my young days, when the father of lord Welby was on the council, you took a couple of drinks before you went up the lane of the mansion. When I was out of work, I went to that man and I asked him for a job on the road. I was given the message that he had nothing. And when I complained about my problems, himself came to the door. He started pontificating that we were a lazy crowd. He would set the dogs on me if I did not go ... Later, when Sean Pearse became our local TD, the situation changed. He told us that we could come to his home with all our problems. He could fix them all. But, mind you, *he* was one of our own. And he knew goddamn well what an ordinary Irishman looked for and where the loot was to be found".

The change of the elite had also important consequences for the power balance between leaders and voters. Prior to this change, the voters had almost no bargaining power *vis-à-vis* their leaders. They were "locked-in electors", that is, they were not free to give their votes to whom they wanted. Usually they acted according to the wishes of those who controlled their means of subsistence, the landlord-politicians. Under their new leaders, the revolutionary elite, however, they improved their bargaining position because these persons were "men of their own station" who did not control their means of subsistence.

Thus, with the change of the political elite the road for approaching the leaders was cleared, and the bargaining power of the voters increased.

Although the freedom fighters took possession of the seats in both the central government and the county councils, and acted as described above, considerable differences are to be found between the machines of TDs and MCCs. Apart from differences in size (a TD's machine was larger), they differed structurally and in the intensity of the transactional content. The men with the best national records, the "brass" of the fighters, entered the Dail, whereas the "gunmen" in the lower echelons obtained seats in the county councils. The leaders of the first category were almost automatically elected, and for some time re-elected, on their national record. As providers of prizes, however, they were in a less favourable position because relatively few problems of the voters were dealt with by the central bureaucracy. Moreover, they acted almost exclusively as brokers since they did not command the prizes asked for. In short, their machines consisted of two clearly differentiated elements, a prize producing segment which was rather small, and a prize consuming one. Both segments were connected by the TD, who

186

acted as broker. The MCCs, on the other had, were not only forced to render favours in order to obtain votes because of their less destinguished records, they were also more often consulted by voters because the majority of the problems were county council matters. They were also in a better position to obtain prizes as policy making and administration were to a great extent in the same hands. In sum, the MCC's machine was rather small, it had a strong transactional element, and in addition to a brokerage role its leaders occupied a strong position as patron.

Expansion of Local Government Services; Competing Revolutionary Elite

In the early thirties, when the country settled to more tranquile and constitutional politics, the goverment's tasks increased rapidly. Especially county government expanded its services with notable speed. Local welfare services were inproved and expanded, and the war damaged infrastructure was repared. As a result of this expansion the influence of the MCCs increased. They became powerful patrons in the countryside. With this expanded power they attempted to climb the political ladder to the Dail. Many called on influential persons in the area, soliciting their help. They renewed old bonds and promises, and they showed by their calls that the recipients were men of influence whose help was needed and who might expect the best services of the candidate if elected. The TDs, on the other hand, who had entered the Dail on their national records, observed that ideology and regional hero-worship were no longer enough for a safe seat. They realized that a councillorship was a very effective means for attracting support. Consequently, they threw themselves in the "rat race", as it was described to me, of local government elections. They also approached locally influential persons for rallying supporters. The result of this competition between TDs and MCCs was threefold. Firstly, the need for supporters forced the increased number of candidates to compete with one another to create larger clienteles. Consequently, the bargaining power of many voters increased. Secondly, a pattern emerged which is typical to-day. That is, increasingly TDs began to occupy seats in the county councils, and started considering these as the basis for their power. Thirdly, local power brokers began to manifest themselves.

The Diminishing Power of the MCCs

As a result of the attacks of the TDs on their power basis, many MCCs lost their seats. Two other factors decreased the influence of the MCCs as a category. The first was the introduction of a managerial system into county government in the mid-fourties. It separated administration and policy making. Administration came into the hands of centrally appointed officials, while policy making only was reserved for the MCCs.

A second factor curbed the power of the MCCs indirectly. After the second world war, the Irish government adopted a policy of increasing bureaucratic centralization and introduced a large scale welfare policy.[9] This expanded the field for operations of the TD: new prizes became available for his clientele. Moreover, it enabled him to deal with constituents' problems more efficiently than his rivals, the MCCs, because many cases were now decided in Dublin.

In sum, as a result of the managerial system and the national government's post-war policy, the TD's influence increased, whereas that of the ordinary MCC diminished. From a powerful patron the latter became downgraded to a broker whose clientele was increasingly dependent upon a large category of prize producers. Consequently, his machine became similar in composition to that of the TD.

The Post-Revolutionary Elite

The increasing transactional content in the relationship between leaders and supporters was strengthened even further when the revolutionary elite disappeared. These national figures have almost been eliminated from the scene by the passage of time.[10] Their successors, the political elite of to-day, belong to the same socio-economic categories but they lack a national record with which to attract supporters. Therefore, they, more than their predecessors, are compelled to build up a following by rendering as many services as possible. But since the powerbase of to-day's TD, like that of the MCC, is predominantly located in the sphere of local government, the TD is in fact compelled to poach in the preserve of the MCC. To do this, and to keep his very large flock together, he creates a circle of quasi-professional intermediaries. This, however, has generated a third competitor in the arena that not only threatens the MCC's position but also the TD's. As the intermediary creates his own small machine, he is thus also a broker. He may at any time hive off from the machine of his boss, start an independent life, and try to obtain a seat in the county council. If he succeeds the TD loses part of his own machine and must look for ways to make up for the loss. He generates new brokers or takes them over from other TDs. Moreover, the ex-local broker replaces a sitting MCC who therewith loses most of his machine.

Thus, creating local brokers has generated a chain of reactions in the political field, and has increased the transactional element in the relationships. Again, the emergence of these new roles has brought about a fundamental structural difference between the machines of the TD and the MCC which is characteristic of the present-day political field.

Revisions of Electoral Districts

A final factor has to be mentioned which plays an important role in keeping machine-style politics going. This factor is the regular re-mapping of the constituencies, branded by the opposition as gerrymandering. The constitution requires the constituencies to be revised at least once every twelve years so that the ratio between the number of seats and the electorate stays roughly the same. This rule of the political game provides the governing party with a splendid opportunity for systematically revising the boundaries in accordance with its own interests. The Fianna Fail party, which was in power for all but six years from 1932 until 1973, made ample use of this opportunity.[11] Since its foundation in 1926, Fianna Fail's strongholds have been the poor western areas. These areas, however, have been steadily losing population through emigration. In contrast, the population of Dublin and its surroundings has been increasing rather rapidly. In order to keep its power, Fianna Fail has been carving up the mid and eastern areas. Although primarily intended to weaken opponents, Fianna Fail TDS have also been victims of these revisions, politicians regularly lose parts of their domains, and to make up for these losses, they must infiltrate "new" areas. The most efficient way to do this is by building up a circle of local brokers. Illustrations of these tactics were given in chapters six and seven and in part three of this book.

Thus, revisions of the constituencies foster machine politics; indeed, they keep the entire machine political field in motion.

Two interesting conclusions can be drawn from this historical overview of Irish politics, and from what was described in previous chapters. One has to do with the equilibrium model of which both Bailey and Barth – authors upon whose ideas I have leaned in this study – have not been able to free themselves, though they attempted to do so. The analytical value of this model, I will argue, is unsatisfactory because it bars our understanding social change. The second conclusion is about a widely held notion that machine politics is inversely correlated with a society's level of centralization and bureaucratization. I deal with these in this order.

II. THE EQUILIBRIUM MODEL AND THE STUDY OF SOCIAL CHANGE

The equilibrium model presents society as a system which is in a relatively stable situation. Conflict is regarded as something that can either be resolved within the existing system and thus does not change it, or if this is impossible, moves society towards a new social equilibrium. Again, conflict is frequently seen as something coming from outside the social system. This view does not preclude the notion of processes that are at work in society, nor does it deny social change. However change is frequently seen as something abnormal, which disturbs the normal situation abruptly and drastically. And processes are often viewed mainly as repetitive or circular.

This model, like any model, is of course an abstraction of reality. It is an "as if situation" as Gluckman, one of its main protagonists, has observed.[12] Consequently, it cannot be said to be right or wrong; what can be questioned however is its analytical value. And the point I want to raise

189

here is that this model abstracts too much from reality with the result that it cannot adequately explain the processual nature of reality.

A basic characteristic of reality is that social phenomena are constantly in motion; they shift and change and are thus processes. Domestic families, for example, are constantly changing in personnel: parents die and children mature; and clashes change the relation between partners. Although the adherents of the equilibrium model (especially the "structuralists" among them) acknowledge these changes, they abstract from them, consider them as elements of circular or repetitive processes, and argue that the basic pattern of the family remains the same. And exactly this prevents them from obtaining more insight in actual situations and from understanding and explaining how and why social forms are now as they are.

The disadvantages of the equilibrium approach become clear in a comparison with my (non-equilibrium) approach of machine-style politics. If I had argued in this chapter like the adherent of the equilibrium model, I would have concluded that political machines developed early this century and that since then the situation has been characterized by a continuous rise and fall of machines. However, by placing the phenomenon against the background of historical time, more could be given than a rather crude picture of a repetitive process of the rise and fall of machines. I was able to discover and explain significant changes in the role of the machine leaders, in the power balance between TDs and MCCs, the size and composition of the machines, and in the nature of the relations between leaders and supporters.

These changes are not "radical" in the "equilibrist's" sense, yet they are significant. Moreover, they are non-circular and lead in a certain direction. Indeed, this is how most change occurs. And only be care fully studying these small (historical) changes, step by step, we can obtain an adequate understanding of the origin, development and disappearance of social forms.[13] Indeed, how else but by these small, almost unnoticed, changes do revolutions originate, and how else could they be explained adequately but in terms of these small *accumulating* changes? In their attempts to be accepted as "scientists", anthropologists have leaned too heavily upon the natural sciences which deal with a subject matter that is quite different from human societies. The equilibrium model is one of the miscarriages of this emulation of the "hard" sciences.[14]

Barth also emphasizes the necessity of dealing with change not as a counterpart of stasis or a stable equilibrium, but as an integral characteristic of social phenomena. Rather than describing two points in time and then relying on extrapolation between these two states to indicate change, Barth observes that we must analyse the events of change themselves. To that end we must look upon social forms "as the epiphenomenon of a number of processes", and concentrate our analysis "on showing how the form is generated".[15] "The determinants of the form", writes Barth, "must be of a variety of kinds. On the one hand, what persons wish to achieve, the multifarious ends they are pursuing, will channel their behaviour. On the other hand, technical and ecologic restrictions doom some kinds of behavior to failure and reward others, while the presence of other actors imposes strategic constraints and opportunities that modify the allocations people make and will benefit from making".[16]

Barth's ideas are stimulating, and I have used them in this study. However, he over-emphasizes the role of the individual as a generator of social forms, and he does not give due attention to the larger long-term processes that take place in society. According to Barth change is the outcome of individual actions that are moulded by those of others, together with technical and ecological factors. It must be emphasized, however, that historical processes, which are largely beyond the control of the individual actors, equally contribute to the generation and change of social forms. Indeed, only the combination of these two can give an adequate picture of the on-going processes in society. The necessity of dealing with these processes for understanding the generation and change of social forms has been clearly illustrated in this study. Only by giving them proper weight I was able to describe the changes in the size and composition of the machine, of the role of the leader, and the structural change in the power balance between TDs and MCCs. These changes, as explained, are the outcome of larger society-wide processes of bureaucratization and centralization. The results of Barth's neglect of larger historical processes are clearly illustrated in his essay on politics of the Swat Pathans.[17] In this study the author does not give due attention, for example, to the influence of colonizing Britain on the widening of economic inequality which reinforced the political power of the rich. Consequently, Barth portrays Swat politics as an equilibrium system of homologous competing political blocs which is maintained through a cyclical aggregation and dispersal of landed property and power. In terms of processes and change, therefore only repetition and circulation are presented which have no beginning and no end, but are just there.[18]

More can be said about the equilibrium model and its incapability of adequately dealing with change. One of the main obstacles to a better understanding of change is the widely held notion of protagonists of this model that conflict is abnormal and comes from outside the system. This is probably the result of the equally deeply rooted idea that conflict in a particular political structure takes place between approximately evenly matched groups according to a set of accepted rules assuring that competition stays within reasonable limits. Since these lines of thought are clearly found in Bailey's analytical framework, much of which has been used in this study, they deserve some more attention.[19] Bailey looks upon politics in terms of games, rules and prizes. His central question is: Why does order exist in situations which are characterized by competition? Rather than referring to power as a regulator of social relations, Bailey seems to observe: Because there is consensus about the rules that regulate the political game. Changes in the game, according to Bailey, are the result of the changing environment. The political structure adapts itself to this changing environment via new pragmatic rules which gradually assume a normative character. Where this adaptation fails Bailey speaks of a "total breakdown". In that case the game turns into fight; a rather vague notion which is nowhere in his book sufficiently clarified.

Several objections can be raised against these views. To begin with, Bailey's argument is almost tautological. The existence of order, orderly competition, is 'explained" in terms of norms for this behavior.[20] Secondly this basic view prevents Bailey from observing that internal inconsistencies occur in all systems, and that change is therefore also generated by these (internal) inconsistencies. Examples of such inconsistencies and their consequences for changes have been amply described in this study. The TD's official task, looking after the population's interests in the Dail, and the fact that support has to be attracted mainly by rendering services which belong to the sphere of local government, constitute a case in point. This inconsistency is one of the main causes of the generation of local brokers who contribute a great deal to the continuous changes in the power balance between TDS.

Closely associated with the previous point is my criticism on Bailey's basic assumption that political groupings are almost always in balanced opposition. That is, that groups are more or less equally matched and accept the rules of the game. On the basis of my descriptions in previous chapters I conclude that this is a false assumption which bars our understanding of real competitive processes. Machine political groupings in Patricksville, for example, appeared to disagree frequently over the rules of the game, and they differed considerably from each other in terms of resources and in organizational structure and strategy. Indeed, their position changed considerably during the period that has been investigated. Thus a process of everchanging power balances came to the forefront.

To conclude, Bailey's analytical framework contains valuable elements for a systematic analysis of the interrelationship between political and parapolitical structures. However, his emphasis that rules are the ultimate source of order, indeed, the very emphasis on order, causes him on many occasions to fall into the trap of the functionalist' equilibrium model. This model, as argued, bars our understanding reality because it abstracts too much from reality. It reduces on-going historical processes to static phenomena, or at best to repetive processes. Consequently, it cannot explain the origin, development and disappearance of social forms. In order to deal with society as an on-going process, which it actually is, two closely connected notions must gain in importance in our discipline and be worked out theoretically. One is that social forms are the product of *both* individual actions *and* of long-term, nation-wide processes which enfold largely outside the sphere of influence of the individual actor. The second is that these two, generally conceptualized in static terms of individual and environment or society, should not be treated separately, as polar concepts. Elias has

192

strongly criticized this theoretical dichotomization of individual and environment. He observes that "there is some need for a terminology that indicates more clearly the specific character of the relationship between the two aspects of men to which we refer as society and individual, between the configurations formed by human beings with each other and the human beings in these configurations seen singly. The uniqueness of this relationship demands unique theoretical models and concepts".[21]

III. MACHINE POLITICS, CENTRALIZATION AND BUREAUCRATIZATION

We have seen how machine-style politics developed, and how and why machines changed in structure. Bureaucratization and centralization have downgraded machine leaders to brokers, and have resulted in a rapid expansion of the prize producing segment of their machines.

We can draw another interesting conclusion from this process. Political scientists usually consider the machine as an informal integration or communication mechanism characteristic of developing countries during turbulent times. Anthropologists have dealt with similar phenomena under the label of brokerage. Both types of scholar regard what may generally be called clientelist politics as a function of a society's stage of development.[22] When dealing with this topic they refer particularly to the government's policy of centralization by means of a rapidly expanding bureaucratic apparatus. Roughly they argue as follows: When the centre plants out its bureaucratic units throughout the country, it thereby creates the channels for the population to communicate directly with it. In that case, they argue, political machines (brokerage) becomes superfluous and will disappear, or at best continue to play only a minor role.[23] From my description it is clear that this argument does not hold for Ireland. In that country an increasing centralization and bureaucratization has not led to a decrease in machine politics; indeed, the phenomenon has been increasing. By means of the centre's general development policy ever more fields are created in which brokers can operate.

But it may be objected that I neglect another important factor, namely the development of horizontal, functional ties of class or occupation. Is it not correct, as is sometimes argued, that the development of these horizontal ties diminishes the importance of the vertical ties in political machines?[24] This is not true; horizontal and vertical bonds are not mutually exclusive. Machine political patterns of behavior frequently exist in the relationship between union leaders and followers. They are, so to say, part of the machine political system. Ireland has several large farmers' organizations and trade unions, which are also found in other countries, such as the USA, Brazil and Chile, where machine-style politics are important.[25]

Thus, we may conclude that there is no direct connection between increasing centralization and bureaucratization on the one hand, and a decreasing importance of machine politics on the other. At best we can say that increasing centralization and bureaucratization reduce the power of the machine leader and make machine politics more disguised and thus more difficult to detect. This is clearly so in Ireland, as we have seen before, but it also holds for the USA.[26]

Why then is there no direct connection between centralization, bureaucratization and the fortunes of machine-style politics? We can answer this question if we realize that centralization and bureaucratization are elements of a larger process of increasing communication between a centre and other parts of the society. It is a two-way process, between at leas two parties, and with two communication paths. The centre of any developing country attempts to infiltrate into the lives of the population *directly*, by means of its expanding bureaucratic apparatus. Ideally the other side of the process is that the population makes *more direct* use of the communication channels created by the centre. These two aspects of the process must be distinguished and dealt with separately, for they need not go hand in hand. The centre may well increase its direct influence on the rest of the country through an ever-widening formal system of bureaucratic organization. At the same time, however, the population may continue to communicate with that centre through informal, face-to-face contacts of machines and their broker-leaders. Put differently, increasing communication from the top needs not correspond with similar initiatives from the bottom. Factors, specific for each country, may be at work which encourage resistance from the bottom to straight communication with the top and help to maintain machine politics. For Ireland this is the strong particularism and parochialism of politicians, bureaucrats and voters. These cultural traits are kept alive because Ireland is basically still a pre-industrial society of small farmers. As Chubb observes: "Country people are strongly locally oriented and they set great store by face-to-face contact. . . . (These) smallholders and their families are conservative, unimaginative, shrewd in the short run, and individualistic".[27] Indeed, the mechanics and implications of the electoral system support these attitudes. Thus, there is an interplay between the working of the electoral system and the population's particularistic world view; the two reinforce each other. The population expects the politicians to act as brokers, and the electoral system reinforces these expectations, because it compells the latter to play this role.

IV. THE FUTURE

Some remarks can be made about future developments of Irish machine politics, though I am treading here slippery ground. To begin with, it is likely that machine politics at the TD level will increase in importance compared with that at the MCC level. If the central government continues its present policy of centralization, the MCCs will be faced with a shrinking bag of prizes. In that case the voters will look ever more for support that can only be given by the TDs. Also, to-day's local brokers may then become al-

194

most superfluous, for their role can be taken over by MCCs. However, there are limits to this development because it is highly impractical, and organizatorically almost impossible, to have Dublin arrange and administer everything concerning local government. A certain number of activities must be carried out by local government: repairing roads, drainage and sewerage systems, to mention but a few.

More general remarks can be made about the future. What, for example, will happen when Ireland urbanizes rapidly; will machine politics then disappear? Huntington has analyzed the impact of this process on clientelist politics in developing countries.[28] According to him political modernization involves several alternative cycles of change in rural-urban power and stability. After a period of mobilization of a peasant base of support, which he calls the "green uprising", eventually, in the course of overall modernization, the growth of the cities becomes a destabilizing phenomenon. Huntington goes on: "If revolution is avoided, in due course, the urban middle class changes significantly; it becomes more conservative as it becomes larger. The urban working class also begins to participate in politics but it is usually either too weak to challenge the middle class or too conservative to want to do so. Thus, as urbanization proceeds, the city comes to play a more effective role in the politics of the country, and the city itself becomes more conservative. The political system and the government come to depend more upon the support of the city than upon that of the countryside. Indeed, it now becomes the turn of the countryside to react against the prospect of domination by the city".[29] Thus, the general pattern, as demonstrated by Huntington, seems a spiral: a rise and fall of rural-based machine politics. Where the political culture is a carrier of machine political patterns of behavior – and this will be so in Ireland for as long as the electoral system is maintained – the disintegration of rutal based machine politics does not mark the end of the generic pattern. Indeed, urban based machine politics may proliferate. They will be more subtle and disguised, but they will function in basically the same way.

Although Huntington's model does not hold in every detail for Ireland this country has never had an urban based power system – it might shed some light on Ireland's future developments. The Irish Republic has not yet reached the second stage of Huntington's development model, but certain trends suggest that the country is on its way to that stage. The population of the eastern part of Ireland grows rapidly whereas that of west and central Ireland is declining. The conurbation of Dublin and Cork, and the Shannon area are expanding rapidly, and their newly established industries are attracting ever more countrymen. The result of this urbanization might more strongly be felt in the political sphere if the government had not taken steps to slow down this "destabilizing" tendency. As has been observed, the government systematically favours political representation of the countryside by means of revisions of the constituencies. It attempts also to slow down emigration from the west through a number of rural development programs. Despite these measures, however, urbanization proceeds. Therefore, it is quite possible that machine politics will become more important in urban areas as they become populated by people with a rural background. This might result again in increasing rural unrest and dissension with the government's policy and budgetary priorities for the urban areas. The first signs of this tendency may already be found in the increasing activities of the rural based IRA. Together with small farmers' organizations this underground army attempts to draw the attention of the "Dublin brass" to problems of the rural parts of Ireland. The process described by Huntington is, however, still far from nearing its end. The countryside is still dominant, and rural machine-style politics prevail and flourish.

V. MACHINE POLITICS AND THE TROUBLES IN NORTHERN IRELAND

The republican issue, the amalgamation of Northern and Southern Ireland into a republic, is very much alive again. What are its consequences for machine politics in the Irish Republic? Some tentative remarks can be made. To begin with, it is likely that the old enmities between pro and anti-Treaty adherents, roughly running parallel to Fine Gael and Fianna Fail, will flare up again. Indeed, I have received information about clashes between Fianna Fail die-hards and Fine Gael members in the area where I conducted field work. They are the result of Fine Gael adherents informing the police of Fianna Fail members being involved in drilling activities of the IRA. And in Patricksville troubles may also flare up again when some five men, who have joined the IRA in the North, come back to their town. Thus far, however, no open conflicts have broken out. The revitalization of the traditional hostilities will provide the politicians with new ideological means to keep their voters tied to them. More generally, the existing party loyalties may gain in importance.

On the other hand however – and this is a second point to be made – it must be remembered that some 50 years have passed since the present cleavage between Fianna Fail and Fine Gael developed. Since that time, and particularly because Fianna Fail was in power up to February 1973, a cleavage inside the Fianna Fail party itself has developed. Many of those who have been able to improve their positions under Fianna Fail's administration are no longer interested in republicanism; they want peace and good relations with England. This category of Fianna Fail supporters is now confronted by a hard core of republicanists in Dublin and elsewhere: ex-ministers and other leading politicians. This cleavage inside the party manifested itself clearly in 1970, with the gun-running affair which headed many newspapers on the Continent, and in which allegedly some ministers were involved. The result was that the prime ministers purged his Cabinet from this ultra-republicanist element. These sacked politicians and their TD-friends are of course dangerous for Fianna Fail's position. Indeed, some were involved in establishing a new republican party (1972) which might well expand under the present circumstances and which may damage Fianna Fail's position. During the general elections in February 1973, both the establishment of *Aontacht Eireann*, as the new republican party is called, and the purging of some leading politicians have had fatal consequences for Fianna Fail. It lost its power position because it was incapable of obtaining an absolute majority in the Dail. A coalition of Fine Gael and Labour was established. Thus, on the one hand, the present troubles in Northern Ireland may consolidate party loyalties. On the other hand they are a source of strains which may lead to increasing factionalism between machine leaders and their supporters.

Finally, the escalating violence in the North may bring back to the Republic the violent politics of the twenties' and thirties'. But now it may assume more organized forms. Machines have been tested and perfected since that time, and they are very suitable for manipulating violence. Indeed, if a merger between Northern Ireland and the Republic becomes a fact, it is likely to cause war in which political machines will be the organizational corner stone for violent actions.

Notes

NOTES TO INTRODUCTION

1 The term village-outward study is from Mayer (1962).
2 This is Easton's view as reproduced in Bailey (1968 : 281).
3 Bailey, 1969.
4 Although the book was not yet published when I prepared my field work, I was fortunate to be able to study the manuscript.
5 In a highly interesting volume, Bailey (1971) has recently dealt with this theme.

PART ONE

NOTES TO CHAPTER ONE

1 Senior, 1968 : 59.
2 Pomfret, 1930 : 141.
3 C.f. Curtis, 1961 : 400.
4 The Parliamentary Act of 1911 practically ended the veto of the House of Lords. Through this Act a Bill should automatically become law within two years.
5 Quoted in Coogan, 1966 : 12.
6 Appendix I gives the proclamation in detail.
7 Curtis, 1961 : 409.
8 This stemmed from the settlement of the land question by the Land Acts of 1891 to 1909. The state bought out the landowners by means of government loans, and distributed their former property among the Irish peasantry. The government stock, given the landowners in exchange for the land, bore three per cent interest. The rent, paid by the new Irish owners, was called "land annuity"; the government collected it as a defrayal of the interest charge. In the Treaty England proposed that the Free State should collect the land annuities and send them to Britain.
9 Desmond Williams, 1967 : 26.
* In this book by Ireland I mean the 26 counties, the present Irish Republic.
10 Unless stated otherwise, statistics are derived from *The Statistical Abstracts, 1965*. Today Ireland has the lowest population density in Europe: 130 to the square mile.
11 For the population structure see e.g. Breathnach (1965 : 19) who observes that as a consequence of the many old people the dependency rate is high: in 1961, for every 100 persons of working age there were 78 of dependent age.
Between 1926 and 1966, more than one million people emigrated.
12 Freeman, 1960 : 127.
13 Home assistance is given by the local authorities; the dole is the popular word for the unemployment assistance provided by the state.
14 C.f. Coogan, 1966 : 151.

15 Although slightly outdated and certainly not in all respects typical for the whole of Ireland, Arensberg (1959), and Arensberg & Kimball (1968), who did field work some forty years ago, give an interesting picture of the town-country relationship of which many elements are still to be found.

16 Generally the following division in categories is used: small farms 1-30 acres; medium-sized farms 30-100 acres; large farms over 100 acres. About 60 per cent of all farms is in the small-farm bracket.

17 For details see Scully, 1965.

18 C.f. Scully, 1965; Walsh, 1968; Breathnach 1965 to mention but a few. Also Arensberg & Kimball (1968) mentioned these factors as outstanding.

19 More girls than boys leave the countryside. Many of them prefer a job in the towns as a nurse, housekeeper, or servant in a hotel or shop to a dull life in the countryside. Therefore, in the rural areas there are 600 girls between 20 and 24 to every 1,000 men.

20 *The Irish Catholic Directory*, 1969.

21 *The Irish Catholic Directory*, 1969. For comparative data on other countries, see Blanchard (1963).

22 Blanchard (1963 : 53) observes that the Church has few landed properties which also provide revenues. The main portion of Church property is in species and in transferable stock: state loans, for example. Convents formerly invested in railways, but their economic decline dealt a severe blow to the monastic resources. The same author, however, observes that there is an increasing tendency to transfer rural estates and properties to the teaching orders, since the hereditary owners are no longer able to keep the large country houses and properties.

23 Blanchard, 1963 : 48-58.

24 *Constitution of Ireland*, Article 44; 1, 2.

25 Blanchard, 1963 : 68.

26 Whyte (1960, passim) observes that the priests often acted as vote brokers. They took their place in the political arena because there were few Irish leaders by birth or with a university training; priests were a uniting link between the voters and the candidates.

27 Blanchard, 1963 : 81.

28 Some years ago, the Language Freedom Movement was founded to put an end to the compulsory and discriminating government policy relative to the language. The allegation that Fine Gael is behind it, is based on the fact that a number of the top leaders are Fine Gael members or supporters.

29 For some curious reasons the 1961 Census returns on the subject were never published.

30 C.f. Coogan, 1966 : 277; c.f. also Bowyer Bell, 1970.

31 Quoted from a regional newspaper, dated August 28, 1968.

NOTES TO CHAPTER TWO

1 TD is an abbreviation of the Irish *Teachta Dala*, Member of Parliament; term of address is Deputy, term of reference TD.

2 Coogan, 1966 : 140.

3 When the term parish is used in Ireland, it invariably means the ecclesiastical (Catholic) parish.

4 Chubb, 1964 : 261.

5 For more details on the central-local relationship see Collins, 1963; Meghen, 1965; Garvin, 1963.

6 The rates are a form of local tax, calculated on the value of a property. Each year every county calculates, on the basis of its financial needs, the "rate in the pound". For example, premises with a rate-valuation of £ 2 would pay £ 6 a year in rates if

the local authority rate was sixty shillings in the pound. Of late the county administrative system has increasingly been criticized as outdated. The major points were the unequal division of financial burdens on the various counties. A county with a small population would either have to pay too much per head for public amenities or have but second rate facilities. The latter, in fact, is generally the case. The serond point is that the rate system operates as a disincentive to improvement of property (c.f. e.g. Robins, 1961).

7 Chubb (1964 : 213) and others have explained this in terms of the involvement of the electorate in the Treaty-issue. Moreover, three other important arguments are frequently mentioned. Firstly, Catholicism in Ireland is very conservative and looks upon socialism as something ugly and dangerous. Secondly, the farming community, conservative in outlook like most farmers, is afraid of the socialist ideas. Thirdly, Ireland is industrially underdeveloped. Consequently, there is no large working class, which is the basis of socialist parties in industrialized countries.

8 Chubb, 1969 : 453.

9 Results published in *Nusight*, October 1969, December 1969, April 1970.

10 Chubb (1969 : 457) estimates the figures of paid up members for Fianna Fail between 40,000 and 50,000; for Fine Gail between 12,000 and 15,000; for Labour about 5,000, but he observes that accurate figures are not available.

11 Duverger, 1967; Hogan, 1945; Lakeman, 1970; Mackenzie, 1967; O'Leary, 1961; McCracken, 1958, to mention but a few.

12 As far as I know Boissevain's study on rural Malta (1965) is an exception. Although this author is mainly concerned with other aspects of the political field, in a few pages he deals with the implications of the Maltese election system. For Ireland articles of Chubb (1963) and Whyte (1966) are only impressionistic.

13 A detailed illustration of the system is given in Appendix II.

14 This is the Droop quota. It is: one vote more than the number obtained by dividing the total number of valid votes by one more than the number of seats to be filled.

15 Lakeman, 1970 : 104.

16 Most of these points are mentioned by Lakeman (1970).

17 Lakeman, 1970 : 161.

18 Duverger, 1967 : 245.

19 Duverger (1967 : 245), Mackenzie (1958 : 72-3), and Lakeman (1970 : 161) make observations of this sort.

20 Both Boissevain (1965 : 132) for Malta and Chubb (1969 : 452) for Ireland mention this tendency. For detailed arguments see Lakeman (1970 : 161-3).

21 C.f. e.g. Whyte, 1966 : 19; Chubb, 1963, passim, and 1959 : 203.

22 Boissevain, 1965 : 131.

23 This happened on a large scale in one constituency during the 1969 Dail elections. The candidate in case won with a landslide, he headed the poll, but with the result that the second candidate of the party was eliminated. The successful candidate expected to obtain a post as a junior minister, and bought a new suit in anticipation. Unfortunately, however, the prime minister punished him by not giving him the "prize".

24 Chubb, 1963 : 285 (italics mine, B.).

25 This is underlined by the deliberate policy of party headquarters in advising selective use of items from the party programme. *Coras Bua*, Fianna Fail's election handbook, observes in this connection: "Constituency publicity should be directed solely to matters of local concern ... The address should emphasize the main points of Fianna Fail policy as it affects the constituency ..." (p. 16).
In Appendix III a personal letter from a candidate to each voter in his constituency is given to illustrate this parochialism.

26 Chubb (1959 : 212) also notices this paradox which he refers to as a "confusing interplay of these two basic features in Irish politics". The party loyalty during Dail elections is clearly illustrated by Chubb (1971 : 157). This author observes:

200

"Throughout the history of the state never fewer than six and usually seven or eight out of ten of all electors have supported one or the other of the two major parties and another one has supported the Labour Party. Moreover, analyses of the results of the elections of 1957, 1961, and 1965 show that almost all electors who gave their first preferences to major party candidates gave their second preferences to other candidates of the same party. For Fianna Fail it was 88.0 per cent in 1957, 83.3 per cent in 1961, and 88.2 per cent in 1965; and for Fine Gael it was 82.0 per cent in 1957, 80.6 per cent in 1961, and 85.5 per cent in 1965".

For local government elections I found out from one county that for a period of about 15 years circa 55-70 per cent of the transfers were given to fellow party candidates only.

27 Of course, this does not mean that politicians will not try to attract support from other parties.

PART TWO

NOTES TO CHAPTER THREE

1 An assistant county manager gave me a striking example of this lack of interest on the side of the MCCs in the council's financial policy. About six years ago, some £ 12,000 was not spent from the budget by the end of the year. Since then, each year the manager uses some money from this amount for irregular expenses without however giving an account of the purposes. This means that every year the financial statement shows a surplus of something less than the original £ 12,000, but no MCC has ever asked for information on this curious decrease.

2 Quoted from Chubb (1964 : 172).

3 C.f. Whyte, 1966 : 14. During the 1969 general elections I traced five cases in which one of the main causes of defeat was neglecting this work.

4 When I interviewed and questioned politicians about this point, I found that questions relative to the local government administration represented between 60 per cent and 85 per cent of the total cases they handled.

5 Through interviews and a general questionnaire I found that the numbers of questions range from 50 to well over 200 weekly.

6 The Department of Lands deals with the distribution of land; part of its activities consists of redistributing land that the state buys from English and Irish absentee landlords. Gaeltacht is the name for the Irish speaking areas, mainly on the western sea board, which are problem areas because they lack natural resources and their holdings are very fragmented. A special department deals with Gaeltacht problems.

7 *Dail Debates*, 10 July 1962, col. 1843.

8 Jobs ranked third in the answers to my questionnaire, after social welfare help and unemployment relief.

9 The Irish *Taca* menas support; it is the name of Fianna Fail's election fund. Until recently, everybody who paid £ 50 or more per year could become a Taca member which, it is alleged, gives him certain facilities. In 1969 the membership fee was reduced to £ 5.

10 *Nusight,* November 1969 : 6.

11 Mayer, 1967; Boissevain, 1969.

12 Chubb, 1964; Whyte, 1966.

13 Boissevain, 1966; 1965; Kenny, 1960.

14 Blok, 1969; Bailey, 1969 : 167-76; Weingrod, 1968; Silverman, 1965, to mention but a few.

15 Silverman, 1965.

16 Whyte (1966) comes to this conclusion on the basis of information gathered through questionnaires.

17 C.f. e.g. McCracken, 1958, Ch. VII, and Whyte, 1966. Both authors attempt to answer part of this question but they do not do it satisfactory. Whyte, for example, describes various "routes of entry to the Dail". He concludes that "local connections are overwhelmingly important in Irish politics" (p. 32), but he does not explain *why* this is so.

18 Cohan, 1970; McCracken, 1958; Whyte, 1966.

19 C.f. Chubb (1971 : 288) who gathered statistical data about all Irish county councils between 1960 and 1967.

20 This leads Whyte (1966 : 38) to observe that "Ireland must be a fairly homogeneous society if its three main parties have developed so many characteristics in common while approaching to their respective electorates".

21 Arensberg, 1959 : 71-146 (passim); Arensberg & Kimball, 1968 (passim).

22 C.f. e.g. Malta and Sicily (Boissevain, 1965, and 1966); Greece (Campbell, 1967); and the same holds for present-day Northern Ireland.

23 C.f. Whyte, 1958; Thornley, 1964; Cruise O'Brien, 1957.

24 By personal network Boissevain means an egocentric interaction system which is in principle unbounded.

25 Boissevain, 1973 : Ch. 2.

26 C.f. Whyte, 1960.

27 "Grapevine" has various connotations in Ireland: gossip which spreads around and increases in content, but also network of personal contacts.

28 Bax, 1970.

29 For the last 15 years I traced 34 MCCs in one county only who had been local brokers; for the 18th Dail I traced 52 out of a total of 88. In both cases there might have been more.

30 C.f. McCracken, 1958: Ch. VII; Cohan, 1970: Ch. VII and VIII.

31 Almost 60 per cent of all Irish ministers from 1922 have been professional men.

NOTES TO CHAPTER FOUR

* The argument presented in this chapter and the next one owes a great deal to Bailey's penetrating theoretical analysis of leaders and teams as set out in chapters 3 and 5 of his *Stratagems and Spoils*.

1 Bailey, 1963 : Ch.6.

2 Bryce (1914, Ch.LX-LXII), for example confines machine to party organization – the array of committees and conventions at all levels of government concerned with party business. Key, Jr. (1952 : 337) describes machine as " . . . the inner core of the party". See also Sait (1933 : 659), and Merton (1963 : 70-76).

3 E.g. Scott, 1970 : 551; Wilson, 1961 : 370.

4 Banfield & Wilson, 1966 : Ch.9.

5 Scott, 1972 : Ch.6-9.

6 Bailey (1963 : 152), for example, observes: "The machine consists, in fact, of a network of key individuals . . .". C.f. also Sait (1933 : 659).

7 Term derived from Scott (1972).

8 The only exception that I know of is the *Cosa Nostra* as described by Maas (1969), though this is not primarily a *political* machine.

9 Metaphor derived from Gottfried (1972).

10 C.f. Bailey (1963 : Ch.6) who speaks of electoral machines. See also Mayer (1966).

11 Chubb (1959 : 202) observes the same when quoting a politician whom he asked for the most effective methods of electioneering. This politician said: "Canvassing and public speaking are in my view the most effective methods of electioneering but the service which a candidate gives to his constituents prior to the election determines in a very large measure the vote he secures in an election".

12 C.f. e.g. Mandelbaum (1965), Gosnell (1968), and White (1933).

13 This is certainly the result of political influence; not, however, of the straight American type but of a kind which I describe shortly.

14 In two regional local government offices I was so lucky as to be able to investigate this point. Eighty per cent and about 65 per cent respectively of the personnel had asked a politician for help in getting their jobs or for (internal) promotions.

15 For the civil service the secretary of the department concerned informs the CSC.

16 From information obtained from two regional offices it appeared that the number of persons in temporary service was considerable. In one office it was about 25 per cent and in the other over 30 per cent. This is largely due to the rather poor financial situation of local government and to pressures from the central government's Department of Local Government. The county councils receive annually from this department a certain amount of money to cover their expenses. The rest must be covered by local taxations. The county council tries to keep these rates as low as possible in order not to become unpopular with the electorate. Furthermore, county government is under severe pressure from the Department of Local Government not to expand its personnel, for each extra man is a drain on its budget. And for each extra (non-temporary) place, local government needs the special approval of the central department. Consequently, local government has developed a policy of attracting persons on a temporary basis which has financial advantages. First, temporary employees can be paid less, that is, under the normal scale of wages. Second, permanent occupations carry a pension and these pensions are an extra burden on the budget. In addition, it is easier to obtain permission for filling temporary post because there is always place on the budget for these extra expenses. A final reason for the many persons in temporary service has to do with Parkinson's law. A number of people are attracted temporarily during an emergency period or for a certain task. When this is finished a demand has grown, so to speak, for the continuation of their labour. These people seem to be indispensable now. Having brought them in, the administration suddenly sees that there is sufficient work to keep them going. Now, however, it is difficult to make them permanent and thus they continue to be temporary for years.

17 Chubb (1963 : 275) observes that 70 per cent of the ordinary TDs is also a member of a local authority, and for the 19th Dail (1969) it appeared that this percentage had increased to about 78.

18 In the county where I conducted my fieldwork all TDs have a circle of helpers, and I know the same is true of other TDs in the country.

19 A hatchetman is a person, as an informant explained, who uses the hatchet to keep the paths to the grass roots open for a TD. Several informants told me that the term tout is borrowed from the bookmaker's helpers who try to sell as many tickets as possible at the horse races. It is interesting to note that the *Oxford English Dictionary* describes tout or touter as a person employed in spying out movements and condition of horses in training.

20 These are not merely theoretical dangers: in county Tallow I was able to establish that during the last 15 years more than 60 per cent of the MCCs had tried to be nominated at Dail conventions.

21 Bailey, 1963 : 151.

22 I have detailed information on 37 local brokers, but some data on another 41 persons who have once been local brokers also seem to confirm my argument.

23 Eight out of the 37 have improved their position considerably through getting better jobs.

24 Bailey (1963 : 151-4), Sait (1933 : 659), Wilson (1961 : 270-1), to mention but a few, describe the political machine as a pyramid.

NOTES TO CHAPTER FIVE

1 See for an example Appendix III.

2 In the Fianna Fail club in the town where I lived almost all members had improved their position considerably just by joining the club.

3 This case however is not an exceptional one. In my county I detected other broker's brokers with broadly the same career pattern and functions. Moreover, I traced 34 MCCs in the same county who over the last 15 years had once been local brokers.

4 Bailey, 1969 : 79; c.f. also Caplow, 1968.

NOTES TO CHAPTER SIX

* My thinking about the construction of this chapter and the next one, as well as the way of analysing my data, has been influenced by Barth (1963, 1966) and Van Velsen (1969). Especially Van Velsen emphasizes the necessity of giving a detailed account of sequences of events, or actions in an actual situation, in order to understand the process of reality.

1 There were about two-and-a-half quotas for Fianna Fail during the previous elections, which is enough for only two seats. The quota, it will be remembered, is one vote more than the number obtained by dividing the total number of valid votes by one more than the number of seats to be filled. On the basis of the numbers of votes which were cast for a particular party in a certain electoral district during previous elections, one can predict roughly how many candidates of this party will be elected.

2 The GAA promotes gaelic sports; one of them is hurling, which looks superficially like hockey.

3 Although I had many discussions with Dwane, he always circumvented my questions on this set-up. Later, the details were given to me by Dwane's legal advisor, one of my key-informants on matters concerning constituency politics.

NOTES TO CHAPTER SEVEN

1 I do not want to suggest that Dwane married this woman for political purposes. I only conclude that his marriage had important political consequences.

2 An action set is an egocentric interaction system; actors in the set are mobilized by an ego (in this case the machine leader) on various bases and for a particular purpose which is decided upon by the ego.

3 Tallyman is a popular name for a member of a politician's machine who is in charge of checking the count of a particular polling district. When the ballot papers of a district are opened, he counts the votes for his boss and also who are marked as second on the papers. This is not done for pure curiosity but in order to obtain a better insight, per district, of a politician's voting strength, for figures are not broken down to polling district level. A politician has as a rule many tallymen. Usually they are local brokers, men who know the area well.

PART THREE

NOTES TO CHAPTER EIGHT

1 I use for both the neutral term of church.

2 Muintir is an abbreviation of the Irish word *Muintir na Tire* which means literally People of the Countryside. It is a national organization for the development of rural communities.

3 Source: Central Statistics Office, Dublin.

4 Depending upon the circumstances, a man obtains (1969) unemployment assistance of 38 sh to maximally 66 sh a week.

5 Patricksville is situated in one of the richest regions of Ireland where "ranching"

(beef producing) and "dairying" (milk producing) together constitute the agricultural economy.

6 According to Irish standards, a farm under 50 acres is small.

7 Source: Central Statistics Office, Dublin.

8 "Friend" has various meanings and the context in which it is used determines the exact connotation A "friend of ours" is always a relative though a distant one. A "friend of mine" is never a relative but denotes a relationship of a transactional nature: a person with whom one curries favour for prizes. It resembles thus the way in which Americans use the word friend. Someone with whom you have an intimate, emotional relationship is usually described as "a real great friend of mine", or "a great friend of mine".

9 These authors describe in detail the kinship and credit relations between farmers and shopkeepers in County Clare (cf. Arensberg, 1959 : 146-81, and Arensberg & Kimball, 1968, passim). Their classic study, based on material from the early 1930s, has been widely accepted as the universal model for rural Irish life. This idea seems to endure with the reissue of their book which is basically unmodified.

10 The detailed description of the institution of the dowry by Arensberg (1959, chapter 3), and Arensberg & Kimball (1968, chapters 6, 7, 8) gives a picture which holds also for the rural part of Patricksville.

11 A crowd, or a *dream* in Irish, is an extended family. It embraces ego's siblings, his parents and their siblings and children, ego's own children, and his grandparents. Affines however are excluded.

12 The ban has been dissolved in 1972.

13 This situation stands in sharp contrast to the city-orientation in Mediterranean Europe (cf. e.g. Julio Caro Baroja, 1963). An important determinant for this difference is, of course, that Ireland has never had cities of any significance. Since ancient times, the Irish elite has lived either in the countryside or in the English cities.

NOTES TO CHAPTER NINE

1 There is no exact description of what constitutes a "section". This has resulted in several problems and clashes as we shall see shortly.

2 Van Hekken & Thoden van Velzen, 1972 : 58.

3 The parish had more organized recreational activities at that date. These constituted however no independent associations but branches of either Muintir or the GAA, and could therefore not be presented to the council of Muintir. Moreover, the Church's voluntary associations were not allowed by the bishop to enter the local political arena.

4 This is the conclusion of Roseingrave (1969 : 1) in his evaluation of Muintir's role in rural Ireland.

NOTES TO CHAPTER TEN

1 Details have been given in chapter six.

2 This phrase is often used to denote that it takes a long time before one can reach something.

3 This process was described in chapter six.

4 The allegations of O'Sullivan were not true. Doherty was determined to enter the ring again in the 1965 general elections.

5 This line of thought is clearly demonstrated in Bailey's analytical framework (Bailey, 1969 : passim).

6 Thoden van Velzen, n.d. : 2.

7 I derived the term flow-system from Thoden van Velzen (n.d. : 2).

1 Historical time is here set off against structural time, a concept from Evans-Pritchard (1940, chapter 3) which refers to succession of events relating to changes in the relationship of social groups.

2 Scott, 1970 (see also Scott, 1972).

3 In a way, particularism can of course be considered both as a cause and as a symptom of corruption.

4 Chubb, 1963 : 273.

5 Cf. e.g. Collins (1963) and McDowell (1964).

6 Although he does not use the term machine, Whyte (1960 and 1965) gives some descriptions from which can be concluded that machine politics existed. Cf. also Hunt (1907, passim).

7 Scott, 1970 : 551. In the same article Scott explains why machines failed to materialize in many new nations though the socio-cultural context was suitable. According to the author an outstanding factor is the lack of electoral pressures because elections had been abolished and the country was represented by one party or a military elite (p.561).

8 Information on the political elite (revolutionary and others) is based both on Cohan (1970), who conducted a detailed investigation into differences in political style and career patterns, and my own field work.

9 Chubb observes that the civil service more than doubled in personnel between 1940 and 1965.

10 In 1965, only 15 TDS out of 144 were still in this category, and after the general elections of 1969, their numbers decreased further.

11 Drafts have been made in 1923, 1935, 1947, 1959, 1961, 1968.

12 Gluckman, 1968 : 219-37.

13 If we put change in the centre of our analysis, the problems of distinguishing between changes of the system and changes with the system, as have been explored by Parsons (1951 : 481), become also less relevant.

14 It is only against this background that Gluckman's rather derogatory remarks can be understood when he describes history as "the quite different form of narrative (as against institutional analysis) . . ." (Gluckman, 1968 : 224).

15 Barth, 1967 : 663.

16 Barth, 1967 : 662-3.

17 Barth, 1959a.

18 For a penetrating criticism on Barth's market-type and a-historical analysis see Talal Asad (1972).

19 I am referring here to Bailey's *Stratagems and Spoils*, but many ideas in that book are also found in his earlier studies. Cf. e.g. Bailey, 1960 and 1963.

20 This is the more striking since Bailey himself has criticized explanations of relations and social forms in terms of norms and values. Cf. e.g. Bailey 1964, and 1965 where he refers to"the mystique of consensus".

21 Elias, 1969a : 141. Cf. also Elias, 1970.

22 The term clientelist politics has been derived from Powell (1970).

23 Cf. e.g. Silverman, 1965; Blok, 1969; Weingrod, 1967/8; Key, Jr., 1952; Mandelbaum, 1965; Scott, 1970 and 1972.

24 Cf. e.g. Wertheim, 1969; Huizer, 1965; Scott, 1970.

25 Cf. e.g. Gosnell, 1968; Mandelbaum, 1965, and Gottfried, 1962 (for the USA); Galjart, 1964 (for Brazil), and Lehmann, 1971 (for Chile).

26 An interesting illustration is given by Maas (1969, especially pp.9-20).

27 Chubb, 1971 : 51-2.

28 Huntington, 1968, particularly the first and last chapters.

29 Huntington, 1968 : 77.

The Proclamation of the Irish Republic, Easter 1916

POBLACHT NA H EIREANN

THE PROVISIONAL GOVERNMENT OF THE IRISH REPUBLIC TO THE PEOPLE OF IRELAND

IRISHMEN AND IRISHWOMEN: In the name of God and of the dead generations from which she receives her old tradition of nationhood, Ireland, through us, summons her children to her flag and strikes for her freedom.

Having organised and trained her manhood through her secret revolutionary organisation, the Irish Republican Brotherhood, and through her open military organisations, the Irish Volunteers and the Irish Citizen Army, having patiently perfected her discipline, having resolutely waited for the right moment to reveal itself, she now seizes that moment, and, supported by her exiled children in America and by gallant allies in Europe, but relying in the first on her own strength, she strikes in full confidence of victory.

We declare the right of the people of Ireland to the ownership of Ireland, and to the unfettered control of Irish destinies, to be sovereign and indefeasible. The long usurpation of that right by a foreign people and government has not extinguished the right, nor can it ever be extinguished except by the destruction of the Irish people. In every generation the Irish people have asserted their right to national freedom and sovereignty; six times during the past three hundred years they have asserted it in arms. Standing on that fundamental right and again asserting it in arms in the face of the world, we hereby proclaim the Irish Republic as a Sovereign Independent State, and we pledge our lives and the lives of our comrades-in-arms to the cause of its freedom, of its welfare, and of its exaltation among the nations.

The Irish Republic is entitled to, and hereby claims, the allegiance of every Irishman and Irishwoman. The Republic guarantees religious and civil liberty, equal rights and equal opportunities to all its citizens, and declares its resolve to pursue the happiness and prosperity of the whole nation and of all its parts, cherishing all the children of the nation equally, and oblivious of the differences carefully fostered by an alien government, which have divided a minority from the majority in the past.

Until our arms have brought the opportune moment for the establishment of a permanent National Government, representative of the whole people of Ireland and elected by the suffrages of all her men and women, the Provisional Government, hereby constituted, will administer the civil and military affairs of the Republic in trust for the people.

We place the cause of the Irish Republic under the protection of the Most High God, Whose blessing we invoke upon our arms, and we pray that no one who serves that cause will dishonour it by cowardice, inhumanity, or rapine. In this supreme hour the Irish nation must, by its valour and discipline and by the readiness of its children to sacrifice themselves for the common good, prove itself worthy of the august destiny to which it is called.

Signed on Behalf of the Provisional Government,

Thomas J. Clarke,

Sean MacDiarmada,	Thomas MacDonagh,
P. H. Pearse,	Eamonn Ceannt,
James Connolly.	Joseph Plunkett.

Proportional Representation: Method of Counting Votes
(Taken from *Córas Bua*)

Let it be assumed that it is a three member constituency and that there are six candidates. The voting papers are examined and the valid papers are arranged in separate parcels under the names of the candidates, marked with the figure 1.

1st Count
Each separate parcel is counted and each candidate is credited with one vote in respect of each paper on which a first preference has been recorded for him. The result of the count may be assumed to be as follows: –

A	4,159
B	1,957
C	3,105
D	1,754
E	754
F	1,205
	12,934
Spoiled Votes	64
Total	12,998

The number of ballot papers was 12,998 but the total valid vote was 12,934.

Fixing the Quota
The quota is arrived at by dividing the number which exceeds by one the number of seats to be filled. In this case the number of seats to be filled is *three* to which one is added. The total valid poll is divided by *four* and 3,234 (3,233 increased by one, disregarding fractions) is the quota, that is, the number of votes required to elect a candidate.
    "A" votes exceed the quota and he is declared elected.

2nd Count
"A" has a surplus of 925 and this must be transferred. All "A's" 4,159 papers are examined and arranged in separate sub-parcels according to the

209

second preferences appearing thereon. A separate sub-parcel is also arranged of those papers on which no second preference is shown and which are therefore non-transferable. The result is that "A's" second preference is shown for:

B on	255 papers
C on	2,062 papers
D on	154 papers
E on	1,676 papers
F on	Nil papers
Total transferable	4,147
Total non-transferable	12
Total of "A's" papers	4,159

Since the total number of transferable papers (4,147) exceeds the surplus (925) only a portion of each sub-parcel can be transferred. The number of papers to be transferred from each candidate's sub-parcel is arrived at by multiplying the number of papers in the sub-parcel by the surplus (925) and dividing the result by the total transferable vote (4,147).

The method is as follows: –

B's sub-parcel contains 255 papers
His share of the surplus is $\dfrac{255 \times 925}{4,147} = 57$

C's sub-parcel contains 2,062 papers
His share of surplus is $\dfrac{2,062 \times 925}{4,147} = 460$

D's sub-parcel contains 154 papers
His share of surplus is $\dfrac{154 \times 925}{4,147} = 34$

E's sub-parcel contains 1,676 papers
His share of surplus is $\dfrac{1,676 \times 925}{4,147} = 374$

Total   925

This calculation contains fractions and since only whole papers can be transferred the largest fractions are recorgnized as a unit.

Result of 2nd Count
The state of the poll at the conclusion of this transfer is as follows: –

210

```
A . . . . . . . . . . . . . . . . . 3,234 ELECTED
B . . . . . . . . . . . . . . . . 1,957 plus  57 = 2,014
C . . . . . . . . . . . . . . . . 3,105 plus 460 = 3,565
D . . . . . . . . . . . . . . . . 1,754 plus  34 = 1,788
E . . . . . . . . . . . . . . . .   754 plus 374 = 1,128
F . . . . . . . . . . . . . . . . 1,205 plus Nil = 1,205
```

"C" being 331 votes in excess of the quota is declared elected.

3rd Count

"C's" surplus of 331 has now to be transferred. For the purpose the parcel of 460 votes transferred to him from "A's" surplus is re-examined and sorted according to the third preferences indicated on each paper. The result is found to be as follows: –

```
B  plus            46
D  plus            32
E  plus           354
F  plus            14

Total transferable 446
Non-transferable    14

                   460
```

The number of papers to be transferred from each sub-parcel is ascertained by multiplying the number of papers in the sub-parcel by 331 (the surplus) and amending the result by 446 (total transfer). The highest fraction is regarded as a unit. The number of papers to be transferred is as follows: –

```
B . . . . . . . . . . . . . . . . 2,014 plus  34 = 2,048
D . . . . . . . . . . . . . . . . 1,788 plus  24 = 1,812
E . . . . . . . . . . . . . . . . 1,128 plus 263 = 1,391
F . . . . . . . . . . . . . . . . 1,205 plus  10 = 1,215
```

4th Count

As no candidate reached the quota and as one seat still remains to be filled the Returning Officer eliminates the candidate with the smallest number of papers and proceeds to distribute. "F's" parcel of 1,215 papers are all, therefore, examined. It is found to contain 1,094 papers in which "D" is the next preference, and 110 on which "B" is next preference. On 11 papers no further preference is marked. The poll now stands as follows: –

```
A . . . . . . . . . . .    3,234   Elected
B . . . . . . . . . . .    2,158
C . . . . . . . . . . .    3,234   Elected
D . . . . . . . . . . .    2,906
E . . . . . . . . . . .    1,391
Non-transferable . . . . .    11

                          12,934
```

5th Count

No further candidate having reached the quota the Returning Officer proceeds to eliminate "E" and distribute his 1,391 papers. All "E's" papers are examined. "B" is marked as next preference on 856 papers and "D" is marked as next preference on 414. No further preference is marked on the remaining 121 papers. "D's" total now exceeds the quota and he is declared elected to the last seat.

The total counting procedure is reproduced in the following table:

Result of Poll and Transfer of Votes.

Total electorate — 12,998

Number of valid votes — 12,934

Constituency ....

Seats: 3

Quota: 3,234

Names of candidates	1st count	2nd count		3rd count		4th count		5th count	
		Transfer of A's Surpl.	Result	Transfer of C's Surpl.	Result	Transfer of F's votes	Result	Transfer of E's votes	Final Result
A	4,159	–925	3,234	—	3,234	—	3,234	—	3,234 (1st El.)
B	1,957	57	2,014	34	2,048	110	2,158	856	3,014
C	3,105	460	3,565	–331	3,234	—	3,234	—	3,234 (2nd El.)
D	1,754	34	1,788	24	1,812	1,094	2,906	414	3,320 (3rd El.)
E	754	374	1,128	263	1,391	—	1,391	–1,391	
F	1,205	nil	1,205	10	1,215	–1,215	—	—	
Non-transferable papers	—	—	—	—	—	11	11	121	132
Total	12,934	—	12,934	—	12,934	—	12,934	—	12,934

212

"Personal Letter" of Sean Dwane to His Electors

To My People in North East Tallow

Four years ago you gave me, an unknown and untried candidate, your generous and wholehearted support in electing me to Dail Eireann. My only qualifications, at that time, were that I was born, and have lived all my life, in North East Tallow, and that there was a tradition of service to the Nation in my family. My father answered his country's call in the struggle for freedom, and the hardships and imprisonment which he endured in 1921 led to his early death. My uncle, Tim O'Driscoll of Kilronan, was shot dead by the Black and Tans in March of 1921. I had lived and worked all my life in North East Tallow but I had little other qualifications for public life. I am proud and grateful of the honour which my people conferred on me in electing me in 1965.

When I sought your votes at that time I was not un-acquainted with many of the problems with which our people had to contend. As Secretary of the F.C.F. farmers' association I had for years been brought into daily contact with the difficulties of those who worked on our land and in our factories; of traders and workers of different categories in our towns and villages and of the manner of life of a very big cross section of our people of varying ages and groups across the length and breadth of North East Tallow. I did not need to be convinced of the problems with which those who were trying to bring up families were faced. My own six children were sufficient to bring those problems to my notice; and my interest in the provision of expanded educational and employment opportunities was the same as that of any father or mother for whose vote I asked.

Since my election, four years ago, the priority needs of my constituents have become more and more apparent to me, improvement of housing, sewerage and water needs, employment and the developement of industry and the social services. I have had everyday contact with workers, farmers and leaders of industry, and I believe I understand their problems. I have found employment for workers from all over North East Tallow, in the areas supplying agricultural products to the Streamtown factory. I have provided work at home for men who would otherwise have to emigrate. I have provided assistance for farmers who would have had to restrict production. I have worked amongst the people, with the people, and for the people, and in all my work on your behalf I have enjoyed the fullest assistance from Local Authorities and their Officials, Local Development Associations, Parish Councils and other voluntary bodies and organisations.

To-day, at the age of forty-two years, I am again seeking the honour of representation for this constituency, in the full consciousness of its needs, and of the great work of those who have gone before us. The last Minister, in any Government, to represent this constituency was the late Sean Pearse, who knew and understood the needs of his people, and whose life's work for the people is a head-line for any candidate who aspires to represent this constituency. The area in which we live has earned a reputation for courageous and efficient development, in farming and in the industries dependent upon farming, as well as in a wide range of other industrial undertakings and in representing you in Dail Eireann I want to see this constituency make even greater strides than it is making now, and I want to follow this example of people like Sean Pearse to ensure that the area in which we live becomes more and more prosperous and to see our friends and neighbours attain a better life, irrespective of creed, class, party, occupation or way of life. In the sphere of farming I have seen this area of ours advance to the status that most other areas might well envy. The great industries based on the land continue to expand and thus provide a market for the produce of all who depend on agriculture for a living, whilst enabling workers to establish homes and rear families in their own country. The most pressing problem with officialdom at the present time is the proposed downgrading of the County Hospital and the removal of a vital amenity from the area. The centralization of hospital services may make for greater efficiency, but distant efficiency will not save the life of one child and the lives and well being of my people are my special concern. I pledge myself that so long as I represent this constituency the needs of my people will never take second place to administrative efficiency; and I will leave no stone unturned and will use every means at my disposal to ensure that Streamtown County Hospital will not alone retain its present status but will expand its present amenities to meet the needs of my people in a growing community.

The gap between government Departments and rural Ireland is wide and I have had no small part in persuading officialdom to speed up the provision of Grants and the sactioning of projects for main and secondary road improvements, roads for farmers, urban roads, telephone and postal facilities, transport amenities for town and country, and grants for workers, farmers, traders and others.

I am asking you to renew the honour which you first conferred on me in 1965, and I believe I can best serve the interests of all who may support me by standing as a Fianna Fail candidate. I believe that the progress of North East Tallow, in every sphere of activity, owes most to the policies of Fianna Fail and can continue to prosper only under a Fianna Fail Government.

I hope, if elected, to be worthy of your trust, ever conscious of your

214

problems and always watchful in your interests, to serve you faithfully and impartially; to avail of every opportunity to foster the welfare of the people of this constituency, to redress communal or individual grievances and always to be at your disposal and to be worthy of the honour and trust you place in me.

MEN AND WOMEN OF NORTH EAST TALLOW make your own and your country's future secure. VOTE FIANNA FAIL, FOR ME SEAN DWANE.

Bibliography

Adams, Richard N.
1966   Power and Power Domains. *America Latina*, 9 : 3-21.
1970   Brokers and Career Mobility Systems in the Structure of Complex Societies. *Southwestern Journal of Anthropology*, 26 : 315-27.
Anderson, Robert T.
1971   *Traditional Europe. A Study in Anthropology and History*. Belmont, California: Wadsworth Publishing Company.
Arensberg, Conrad M.
1959   *The Irish countryman. An Anthropological Study*. Gloucester, Mass.: Peter Smith. First published in 1937.
Arensberg, Conrad M. & Solon T. Kimball
1965   *Culture and Community*. New York: Harcourt, Brace & World.
1968   *Family and Community in Ireland*. Cambridge: Harvard University Press. First published in 1940.
Asad Talal
1972   Market Model, Class Structure and Consent: A Reconsideration of Swat Political Organization. *Man* (NS), 7 : 74-94.

Bailey, F.G.
1960   *Tribe Caste and Nation*. Manchester: Manchester University Press.
1963   *Politics and Social change. Orissa in 1959*. London: Oxford University Press.
1964   Two Villages in Orissa (India). In: Max Gluckman (Ed.), *Closed Systems and Open Minds: The Limits of Naïvity in Social Anthropology*. London: Oliver & Boyd.
1965   Decisions by Consensus in Councils and Committees: with special Reference to Village and Local Government in India. In: Michael Banton (Ed.), *Political Systems and the Distribution of Power*. (ASA monographs, No. 2), London: Tavistock Publications.
1968   Parapolitical Systems. In: Marc J. Swartz (Ed.), *Local-Level Politics. Social and Cultural Perspectives*. Chicago: Aldine Publishing Company.
1969   *Stratagems and Spoils. A Social Anthropology of Politics*. Oxford: Basil Blackwell, Pavilion Series.
1971   *Gifts and Poison. The Politics of Reputation*. Oxford: Basil Blackwell, Pavilion Series.
Banfield, E.C. & J.Q Wilson
1966   *City Politics*. Cambridge (Mass.): Harvard University Press.
Barnes, J.A.
1968   Networks and Political Process. In: Marc J. Swartz (Ed.), *Local-Level Politics. Social and Cultural Perspectives*. Chicago: Aldine Publishing Company.
Baroja, Julio Caro
1963   The City and the Country: Reflexions on Some Ancient Commonplaces. In: Julian Pitt-Rivers (Ed.), *Mediterranean Countrymen. Essays in the Social Anthropology of the Mediterranean*. The Hague: Mouton & Co.

216

Barth, Fredrik
1959a *Political Leadership among the Swat Pathans*. London: Athlone Press.
1959b Segmentary Opposition and the Theory of Games. A Study of Pathan Organization. *Journal of the Royal Anthropological Institute,* 89 : 5-21.
1967 On the Study of Social Change. *American Anthropologist,* 69 : 661-70.
1963 (Ed.) *The Role of the Entrepreneur in Social Change in Northern Norway*. Bergen-Oslo: Norwegian Universities Press.
1966 *Models of Social Organization*. Royal Anthropological Institute Occasional Paper No. 23, London.

Bateman, John
1971 *The Great Landowners of Great Britain and Ireland*. New York: Humanities Press. First published in 1876.

Bax, Mart
1971 Patronage Irish Style; Irish Politicians as Brokers. *Sociologische Gids,* 17 : 179-91.
1971 Kiesstelsel en leider-volgeling relaties in Ierland. (Electoral System and Leader-Follower Relationships in Ireland) *Mens en Maatschappij,* 46 : 366-75.
1972 Integration, Forms of Communication, and Development: Centre-Periphery Relations in Ireland, Past and Present. *Sociologische Gids,* 19 : 137-44.

Bestic, Alan
1969 *The Importance of Being Irish*. London: Cassell & Company.

Bienen, Henry
1968 *Violence and Social Change*. Chicago: University of Chicago Press.

Blaney, Neil T.
1965 The Role and Function of the Councillor. *Administration,* 13 : 73-7.

Blanchard, Jean
1963 *The Church in Contemporary Ireland*. Dublin: Clonmore & Reynolds.

Blanshard, Paul
1953 *The Irish and Catholic Power*. Boston: Beacon Press.

Blau, Peter M.
1964 *Exchange and Power in Social Life*. New York: John Wiley & Sons.

Blok, Anton
1969 Variations in Patronage. *Sociologische Gids,* 16 : 365-86.

Boissevain, Jeremy
1965 *Saints and Fireworks. Religion and Politics in Rural Malta*. London: The Athlone Press.
1966 Patronage in Sicily. *Man* (NS), 1 : 18-33).
1969a Patrons as Brokers. *Sociologische Gids,* 16 : 379-86.
1969b *Hal-Farrug. A Village in Malta*. New York: Holt, Rinehart & Winston.
1971 Democracy, Development and Proportional Representation: A Sicilian Case. *The Journal of Development Studies,* 8 : 79-90.
1974 *Friends of Friends. Networks, Manipulators and Coalitions*. Oxford: Basil Blackwell, Pavilion Series.

Bowyer Bell, J.
1970 *The Secret Army. A History of the IRA, 1916-1970*. London: Anthony Blond.

Breathnach, Tomàs
1965 The Social and Economic Position of Western Areas. In: George F. Thomason (Ed.), *Report and Papers of an International Seminar on Western Development*. Tipperary: Muintir na Tire Rural Publications.

Bromage, Arthur W.
1961 *The Council-Manager Plan in Ireland*. Dublin: Public Management.

Brown, Thomas N.
1953 Nationalism and the Irish Peasant, *Review of Politics,* 15 : 403-45.

Bryce, T.
1914 *The American Commonwealth*. New York: The MacMillan Company.

Byrne, Patrick F.
1967 *Witchcraft in Ireland*. Cork: The Mercier Press.

Campbell, J.K.
1967 *Honour, Family and Patronage. A Study of Institutions and Moral Values in a Greek Mountain Community*. Oxford: Clarendon Press. First published in 1964.
Caplow, Theodore
1968 *Two Against One, Coalitions in Triads*. Englewood Cliffs, N.J.: Prentice-Hall.
Chubb, Basil
1954 Vocational Representation and the Irish Senate. *Political Studies*, 2 : 97-111.
1957 The Independent Member in Ireland. *Political Studies*, 5 : 131-39.
1959 Ireland 1957. In: D.E. Butler (Ed.), *Elections Abroad*. London: MacMillan & Company.
1964 *A Source Book of Irish Government*. Dublin: Institute of Public Administration.
1963a Going about Persecuting Civil Servants: The Role of the Irish Parliamentary Representative. *Political Studies*, 11 : 272-86.
1963b *The Constitution of Ireland*. Dublin: Institute of Public Administration.
1968 *The Government: An Introduction to the Cabinet System in Ireland*. Dublin: Institute of Public Administration.
1969 The Republic of Ireland. In: Stanley Henig & John Pinder (Eds.), *European Political Parties*. London: Allen & Unwin.
1971 *The Government and Politics of Ireland*. London: Oxford University Press.
Cohan, Alvin S.
1970 *Revolutionary and Non-Revolutionary Elites: The Irish Political Elite in Transition; 1919-1969*. Unpublished Ph.D. Thesis, Athens: University of Georgia.
Cohen, Abner
1969 Political Anthropology: The Analysis of the Symbolism of Power Relations. *Man* (NS), 4 : 215-35.
Collins, John
1963 *Local Government*. Revised by Desmond Roche. Dublin: Institute of Public Administration.
Comerford, Maire
1969 *The First Dail, January 21st 1919*. Dublin: Joe Clarke.
Connell, K.H.
1968 *Irish Peasant Society. Four Historical Essays*. Oxford: Clarendon Press.
Coogan, Timothy Pat
1966 *Ireland Since the Rising*. New York: Pall Mall Press.
1970 *The* I.R.A. New York: Pall Mall Press.
Coser, Lewis A.
1970 *Continuities in the Study of Social Conflict*. New York: The Free Press.
Coyne, Edward J.
1958 The Small Farm in Irish Agriculture. *Studies*, XLVII : 1-20.
Cruise O'Brien, Conor
1957 *Parnell and His Party, 1880-90*. Oxford: The Clarendon Press.
Curtis, Edmund
1961 *A History of Ireland*. London: Methuen University Paperbacks.
Cullen, L.M.
1968 *Life in Ireland*. London: B.T. Batsford.

Dowling, P.J.
1968 *The Hedge Schools of Ireland*. Cork: The Mercier Press. First published in 1935.

218

Duverger, Maurice
1967 *Political Parties. Their Organization and Activity in the Modern State.* London: Methuen & Co. First published in 1954.

Edwards, Owen Dudley (Ed.)
1969 *Conor Cruise O'Brien Introduces Ireland.* London: Andre Deutsch.

Elias, Norbert
1969a Sociology and Psychiatry. In: S.H. Foulkes & G.S. Prince (Eds.), *Psychiatry in a Changing Society.* London.
1969b *Ueber den Prozess der Zivilisaton. Soziogenetische und psychogenetische Untersuchungen.* Bern-München: A.G. Franke Verlag.
1970 *Was ist Soziologie?* München: Juventa Verlag.

Elias, Norbert & John L. Scotson
1965 *The Established and the Outsiders. A Sociological Enquiry into Community Problems.* London: Frank Cass & Co.

Farell, Brian
1969 The New State and Irish Political Culture. *Administration*, 17.
1971 Dail Deputies: "The 1969 Generation". *Economic and Social Review*, 2 : 309-25.

Fennell, Desmond (Ed.)
1968 *The Changing Face of Catholic Ireland.* London: Geoffrey Chapman.

Fennell, Rosemary
1961 The Economic Problems of Western Ireland. *Studies*, 50 : 385-402.

Finlay, Ian
1966 *The Civil Service.* Dublin: Institute of Public Administration.

Fitzgerald, Garret
1961 *State-Sponsored Bodies.* Dublin: Institute of Public Administration.
1968 *Planning in Ireland.* Dublin: Institute of Public Administration.

Frankenberg, Ronald
1957 *Village on the Border. A Social Study of Religion, Politics and Football in a North Wales Community.* London: Cohen & West.

Freeman, T.W.
1960 *Ireland: A General and Regional Geography.* London: Methuen & Co.

Galjart, Benno
1964 Class and "Following" in Rural Brazil, *America Latina*, 7 : 3-23.

Garvin, J.
1963 Local Government and Its Problems. *Administration*, 11 : 224-41.

Garvin, Thomas
1969 *The Irish Senate.* Dublin: Institute of Public Administration.

Gluckman, Max
1968 The Utility of the Equilibrium Model in the Study of Social Change. *American Anthropologist*, 70:219-37.

Gosnell, Harold F.
1968 *Machine Politics. Chicago Model.* Chicago: The University of Chicago Press. First Published in 1937.

Gottfried, Alex
1961 *Boss Cermak of Chicago: A Study of Political Leadership.* Seattle: University of Washington Press.
1972 Political Machine. In: David L. Sills (Ed.), *Internal Encyclopedia of the Social Sciences*, Vol 11, pp. 148-52. New York: MacMillan.

Healy, John
1968 *The Death of an Irish Town.* Cork: The Mercier Press.

Hekken, P.M. van & H.UE. Thoden van Velzen
1972 *Land Scarcity and Rural Inequality in Tanzania. Some Case Studies from Rungwe District.* The Hague: Mouton & Co.
Hertz, Frederick
1957 *Nationality in History and Politics.* London: Routledge & Kegan Paul.
Hogan, James
1945 *Election and Representation.* Cork: The Cork University Press.
Hollnsteiner, Mary R.
1967 Social Structure and Power in a Philippine Municipality. In: J.M. Potter, M.N. Diaz, and G.M. Foster (Eds.), *Peasant Society. A Reader.* Boston: Little, Brown.
Humphreys, A.J.
1966 *New Dubliners.* London: Routledge & Kegan Paul.
Hunt, William
1907 *The Irish Parliament 1775.* Dublin: Hodges, Figgis & Co.
Huntington, Samuel P.
1968 *Political Order in Changing Societies.* New Haven: Yale University Press.
Huizer, Gerrit
1965 Some Notes on Community Development and Rural Social Research, *America Latina,* 8 : 728-144.

Joyce, James
1968 *A Portrait of an Artist as a Young Man.* Middlesex, England: Penguin Books.

Kane, Eileen
1968 Man and Kin in Donegal: A Study of Kinship Functions in a Rural Irish and an Irish-American Community. *Ethnology,* 7 : 245-58.
Keane, John B.
1967 *Letters of a Successful* T.D. Cork: The Mercier Press.
Kenny, Michael
1960 Patterns of patronage in Spain. *Anthropological Quarterly,* 33 : 14-23.
Key, Jr., V.O.
1952 *Politics, Parties, and Pressure Groups.* New York: Crowell.

Lakeman, Enid
1970 *How Democracies Vote. A Study of Majority and Proportional Electoral Systems.* London: Faber & Faber.
Lee, J.M.
1963 *Social Leaders and Public Persons. A Study of County Government in Cheshire since 1888.* Oxford: Oxford University Press.
Lehmann, David
1971 Political Incorporation versus Political Stability: The Case of the Chilean Agrarian Reform, 1965-70, *The Journal of Development Studies,* 7 : 365-95.
Leyton, Elliott
1966 Conscious Models and Dispute Regulation in an Ulster Village. *Man* (NS), 1 : 534-42.
1970 Spheres of Inheritance in Aughnaboy. *American Anthropologist,* 72 : 1378-88.
Lipset, Seymour M.
1963 *Political Man.* London: Hineman.
Lynch, P.
1959 The Economics of Independence. *Administration,* 7 : 91-108.
Lyons, F.S.L.
1951 *The Irish Parliamentary Party 1890-1910.* London: Faber & Faber.
1971 *Ireland since the Famine, 1850 to the Present.* London: Weidenfeld & Nicolson.

Maas, Peter
1969   *The Canary that Sang.* London: MacGibbon & Kee.
Macardle, Dorothy
1968   *The Irish Republic.* London: Corgi Books. First published in 1937.
MacDonagh, Oliver
1968   *Ireland.* Englewood Cliffs, N.J.: Prentice-Hall.
Mackenzie, W.J.M.
1967   *Free Elections. An Elementary Textbook.* London: Allen & Unwin. First published in 1958.
MacManus, Francis (Ed.)
1967   *The Years of the Great Test: 1926-39.* The Thomas Davis Lectures. Cork: The Free Press.
Mandelbaum, Seymour J.
1965   *Boss Tweed's New York.* New York: Wiley & Sons.
Manning, Maurice
1970   *The Blueshirts.* Dublin: Gill & MacMillan.
Mansergh, Nicholas
1965   *The Irish Question: 1840-1921.* London: Allen & Unwin.
Martin, F.X. (Ed.)
1967   *Leaders and Men of the Easter Rising: 1916.* London: Methuen & Co.
Mayer, Adrian C.
1962   System and Network: An Approach to the Study of Political Processes in Dewas. In: T.N. Madan & G. Sarana (Eds.), *Indian Anthropology.* Bombay: Asia.
1966   The Significance of Quasi-Groups in the Study of Complex Societies. In: Michael Banton (Ed.), *The Social Anthropology of Complex Societies.* (ASA Monographs, No. 4), London: Tavistock Publications.
1967   Patrons and Brokers: Rural Leadership in Four Overseas Indian Communities. In: M. Freedman (Ed.), *Social Organization: Essays Presented to Raymond Firth.* London: Frank Cass.
McCaffrey, L.J.
1968   *The Irish Question.* Lexington: The University of Kentucky Press.
McCarthy, Charles
1968   *The Distasteful Challenge.* Dublin: Institute of Public Administration.
McCay, Hedley
1966   *Padraic Pearse. A New Biography.* Cork: The Mercier Press.
McElligot, T.J.
1958   *Representative Government in Ireland: A Study of Dail Eireann 1919-48.* London: Oxford University Press.
McDowell, R.B.
1964   *The Irish Administration, 1801-1914.* London: Routledge & Kegan Paul.
McElligot, T.J.
1966   *Education in Ireland.* Dublin: Institute of Public Administration.
Meghen, P.J.
1965   Central-Local Relationships in Ireland. *Administration,* 13 : 107-22.
Merton, Robert K.
1963   *Social Theory and Social Structure.* Glencoe: The Free Press. First published in 1949.
Mescal, J.
1957   *Religion in the Irish System of Education.* Dublin: Clonmore & Reynolds.
Messenger, John C.
1969   *Inis Beag. Isle of Ireland.* New York: Holt, Rinehart and Winston.
Moody, T.W. (Ed.)
1967   *The Fenian Movement.* The Thomas Davis Lectures. Cork: The Mercier Press.

Moody, T.W. & F.X. Martin (Eds.)
1968   *The Course of Irish History*. Cork: The Mercier Press.
Moore, Barrington
1968   *Social Origins of Dictatorship and Democracy. Lord and Peasant in the Making of the Modern World*. Boston: Beacon Press.
Moss, Warner
1933   *Political Parties in the Irish Free State*. New York: Columbia University Press.

Neeson, Eoin
1967   *The Book of Irish Saints*. Cork: The Mercier Press.
1969   *The Civil War in Ireland, 1922-1923*. Cork: The Mercier Press. First published in 1966.
Newman, Jeremiah
1958   The Future of Rural Ireland. *Studies*, XLVII : 388-409.
Newman, Jeremiah (Ed.)
1964   *The Limerick Rural Survey, 1958-1964*. Tipperary: Muintir na Tire Rural Publications.
Nicholas, Ralph W.
1963   Village Factions and Political Parties in Rural West Bengal. *Journal of Commonwealth Political Studies*, 2 : 17-32.
Norman, E.R.
1969   *The Catholic Church and Irish Politics in the Eighteen Sixties*. Dundalk: Dundalgan Press. Irish History Series, No. 5.

O'Broin, Leon
1966   *Dublin Castle and the 1916 Rising*. Dublin: Helicon Ltd.
1971   *Fenian Fever, An Anglo-American Dilemma*. London: Chatto & Windus.
O'Leary, Cornelius
1961   *The Irish Republic and Its Experiment with Proportional Representation*. Notre Dame, Indiana: University of Notre Dame Press.

Parry, Geraint
1969   *Political Elites*. London: Allen & Unwin.
Parsons, Talcott
1959   *The Social System*. Glencoe: The Free Press. First published in 1951.
Pearse, Padraic
1966   *Political Writings and Speeches*. Dublin: The Talbot Press.
Pomfret, John E.
1930   *The Struggle for Land in Ireland: 1800-1923*. Princeton: Princeton University Press.
Powell, John Duncan
1970   Peasant Society and Clientelist Politics. *American Political Science Review*, 64 : 411-25.

Robins, J.A.
1961   The County in the Twentieth Century. *Administration*, 9 : 88-94.
Rohan, Dorine
1969   *Marriage Irish Style*. Cork: The Mercier Press.
Rooney, Philip
1966   *Captain Boycott*. Tralee: Anvil Books.
Roseingrave, Tomas
1969   *Muintir na Tire: National Director's Report to Annual Congress*. Ennis, mimeo.
Rynne, Stephen
1960   *Father John Hayes. Founder of Muintir na Tire*. Dublin: Clonmore and Reynolds.

Sait, Edward McChesney
1933   Political Machine. In: Edwin R.A. Seligman (Ed.), *Encyclopaedia of the Social Sciences*, Vol 9, pp. 657-61. New York: MacMillan.

Schwartz, Norman B.
1969   Goal Attainment Through Factionalism: A Guatemalan Case. *American Anthropologist*, 71 : 1088-1171.

Scott, James C.
1970   Corruption, Machine Politics, and Political Change. In: Arnold J. Heidenheimer (Ed.), *Political Corruption. Readings in Comparative Analysis*. New York: Holt, Rinehart and Winston.
1972   *Comparative Political Corruption*. Englewood Cliffs, N.J.: Prentice-Hall.

Scully, John J.
1965   The Family Farm in the context of Western Development. In: George F. Thomason (Ed.), *Report and Papers of an International Seminar on Western Development*. Tipperary: Muintir na Tire Rural Publications.

Senior, Hereward
1968   The Place of Fenianism in the Irish Republican Tradition. In: Maurice Harman (Ed.), *Fenians and Fenianism*. Dublin: Scepter Books.

Sheehan, C.
1967   *My New Curate. A Story Gathered from the Stray Leaves of an Old Diary*. Dublin: The Talbot Press.

Silverman, Sydel F.
1965   Patronage and Community-Nation Relationships in Central Italy. *Ethnology*, 4 : 172-89.

Strauss, E.
1951   *Irish Nationalism and British Democracy*. London: Methuen & Co.

Thoden van Velzen, H.U.E.
n.d.   *The Condotieri and the Levellers*. Leiden, mimeo.
1971   *Staff, Kulaks and Peasants: A Study of a Political Field*. Leiden: Afrika Studiecentrum.

Thomason, George F.
1961   *Community Development in Ireland*. Tipperary: Muintir na Tire Rural Publications.

Thornley, David
1964   *Isaac Butt and Home Rule*. London: MacGibbon & Kee.

Trench, W. Steuart
1966   *Realities of Irish Life*. London: MacGibbon & Kee. First published in 1868.

Turpin, D.
1954   The Local Government Service: Consolidating the Service. *Administration*, 2 : 81-94.

Velsen, J. van
1967   The Extended-Case Method and Situational Analysis. In: A.L. Epstein (Ed.), *The Craft of Social Anthropology*. London: Tavistock Publications.

Walsh, Brendan M.
1968   *Some Irish Population Problems Reconsidered*. Dublin: The Economic and Social Research Institute, Paper No. 42.

Walsh, T. (Ed.)
1963   *West Cork Resource Survey*. Dublin: An Foras Taluntais.

Weingrod, Alex
1968   Patrons, Patronage and Political Parties. *Comparative Studies in Society and History*, 10 : 377-400.

Wertheim, W.F.
1969   Patronage als Structureel Verschijnsel (Patronage as a Structural Phenomenon), *Sociologische Gids*, 16 : 362-5.

White, Leonard D.
1933   Spoils System. In: Edward R.A. Seligman (Ed.), *Encyclopaedia of the Social Sciences*, Vol 13, pp. 301-5. New York: MacMillan.

Whyte, John H.
1958   *The Independent Irish Party, 1850-9*. Oxford: Oxford University Press.
1960   The Influence of the Catholic Clergy on Elections in Nineteenth-Century Ireland. *The English Historical Review*, LXXV : 239-59.
1965   Landlord Influence at Elections in Ireland, 1760-1885. *The English Historical Review*, 80 : 740-60.
1966   *Dail Deputies*. Dublin: Tuairim Pamphlet.
1971   *Church and State in Modern Ireland, 1923-1970*. London: Gill & MacMillan.

Williams, T. Desmond
1967   De Valera in Power. In: Francis MacManus (Ed.), *The Years of the Great Test, 1926-1939*. The Thomas Davis Lectures. Cork: The Mercier Press.

Wilson, J.Q.
1961   The Economy of Patronage. *The Journal of Political Economy*, LXIX : 369-80.

Winder, Frank (Ed.)
1959   *P.R. – For or Against?* Dublin: Tuairim Publications.

Wolf, Eric R.
1969   *Peasant Wars of the Twentieth Century*. New York: Harper & Row Publishers.

OTHER SOURCES AND DOCUMENTS

n.d.   Córas Bua. (Fianna Fail's Election Handbook) Dublin: Juverna Press.
1956   Constitution of Ireland. Dublin: Government Publications Sale Office.
1968   Dail Debates. Dublin: The Stationery Office.
-69
1969   Irish Catholic Directory. Dublin: James Duffy & Co.
1966   Irish Central Statistics Office. Census of Population of Ireland. Vol. I: Population – Vol. II: Occupations.
1965   Statistical Abstract. Dublin: Central Statistics Office.
1969   Nusight. Ireland's Newsmagazine. Dublin: Independent Newspapers Ltd.
-70
1964   The Concise Oxford Dictionary of Current English. Edited by H.W. Fowler and F.G. Fowler. Based on the Oxford Dictionary. Fift Edition. Oxford: The Clarendon Press.